CITY AND ENTERPRISE

The European Institute for Comparative Urban Research, EURICUR, was founded in 1988 and has its seat with Erasmus University Rotterdam. EURICUR is the heart and pulse of an extensive network of European cities and universities. EURICUR's principal objective is to stimulate fundamental international comparative research into matters that are of interest to cities. To that end, EURICUR co-ordinates, initiates and carries out studies of subjects of strategic value for urban management today and in the future. Through its network EURICUR has privileged access to crucial information regarding urban development in Europe and North America and to key persons at all levels, working in different public and private organizations active in metropolitan areas. EURICUR closely cooperates with the Eurocities Association, representing about 80 large European cities.

As a scientific institution, one of EURICUR's core activities is to respond to the increasing need for information that broadens and deepens the insight into the complex process of urban development, among others by disseminating the results of its investigations by international book publications. These publications are especially valuable for city governments, supra-national, national and regional authorities, chambers of commerce, real estate developers and investors, academics and students, and others with an interest in urban affairs.

EURICUR website: http://www.euricur.nl

This book is one of a series to be published by Ashgate under the auspieces of EURICUR the European Institute for Comparative Urban Research, Erasmus University Rotterdam. Titles in the series are:

Metropolitan Organising Capacity
Leo van den Berg, Erik Braun and Jan van der Meer

National Urban Policies in the European Union
Leo van den Berg, Erik Braun and Jan van der Meer

The European High-Speed Train and Urban Development
Leo van den Berg and Peter Pol

Growth Clusters and City Marketing in European Cities
Leo van den Berg, Erik Braun and Willem van Winden

Information and Communications Technology as Potential Catalyst for Sustainable Urban Development
Leo van den Berg and Willem van Winden

Sports and City Marketing in European Cities
Leo van den Berg, Erik Braun and Alexander H.J. Otgaar

Social Challenge and Organising Capacity in Cities
Leo van den Berg, Jan van der Meer and Peter M.J. Pol

City and Enterprise

Corporate Community Involvement in European and US Cities

LEO VAN DEN BERG
ERIK BRAUN
ALEXANDER H.J. OTGAAR
European Institute for Comparative Urban Research
Erasmus University Rotterdam

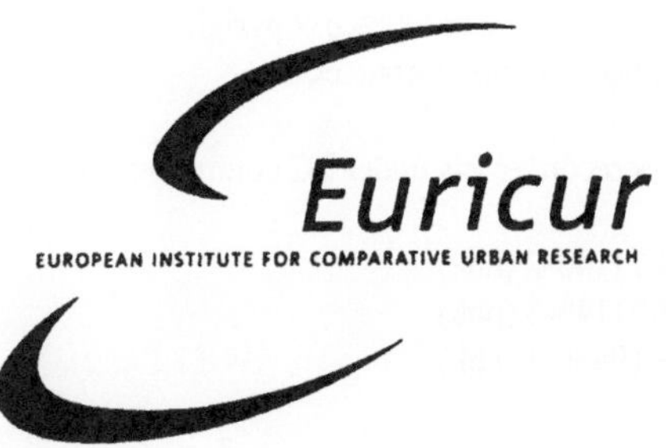

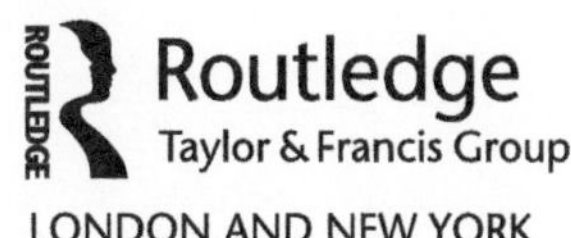

LONDON AND NEW YORK

First published 2003 by Ashgate Publishing

Reissued 2018 by Routledge
2 Park Square, Milton Park, Abingdon, Oxon OX14 4RN
711 Third Avenue, New York, NY 10017, USA

Routledge is an imprint of the Taylor & Francis Group, an informa business

A Library of Congress record exists under LC control number: 2003048162

ISBN 13: 978-1-138-71145-7 (hbk)
ISBN 13: 978-1-138-71143-3 (pbk)
ISBN 13: 978-1-315-19980-1 (ebk)

Contents

List of Figures

List of Tables

Preface

From 2000 until 2002, the European Institute for Comparative Urban Research (EURICUR) has been carrying out two studies on corporate citizenship in Europe and the United States. This book – *City and Enterprise: Corporate Community Involvement in European and US Cities* – contains the results of these investigations. It discusses the changing interests of private firms and the increasing need to develop partnerships between companies and non-private organisations.

The importance of working together also reveals itself in our research activities. Therefore, we should like to thank the following people and organisations for their assistance. First of all, we are grateful to Peter Zimmermann and Giljam Lokerse from accountancy and consultancy firm Deloitte & Touche The Netherlands, who sponsored both projects. Secondly, thanks are due to our contact persons in the various cities, namely Dennis Judd, David Jenkins and Wim Wiewel (Chicago), Christopher Exeter, Peter Davies, David Halley, Ella Ward and Pam Lee (London/Leeds), Bernhard Eller and Klaus Schußmann (Munich), Professor Susan Fainstein (New York) and Professor Alan Artibise (Seattle/St. Louis). Furthermore, we give thanks to all the discussion partners (listed at the end of the chapters) for their valuable input.

A final word of thanks and appreciation goes to Ankimon Vernède for her steady support on behalf of the EURICUR secretariat, and to Mrs Attie Elderson-de Boer for her translation of the original Dutch text.

Professor Leo van den Berg
Drs Erik Braun
Drs Alexander H.J. Otgaar

Rotterdam, March 2003

Chapter 1

Introduction

Introduction

In the past, corporate community involvement[1] was mainly considered a form of philanthropy. From some moral obligation, companies were presumed willing to contribute towards activities that help to solve or alleviate social problems. However, nowadays the argument is gaining credit that corporate community involvement is not (only) a matter of ethics, but (also) of self-interest. That argument may have intriguing consequences for the sustainable development of (major) cities and the relation between companies, local governments and non-profit organisations. For indeed, as companies recognise their interest in the welfare of the city (where their employees, suppliers and customers are situated), they may become inclined to invest in some way in that city's welfare. We assume that the interests of public and private stakeholders tend to converge as companies become aware of their interest in an attractive environment. If that is true, corporate community involvement may bring along a new type of public-private partnership, as an instrument of urban regeneration.

To develop knowledge with respect to corporate community involvement in relation to urban development, the European Institute for Comparative Urban Research (EURICUR) has carried out an international investigation, of which this book is the result. The key question is: what are the (potential) implications of corporate community involvement for the sustainable development of cities and the creation of cross-sector partnerships? To answer that question, we have identified four sub-questions:

1) to what extent do companies show their community involvement, and in what way;
2) what is the relation between the type of company and its social activities;
3) to what degree do companies cooperate with other organisations – and the local government in particular – to give evidence of their social responsibilities and self-interest in an attractive city;
4) what are the factors of failure and success in the process of developing cross-sector partnerships ensuing from corporate community involvement?

Methodology

The investigation was carried out in two stages. In the first, exploratory stage, most attention was paid to the first three questions. By means of literature study, (panel) discussions in the Netherlands and case studies in Chicago, London, Munich and St Louis we analysed the state of the art concerning corporate community involvement (corporate social responsibility) in relation to urban development (Van den Berg, Braun and Otgaar, 2000). From that exploration we learned that, although the interests of city and enterprise often converge, the number of cross-sector initiatives ensuing from corporate community involvement is somewhat disappointing. That is why the second stage of the investigation was mainly orientated towards the fourth question. Through a thorough study of literature on public-private partnerships and case studies in Amsterdam, Leeds, London, New York and Seattle, we identified the main barriers in the translation of common interests into joint initiatives (Van den Berg, Braun and Otgaar, 2002).

With the help of experts in the field of corporate community involvement (including Business in the Community, UK and Samenleving en Bedrijf, The Netherlands) and local contacts (including our sister organisation, the North American Institute for Comparative Urban Research), and by means of literature and the internet, we selected the cities, companies and intermediary organisations that we considered relevant for this investigation. In total, more than 130 people were interviewed. They represent about 40 companies, several governmental bodies and various non-profit organisations. In addition, we used written sources for the empirical research, including scientific papers, policy reports, annual reports and the internet.

With regard to the selection of cities and companies (as 'best practices'), several experts confirmed to us that North America and the UK are in terms of corporate community involvement ahead of continental Europe. Companies in these Anglo-Saxon countries appear to have a long tradition of community involvement and philanthropy in particular. Moreover, these countries do not have, like countries on the European continent, a dominant public sector, which could be an incentive for companies to put in their (voluntary) bit to solve social problems. Naturally, the experts also pointed out that the cultural, political and economic differences between continental Europe and the Anglo-Saxon countries must not be overlooked. To translate the experiences of the USA and the UK into lessons for continental Europe, where the government has assumed most social tasks, is not easy. However, what with the retrenchment of the welfare state and the reduction of taxes (in reaction to world-wide competition) the expectations with respect to the private sector may well change in Europe. Furthermore, European cities and companies would do wise to keep a watchful eye on the developments in North America, since experience has taught us that many American trends after some time will present themselves in Europe as well, if sometimes in a weaker form.

Structure of the Book

This book is composed as follows.

Chapter 2 sketches the research framework of this study. Theories concerning the interests of companies and communities, and dealing with collaboration between public and private actors are combined into several models that help to understand the dynamic relation between city and enterprise.

Chapter 3 discusses projects and initiatives in the Netherlands. We analyse the community involvement activities undertaken by large companies, and the results of two projects: the Consultation Platform for Urban Renewal and the ArenA Initiative.

Chapter 4 is about the experiences in Chicago, where the private sector has a long tradition of community involvement, for instance through interest groups such as The Commercial Club of Chicago. Furthermore, we bring up the progressive ideas concerning corporate community involvement that exist among Chicago-based companies, including McDonald's and Sara Lee.

Chapter 5 takes you along to the English city of Leeds. We analyse the activities of the regional branch of Business in the Community, which is regarded as one of the most active in the UK. Besides, this chapter includes a section on football club Leeds United and its programme entitled Community United.

Chapter 6 deals with the metropolis of Greater London, where economic prosperity goes hand-in-hand with severe problems in the sphere of accessibility, poverty and the environment. This chapter analyses the ability and willingness of the private sector to contribute to a sustainable development of London, and shows the barriers towards cooperation between the public and private sectors.

Chapter 7 contains the experiences of the German city of Munich, with special attention to the social activities of car manufacturer BMW and electronics concern Siemens. Furthermore, this chapter includes an analysis of the project Munich in Artificial Light, a brave attempt to get small and medium sized companies involved in culture.

Chapter 8 tells the story of New York, only two months after the destructive terrorist attack on the World Trade Centre. We analyse the role of banks that have been, and still are, very active in low-to-moderate income neighbourhoods, and the partnerships that pharmaceutical manufacturer Pfizer has created for the benefit of community development around the establishment in Brooklyn.

Chapter 9 is concerned with the city of Seattle, and the social activities of aircraft builder Boeing and coffee retailer Starbucks in particular. Moreover, the chapter identifies the main issues in the Seattle region and the extent to which the private sector is willing and able to deal with these problems.

Chapter 10 comprises the case study of the city of St Louis, which includes an analysis of various intermediary organisations, which defend the public interests of the private sector. Furthermore, we discuss the activities of some companies in the field of community involvement, and the role of interest groups in relation to sustainable urban development.

Chapter 11 confronts the practical findings with the theoretical framework, analysing the barriers in the process of developing strategic cross-sector alliances aimed at a sustainable development of cities. In the end, we formulate some challenges for managers of cities and companies, in reaction to the increasing attention to corporate community involvement.

Note

1 Alternative terms are corporate social responsibility and corporate social involvement. However, to emphasise the relation between companies and their local communities, we prefer to use the terms corporate community involvement and corporate citizenship.

References

Berg, L. van den, E. Braun and A.H.J. Otgaar (2000), *City and Enterprise: Corporate Social Responsibility in European and US Cities*, European Institute for Comparative Urban Research, Rotterdam.

Berg, L. van den, E. Braun and A.H.J. Otgaar (2002), *City and Enterprise: From Common Interests to Joint Initiatives*, European Institute for Comparative Urban Research, Rotterdam.

Chapter 2

Corporate Community Involvement

Introduction

In our view, corporate community involvement implies that a company considers not only the interests of shareholders (profit) but also the interests of society (people) and those of the environment (planet), not only from a moral commitment but also from the conviction that such an approach contributes to the long-term viability of the company. Several recent developments have caused companies to define their interests more broadly than in the past. Indeed, corporate community involvement has become a matter of self-interest, requiring a strategic approach. We assume that in particular cases city and enterprise have the same interests, and may therefore be willing to develop joint initiatives. In this chapter we analyse the road to cross-sector partnerships that ensue from corporate community involvement by looking at the (changing) interests of stakeholders and the factors of success and failure that play a role in the coalition-forming process.

The section that follows is about the interests of companies and the impact of corporate social responsibility on the behaviour of firms. In the third section we pay attention to the interests of local governments and other organisations that may contribute to sustainable urban development. The following section shows that in the road to partnership several stages can be observed. Next we look at the (financial and economic) factors that relate to the question whether cooperation is useful and necessary to achieve the objectives set by the relevant organisations. We then present (social, cultural, psychological, etc.) factors that are relevant because organisations consist of people with their own objectives, norms, values and capacities. The final section summarises and concludes, resulting in a schematic presentation of the coalition-forming process and the identification of four success factors.

The Interests of Companies

There are several theories regarding the objectives and interests held by companies. These theories are inevitably related to the company's accountability (see, for instance, Karake-Shalhoub, 1999; Boudhan et al., 1996). The classical theory assumes that companies aim at making profit (Friedman, 1970). On that score they are beholden to their shareholders. In consequence, they mostly adopt a policy geared to maximum economic performance and maximum shareholder value. Although this theory is increasingly subject to criticism (Goyder (1998), for one, called the maximisation of shareholders value a shortsighted objective), the policy of companies is still undeniably largely determined by shareholders interests. On the other hand, shareholders as well are broadening their perspective, and allowing themselves to be guided more and more by factors which only indirectly and in the long term affect the company's economic performance. That is true in particular of institutional investors such as pension funds. The rise of ethical funds and 'ethical investors' illustrates the trend.

Stakeholder Theories

In the past few decades, theories have been developed by which companies are accountable not only to their shareholders but also to other actors who influence the continuity of the firm. According to Douma and Eppink (1996), companies aim to secure not only their economic viability but also their social viability. The economic viability refers to the (financial) economic performance (with growth, profitability and solvency as primary indicators), the degree of independence and flexibility. Within the objective of social viability, these authors make a distinction between individual (internal) and social (external) acceptance of the company (see Table 2.1).

Table 2.1 An overall hierarchy of objectives

1st level	2nd level	3rd level
Overall viability	Social viability	Social acceptance of the company Individual acceptance of the company
	Economic viability	Growth, profitability and solvency Independence Flexibility

Source: Douma and Eppink, 1996.

In fact, Douma and Eppink – like Post et al. (1999), de Waal (2000), and Karake-Shalhoub (1999) – recognise internal and external stakeholders, or stakeholders in the primary and secondary environments. Karake-Shalhoub (1999) makes a distinction between the stakeholder theory – which assumes that companies are accountable to stakeholders who have a direct interest or direct involvement in the primary (production) process of the organisation – and the social-demandingness theory – which states that companies are also responsible to people and organisations that have an indirect interest or an indirect involvement in that primary (production) process.

The primary stakeholders include on the one hand the suppliers of production factors, such as employees (labour) and financiers (capital), and on the other the buyers of the final products (customers). Shareholders to the primary stakeholders, since they provide funds to the company (they can be seen as financiers). All primary stakeholders can be said to be able instantly to withdraw the company's licence to operate by ceasing to supply production factors or to buy final products. A good relationship with these stakeholders is therefore crucial to the continuity of the enterprise.

Secondary stakeholders determine the social acceptance of the company and thus affect the behaviour of primary stakeholders. It should be noted that relationships often overlap, as secondary stakeholders can also be primary stakeholders. The media, social organisations (non-governmental organisations (NGOs)) and neighbours are such stakeholders. The government, too, is often included in this group, though its role is clearly different, since the government has the power literally to withdraw the licence to operate through legislation.

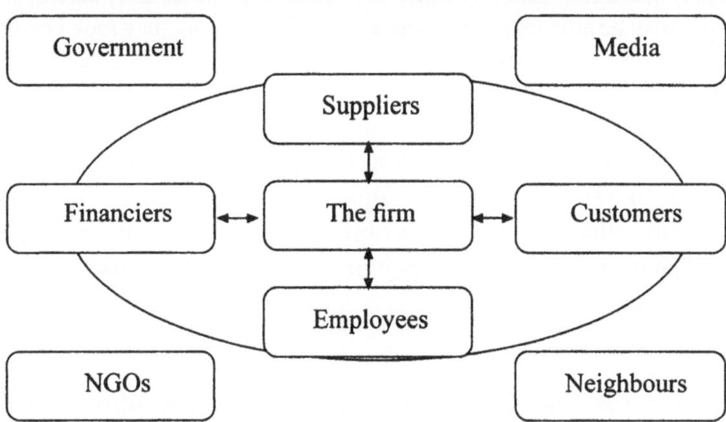

Figure 2.1 Primary and secondary stakeholders

A practical concept that illustrates the broadened objectives, interests and responsibilities of companies, is the triple-p bottom line. By this concept companies are answerable not only for their profit, but also for their relation with society (people) and the environment (planet) (Elkington, 1997). Several companies employ the concept in their annual reports. The three pillars of the triple-p bottom line must not be viewed separately. Increasingly, indeed, companies understand that a good social and ecological performance is a condition for good long-term financial performance.

Corporate Social Responsibility: the Evolution of a Concept

Corporate social responsibility is not a recent phenomenon, although the concept has evolved considerably over recent decades, as has been described by, among others, Carroll (1999). He looks upon Howard R. Bowen as the founder of corporate social responsibility. In *Social Responsibilities of the Businessman* (1953), Bowen pointed out that in their decisions managers should take account of the objectives and values of society. Many definitions have been based, following Bowen, on the principle that managers should make some compensation to society, mainly from a kind of moral obligation. The definitions mostly make an appeal to the individuals rather than the company as a whole, as is apparent from the next fragment:

> Social responsibility, therefore, refers to a person's obligation to consider the effects of his decisions and actions on the whole social system. Businessmen apply social responsibility when they consider the needs and interests of others who may be affected by business actions. In doing so, they look beyond their firm's narrow economic and technical interests (Davis and Blomstrom, 1966, p. 32).

However, in an earlier publication Davis (1960) puts the accent not so much on the moral obligations of people, as on the companies' self-interest. His argument is that socially responsible corporate decisions can be justified by a good chance of long-term economic profit for the company.

The 1990s

In the 1990s, the concept of corporate social responsibility increasingly gained credit, not only from social scientists but also from companies and governments. That is evident for one thing from the foundation of several national and international networks and platforms. According to the Chatham House Forum Report (1996), a growing number of companies communicate their social involvement to gain the loyalty of employees and customers. More than ever before companies exert themselves to ensure their social viability (and thus their economic viability!). Goyder (1998) argues that the 1990s revealed an about-turn in the field of corporate community involvement. Businesses that ignore public opinion run the risk of damaging their reputation, with all the consequences for the loyalty of customers and employees as well as shareholders. The confidence of all these stakeholders is necessary to keep the licence to operate. According to Burke (1999), companies nowadays have to make special efforts to become and remain a 'neighbour of choice'.

In practice, 'incidents' can sometimes stir the social awareness of large companies. Two often-recalled incidents involve the British-Dutch oil concern Shell. In the early 1990s this company became discredited when it wanted to sink the obsolete oil platform Brent Spar into the North Sea. An extensive study had indeed proved that dumping the platform into the sea would have the least damaging effect on the environment. However, Shell's intention provoked not only protests from Greenpeace and negative media attention, but also a massive strike of (mainly German) consumers, and even attacks on petrol stations. Afterwards the oil concern was shown to have been perfectly correct in its calculations (approved by the respected scientific journal *Nature* as well as by an independent Norwegian research agency), but it had failed in its relations with relevant stakeholders. Shell had neglected to sound out the opinion of environmental groups. Two months after the disturbances, Shell even received apologies from Greenpeace: the environmental activists had hugely overestimated the quantity of oil left behind in the Brent Spar. However, Shell's image (notably in Germany) suffered greatly in the process. In 1996, Shell again stumbled into the news. On this occasion Shell was accused of violating human rights in Nigeria, having for many years polluted the living environment of the Onogi people without doing anything for them in return. Shell was even said to have supplied weapons to the national government to suppress revolts of this people. In particular, the death sentence and execution of Ken Saro-Wiwa, the leader of the Ogoni, caused great indignation and action by human rights organisations Pax Christi and Amnesty International.

Fundamental Developments

Many authors (see, inter alia, Elkington, 1997; de Waal, 2000; Boudhan, Vonk and Nelissen, 1996), have pointed out that in recent years certain fundamental developments have stimulated companies to give more attention to their social responsibilities and interests. Burke (1999) refers to external incentives to become a neighbour of choice.

For one thing, consumers are becoming ever more critical in their purchasing behaviour (see, for example, de Waal, 2000), which means that companies have to take account of consumers' preferences as to how products have been manufactured and how the company deals with society (Goyder, 1988). For another, globalisation is bringing companies into contact with the most divergent norms and values (cultures), confronting them with awkward problems in the sphere of the environment and human rights. Thirdly, innovations in information and communication technology (ICT) are reinforcing the media's (potential) role as monitors, making the social behaviour of business companies more transparent (Elkington, 1997). Negative reports tend to have instant effects on the stock market, on which companies have become increasingly dependent in the past decade. A fourth trend concerns withdrawing government, a development manifest notably in Europe and not so much in the USA where the government is traditionally less influential and dominant. As a result of the retreating government and the erosion of the welfare state, space has become available for a greater role of companies in society (Boudhan et al., 1996). Many companies are feeling a greater need for self-regulation now that legislation is not forthcoming. Many of them are also seeking to make further legislation superfluous by their socially responsible behaviour. Moreover, common-interest groups (NGOs) are taking over part of the government's erstwhile supervising role. Organisations like Greenpeace and Amnesty International operate worldwide and in close cooperation with the media. Another result of the government's retreat is that nationwide regulations (the social safety net) are giving way to corporate arrangements. Companies are thus being forced into a more active role in ensuring the individual acceptance of the enterprise. In addition, governments are increasingly looking to private enterprise as partner in projects with a social objective (Elkington, 1997). As early as the 1970s, awareness was growing in the USA that the government could not by itself solve certain problems (Foster and Berger, 1982). A fifth relevant development is the increasing importance of the factor labour in the production process, stimulated by the rise of the service and information society. Especially highly educated employees – but in times of boom also the lower educated – can afford to make greater claims on the employer. Ever more often these claims are referring not only to primary and secondary employment conditions, but also to the social position of the company and the social relevance of the job in question. Employees look upon the company's social behaviour as indicative of the way it treats its own staff.

Approaches to Corporate Social Responsibility

With respect to their social responsibilities, companies may adopt different strategies. Eilbert and Parket (1973) made a distinction between passive and active approaches.

Perhaps the best way to understand social responsibility is to think of it as 'good neighbourliness'. The concept involves two phases. On one hand, it means not doing things that spoil the neighbourhood. On the other, it may be expressed as the voluntary assumption of the obligation to help solve neighbourhood problems.

Carroll (1979), taking up that line of thought, recognised four variants: the reactive, defensive, adaptive and proactive forms of corporate social responsibility, under which businesses seek to ensure their licence to operate by making no mistakes and keeping stakeholders contented (see Boudhan et al., 1996). The social-activist theory suggests that such a defensive strategy is not enough to ensure the achievement of all commercial and social objectives: frequently a company is wise to take one step beyond what stakeholders claim and expect in the first instance. Companies could, for instance, make knowledge and resources available for social projects. Boudhan et al. (1996) call the proactive approach 'real' corporate social responsibility. Burke (1999) considers proactive corporate social responsibility an opportunity to achieve competitive advantages. Burke analyses these opportunities (internal incentives to become a neighbour of choice) with the help of Michael Porter's (1985) 'value chain'.

The difference between passive and proactive can also be illustrated by the 'inclusive view' that Goyder (1998) propagated. In his view, entrepreneurs should be sensitive not only to matters that could jeopardise the future of the company, but also to matters that could strengthen that future. Any relation with a stakeholder represents an opportunity to create synergy. Corporate social involvement may help to attract and motivate staff (Boudhan et al., 1996; de Waal, 2000; Goyder, 1998), to develop new markets and products (expansion of the core business), to improve relations with stakeholders, to obtain access to networks, to identify competitors (Boudhan et al., 1996), and finally to achieve a higher turnover and profit. In sum: commercial and social objectives (in fact, the three pillars of the triple-p bottom line) can no longer be considered in separation. One form of proactive corporate social responsibility is 'corporate social innovation' (Kanter, 1999), which implies companies regarding the social sector as a test area in which they can develop new ideas and markets. By devoting energy to the chronic problems of the social sector, such companies also contribute to their own corporate results. Tackling social problems forces companies to initiate innovations which benefit both the company and the community. When companies approach social needs in that manner, they take a stake in the problems, treating the social project like any other project related to central management, that is to say, they put in their best people and their finest skills.

The role of corporate social involvement in the corporate strategy can be analysed with the help of a model of the London Benchmarking Group (Logan and Tuffrey, 1999). This model divides the (social) activities of companies into four categories: philanthropy ('charity'), community investment, commercial initiatives, and business basics. The triangle of Figure 2.2 shows that the share of charity (in terms of expenditure) is significantly smaller than that of the other categories. This type of activity has hardly any relation at all with the corporate strategy. A company will be inclined to spend more on social activities when the expenditure is regarded as community investment (the company committing itself for some considerable time to a certain social objective), on the assumption that such investment will in time be recuperated. By commercial initiatives, the London Benchmarking Group understands social activities with direct commercial advantages, mostly in the area of marketing. An example is what is called cause-related marketing, by which a company and a good cause jointly set up a campaign to bring the cause to the attention of the public. In theory, the obvious relation with the corporate strategy will raise the budget for this type of activity. However, companies make the greatest social contribution through their core business, by providing employment and supplying products or services. To that category belong investments related to their core business, which are justified both socially and commercially, for instance in the development of products, services or markets.

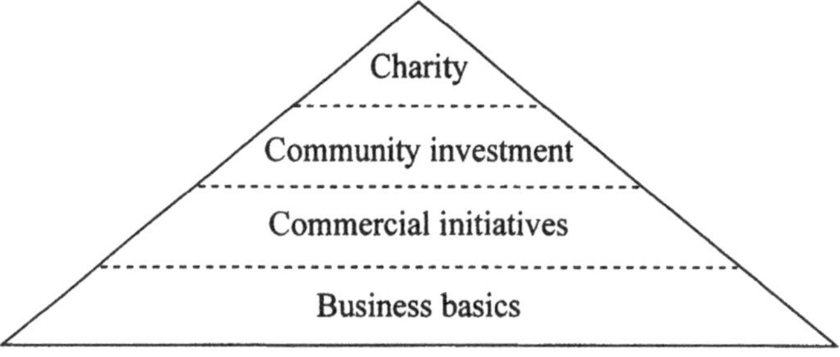

Figure 2.2 The London Benchmarking Group model

Source: Logan and Tuffrey, 1999.

The Local (Urban) Interests of Companies

In the stakeholder theory, the local (urban) community involvement of a company is determined by the relevance of local (urban) stakeholders' concerns and their (possible) influence on the attainment of the company's objectives. These local stakeholders include neighbourhood residents, customers, employees, companies, common-interest organisations, and governments. A group of stakeholders forms the community which companies are supposed to take into account. The relation between a company and a certain community depends, in our model, on the characteristics of the company and the markets on which it is active. The local involvement of a certain company can be explained from the company's intention to improve the relations with one or more primary stakeholders. Developing good relationships with secondary stakeholders is often required to optimise relations with primary stakeholders.

For example: company X participates in an employment project and to that end cooperates with a school. The company is motivated by the wish to establish a good relationship with its employees (primary stakeholders). The relationship with the school (secondary stakeholder) is needed to optimise that with employees. Company Y joins forces with a local residents' corporation so as to communicate better with residents about possible nuisance caused by the company and give the residents opportunities to make their complaints known. The company invests in the relationship with neighbourhood residents (secondary stakeholders) to prevent awkward relations with potential customers and employees or with the government (all of them primary stakeholders).

The distinction between primary and secondary stakeholders is not always clear-cut. Some stakeholders are primary for certain companies or in certain situations, but secondary for other companies or in different situations. To a factory apt to cause nuisance (company Y in the example given above) relations with local government are of crucial importance to retain the necessary licences. If the local government participates in the employment project of which our company X is a partner, a good relationship with the local government is very helpful. Another fact to be kept in mind is that a neighbourhood resident (secondary stakeholder) may at the same time be a (potential) customer or employee, and that the government in some cases is at the same time a customer. Goyder (1998) calls the phenomenon 'overlapping relations'.

Factors that Determine Local Corporate Community Involvement

The local involvement of companies is inspired among other things by the characteristics of the sales market and the product the companies sell. Not only is the size of the market relevant (local companies versus multinationals), but also the distinction between the consumer market and the business-to-business market. The size of the market is determined for one thing by the product sold. Supermarkets, for instance, have a smaller sales area than furniture malls. Competition is another important criterion. Companies operating in a strongly competitive market are in principle more motivated to build up a good relationship with their customers than (quasi-)monopolists. Presumably, moreover, companies will spend more time on their relationship with customers as they find it harder to differentiate themselves at the product level (in other words, as the products in the market become more homogeneous). Petrol and financial services are two markets in which suppliers are hard pressed to compete at the product level. There is also a significant difference between companies in direct touch with the customer (such as the providers of services) and those that have to enlist the services of distributors. Shops have a natural interest in an attractive environment, since their turnover depends directly on the appeal of the shopping centre (or cluster of shops).

The local involvement of companies also varies with the type of employment they provide (function and wage) and the state of the labour market for that type of function. The level of the function, the schooling required, and the salary paid determine to a large extent the maximum acceptable home-to-work distance and hence the maximum physical dimension of the employee community (in Burke's (1999) terminology). On the whole, the higher the income, the greater the distance between home and work employees are willing to accept. Branch offices of banks have a relatively small employee community, whereas their headquarters can reach farther afield for their top staff. Shop assistants are mostly not prepared to travel far from home to work, in contrast to managers of shopping chains.

The relevance of the employee community depends in part on the state of the labour market. A tight labour market drives companies to a more active staffing policy and makes companies aware of their interest in a pleasant living environment for their exacting employees. Additionally, employees increasingly give attention to the social reputation of their (potential) employers. Especially the better paid employees (higher position, higher educational level) want more than just a good salary. Their choice of employer involves consideration of its social performance (people, planet) and they consider active participation in social projects a welcome addition to their daily work. Various companies cooperate with non-profit organisations and/or local government to develop special exchange programmes for their employees.

Managers appear to gain much practical knowledge and experience from working for social organisations. The city functions in such projects as a training ground for gaining real-life experience (Kanter, 1989).

The Spatial Extent of a Local Community

The dimensions of a community of stakeholders can vary from a neighbourhood to the whole world (Goyder, 1998), as is apparent from the division proposed by Burke (1999), who has identified, inter alia, the internet community (the entire world) and the community of surrounding residents (the fenceline community). In contrast to the geographical community, Burke places the common-interest community, comprising people and organisations with similar interests. Interest organisations often try to influence geographically-oriented organisations (like local governments) by the lobby instrument. Actually, thematic interest organisations as a rule address a geographical target area, such as a local neighbourhood, a town, city, region, country or continent.

As explained, the size of the relevant region depends on the characteristics of the company and the markets in which it operates (labour markets and sales markets). Companies whose employees and customers are found in the direct vicinity are most ready to undertake initiatives at the neighbourhood level. Examples of such companies are bank branch offices, shops, and suppliers of low-grade services. Actually, almost all businesses have an interest in an attractive location that is easily accessible to employees and customers. Because the appeal and accessibility of a given location cannot be separated from those of the environment (think, for instance, of a backward region in the vicinity) and from the urban infrastructure, local interests on the neighbourhood level tend to reach beyond the company's direct surroundings.

Of large groups of companies it can be said that their employee and customer communities are at least equal to the region, which has consequences for their local involvement. Among them are to be found, for instance, suppliers of high-grade services (business and financial service providers), utility companies, and corporate headquarters. That type of company has an interest in an attractive city or region because they want to attract and retain highly educated and well paid employees. Moreover, they have their eyes on a wider sales market, which can be achieved by attracting residents, businesses and visitors. In 1981, the Federal Reserve Bank of New York observed that 'many [American] companies have begun to recognize the degree to which the quality of the living environment in the cities and the quality of infrastructure affect their own viability in the long run' (Brooks et al., 1984, pp. 9–10). Already in the 1960s, Baumol (1965) claimed that 'an unappealing environment can jeopardise the continuity of a company, for instance because it becomes harder to recruit the right kind of staff'.

The Limits of Local Involvement: Business Moves

The local involvement of businesses is not unlimited. Indeed, companies can at any time decide to move their activities to another region, so that the urban stakeholders in the 'exiting impact community' (Burke's (1999) terminology) suddenly lose much of their relevance. The underlying motives can be internal and business-like (merger, scale enlargement, etc.), but also external, such as an unappealing location or city. A company's local involvement depends in part on the opportunities and costs of moving, in other words, the degree of inertia. Businesses are apt to trade off the costs of a possible move against the advantages it would entail. Moreover, companies whose suppliers and customers are concentrated in a certain region will be less inclined to move than those that have (potential) primary stakeholders everywhere.

Globalisation, reinforced by innovation in the realm of information and communication technology (ICT), is subjecting more and more companies to a strong (worldwide) deconcentration of stakeholders. ICT enables companies to separate their divisions spatially. Moreover, relations with primary stakeholders can be more and more maintained with modern means of communication, through e-commerce (customers) or the employment of outworkers (staff). However, in several other relationships there is still, despite the digitisation of society, an urgent need for personal contacts. Face-to-face contacts remain vital in particular for so-called high-touch sectors such as fashion, design and art (Hall, 1995). Businesses that are active in these sectors set great store by a good relationship with the customer community, because for commercial success they must keep a close eye on new trends.

The Interests of Governments and other Non-profit Organisations

The previous section showed that companies have a significant measure of interest in a pleasant, accessible and well-organised city. In that respect they enter the domain of an actor whose primary concern is to create just such a city, namely, the (local) government.

Local governments are supposed to serve the general interest in a certain geographical area. First and foremost, local government defends the interests of inhabitants: the primary objective of a local government is to improve the well-being and prosperity of the residents in their city or region (see Van den Berg, Klaassen and Van der Meer, 1990). The interests of the inhabitants cannot, however, be separated from the interests of other actors in the region, such as companies and institutions (schools, hospitals and housing corporations, to name a few), and even actors outside the region, such as companies that are considering to settle in the region and people who visit the region (regularly). Residents naturally need employment (income) and services. In recent decades the notion has also gained credence that governments should also defend the interests of future generations, the children and grandchildren of the present inhabitants. All stakeholders have their own interests, which makes the general interest difficult to define in detail. Local governments mostly weigh the interests by means of the political, democratic mechanism (by the majority of votes cast in parliament). No wonder then that opinions of the exact objectives of local governments vary widely.

In this investigation we have assumed that local governments actively exert themselves for a city that appeals to residents, companies and visitors, and can withstand the increasing competition among cities that is ensuing from globalisation and the growing mobility of people and companies (Van den Berg, 1987; Bramezza, 1996; Van den Berg, Van der Meer and Otgaar, 2000). An attractive city is a city with a sound economy, good internal and external access, and a high-quality living environment (see Figure 2.3). Because the aspects of attraction can influence one another both positively and negatively, an integral approach is advisable (Van den Berg, Braun and Van der Meer, 1997). Since cities consist of neighbourhoods of mutual influence (for instance with regard to their image), most governments also aspire to spatial and social balance in the city. A lack of social cohesion can frustrate economic development. Local governments try therefore to use the fruits of economic growth to revitalise deprived neighbourhoods and fight against unemployment. Because cities are an integral part of the network in which they operate, the interests of governments do not stop at administrative borders: municipalities have an interest in a pleasant region just as regions benefit from an attractive country.

While employees and customers affect companies by way of the markets, governments can do so through rules, laws, subsidies and taxes.[1] With these instruments the government can stimulate, or even oblige, companies to act for the general interest (the government's interest) and to give evidence of local involvement.

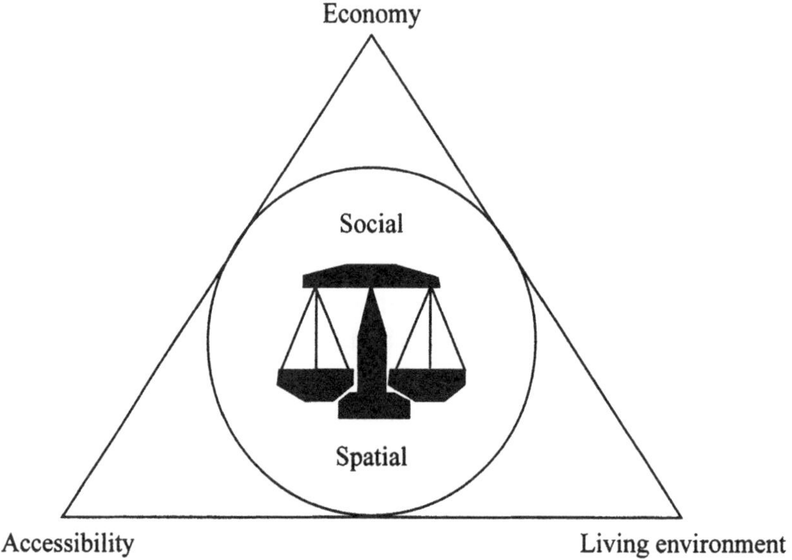

Figure 2.3 Sustainable urban development

Source: Van den Berg, Braun and Van der Meer, 1997, adapted by the authors.

Other Non-profit Organisations

Apart from the government and the private sector, many other organisations can be engaged in partnership for the sake of an attractive city. Think for instance of care providers, educational institutions, housing corporations, social security institutions, residents' associations, chambers of commerce, and fund raisers ('good causes'). The interests of these organisations are so divergent that they can hardly be described as one group. We can identify at least three groups: providers of social services and products, common-interest groups, and fund raisers. Mixed forms of these types of organisations are also possible, for instance a social agency which itself raises funds and lobbies government and private enterprise.

Providers of Social Products or Services

The first group among the 'other organisations' comprises institutions, associations and foundations that offer products and services with a social mission, in the sphere of education (schools, universities), care (hospitals, provisions for the homeless, care for drugs addicts) and housing (housing corporations). These organisations give priority to social above commercial objectives (such as making a profit). The organisations are often (partly) financed from public money (subsidies), but private financing constructions are possible too.

Many of these types of social institutions need to observe elements of policy drawn up by governments. Providers of social services are often under supervision of government, which is supposed to ensure that certain services are available to a certain target group at an acceptable price-quality ratio. For instance, housing corporations are sometimes obliged to provide accommodation first and foremost for the lower-income groups who cannot afford to buy a house. Social organisations are eminently interesting partners for cooperation in urban development and neighbourhood revitalisation.

Common-interest Groups

The second group consists of organisations that defend the interests of certain actors (in the city) and try to influence the policy of authorities, companies and other organisations by pressure or lobbying. Burke (1999) calls these organisations (common) interest groups. Some organisations defend all the interests of one particular group (residents' associations, neighbourhood societies, social security boards, chambers of commerce), others stand up for one specific aspect of 'the general wellbeing', for instance the environment, accessibility, or the urban economy. These organisations are financed privately from membership fees or donations.

Fund Raisers

The third group consists of organisations (mostly foundations) that raise funds for 'good causes'. They act as intermediaries between sponsors (companies, individuals) and social institutions (the 'good causes'). More and more great companies have set up their own foundations, which seek to combine corporate interests with charitable work.

The Road to Cooperation

The second section of this chapter analysed what type of companies have a specific interest in an appealing, accessible and well-organised city. From the observation that the interests of such companies accord with those of governments and other (non-profit) organisations that stand up for the city, the assumption is warranted that the same parties will in many situations also be interested in cooperation. The present describes the process towards partnerships and identifies the main success and failure factors in that process.

On the road to cooperation, several phases can be distinguished. Sanders (2000) recognised a life cycle of cooperative relations: they emerge, develop and terminate. Smith Ring and Van de Ven (1994) divide the birth phase into a stage of negotiation and one of contract. Our analysis refers mainly to the negotiation stage, inseparable though it may be from later stages. While a partnership is being negotiated, parties may include in their considerations possible future amendments of the contract in view of the results (evaluation). A distinction between the negotiation and the implementation stages was made implicitly by the Dutch Board for Domestic Administration (Raad voor Binnenlands Bestuur, 1987) in its advisory note on public-private partnerships, which distinguished conditions for the achievement of public-private partnerships (negotiation) from demands on the partnership itself (implementation). The Dutch State Planning Department (Rijksplanologische Dienst, 1993) identifies four steps: initiative, negotiation, implementation and administration. Klijn and Teisman (2000) name four almost identical phases: the orientation or initial phase, definition and preparation, development and implementation, and the exploitation and maintenance phase. Our attention focuses on the orientation phase that may lead to negotiations.

The first step towards the negotiation phase is that the parties concerned become aware of their motives, that is, their interests. Each party needs to recognise that a given situation (a problem or neglected opportunity) is not ideal for attaining the organisation's objectives. Preston, a consultant of the Royal Commission on Concentration in Canada, looks at the awareness (in his terms, 'awareness and recognition of an issue') of companies as the first step towards social involvement (Clarkson, 1995). Next, either party needs to realise the desirability of (actively) helping to solve the problem or seizing the opportunity, understanding that an investment of that kind is profitable (in the widest sense). Obviously, a partnership cannot be achieved unless the actors concerned understand that cooperation (some form of mutual adjustment, whether or not institutionalised) produces synergy. Naturally, organisations need to get in touch with one another before the actual negotiations start. The relevance of these pre-negotiation steps was confirmed by Fosler and Berger (1982), who subdivided the process towards public-private partnership into two phases: the creation of the right conditions for action, and the actual undertaking of action. One of the most important conditions is that people and organisations recognise the problem (or the opportunity) and go in search of means to 'do something about it'.

At the stage of negotiation, the parties jointly develop expectations about their motives and possible investments, and make an estimate of uncertainties (risks) involved in an agreement which they may conclude. Efforts are made to reduce uncertainties, and to formulate common objectives. At this stage, the participants assess the division of rights and obligations and the credibility of potential partners. Of course, all parties are guided in the negotiations by their own interests and their own objectives. The aspects that matter most are efficiency, effectiveness, usefulness and necessity. At this stage of commitment the wishes of the parties are laid down in agreements about the mutual cooperation, in a formal contract and/or an informal (psychological) contract. The implementation phase (the development phase) then follows, in which the commitments are translated into policy and action. Associates are instructed and practical matters implemented.

In *The Collaboration Challenge* – which focuses on partnerships between companies and non-profit organisations – Austin (2000) mentions three phases in the evolution of cross-sector relationships (the so-called cooperation continuum), phases which refer not so much to the birth as to the maturing of partnerships. In several examples the author describes how partnerships develop from pure charity (the company as donor and the non-profit organisation as recipient) through the transaction phase (in which the relation becomes more strategic and formal by cause-related marketing, sponsoring, licences and paid services) to the integration phase (organisations undertaking more and more joint action and beginning to integrate). Table 2.2 applies a number of criteria to describe the phases.

Our approach focuses on the more strategic partnerships at the transaction and integration stages. From Austin's book, this type of partnership makes considerably more demands on the partners than the purely charitable type. These demands have been included in the seven Cs of strategic cooperation[2] to which we refer in the analysis of success and failure factors that follows.

Economic Factors in the Coalition-forming Process

From a purely economic point of view, partnerships are born when two or more organisations become aware that collaboration is to their advantage. With traditional public-private partnerships (PPP), government(s) and one or more

Table 2.2 The cooperation continuum

Stage	Philanthropy	Transaction	Integration
Commitment	Low	→	High
Interest in mission	Peripheral	→	Strategic
Volume of means	Small	→	Large
Scope of activities	Narrow	→	Broad
Interaction	Incidental	→	Intensive
Management complexity	Simple	→	Complex
Strategic value	Modest	→	Large

Source: Austin, 2000.

companies, jointly strive to attain synergy between commercial and social objectives, so that social and economic added value ensues with both parties investing and sharing the risk. A characteristic of PPP is the expectation that added value will be created when public and private parties collaborate right from the planning stage. Both financial-economic and strategic motives play a role to that end (Krikke, Kooi and Schuur, 1999). Corporate community involvement brings about a more or less new form of PPP, since companies are waking up to their interest in social added value. For a traditional PPP the notion of 'value added' is defined in a narrower manner (often short-term and in financial terms) than for a social PPP.

Company Z considers participating in a public-private partnership aiming at a new city railway line. Now if the PPP is a traditional one, the company would regard its possible participation as a commercial investment, for which only the economic (commercial) added value counts. The company would be answerable only to its shareholders. Participation in a social PPP would be (also) a social investment enhancing the company's relations with customers, employees and other stakeholders. The company would then recognise its interest in an attractive and in particular an accessible city and content itself with a lower or even negative commercial return on its investment. Evidently, even for a social PPP, the company has to answer to its shareholders. In theory, however, shareholders also benefit from good relations with other stakeholders.

An important condition for cooperation is synergy. A partnership can be achieved only if all parties understand that they need the other actors. Partnerships require that the parties recognise their mutual dependence (Stone, 1989). Austin (2000) proposes that the creation of value (one of the seven Cs) should be to the benefit of both organisations, and that there must be a sort of balance. With a social PPP, the creation of added value for the company will often consist of improvement of the environment, which can ultimately (in the long run) yield commercial benefits.

Economic Motives for Collaboration

Several economic motives for collaboration come to mind, most of which can be reduced to economies of scale and scope, or the exchange of knowledge and expertise (economies of skill). Local governments can be said to have an interest in collaboration with the private sector, not only to obtain extra resources (financial contributions, human resources), but also and predominantly on account of knowledge and expertise (Gribling, Van Vliet and Go, 1999; Cahn, 1999). Because cities are increasingly confronted with changes, diversity, fragmentation and a lack of consensus, the need for partnership grows, especially between government and non-public organisations (among which are commercial companies) (Miller, 1998). The cooperative willingness of local governments depends among other things on the number of problems and the size of the available budgets. In the Netherlands, some cities do not feel a strong drive to work together with the private sector because they receive funds from the national government (via the large cities policy, among others) to fight most of their problems. Besides, the government's level of aspiration influences the economic necessity of cooperation.

Companies have an interest in cooperation with the public sector because the government is responsible for the general interest (and thus for the integral approach) (Brooks et al., 1984), and itself possesses knowledge, expertise, (financial) resources, access to networks, and political and legislative power. Admittedly the local government is to many companies not a primary stakeholder, but as a prominent secondary stakeholder crucial for the relationship with primary stakeholders (customers, employees, suppliers). Private enterprise, according to Austin (2000), seeks cooperation with other sectors ('cross-sector collaboration') to enrich its strategy (it enhances relations with stakeholders and conveys to them a strong image); to manage human resources (cooperation is helpful in attracting and retaining employees as well as adding to their capabilities), to reinforce the corporate culture and to generate business (expansion of the core business through networks and access to new markets). Naturally, the drive for profit will always be the main motive of companies (Klijn and Teisman, 2000). In addition, partnerships can generate external resources which otherwise might not have been made available to any individual partner, partners can learn from one another about the nature of the problems and their potential role in that respect, and consider new ways to solve them (Miller, 1998). Bryson and Crosby (1992) claim that knowledge and power need to be shared because no single organisation (public or private) can identify and solve all social and economic problems.

According to Bartelsman, Canoy, Van Ewijk and Vollaard (1998), cooperation is advisable when there is a combination of failing government and failing market, in other words, when neither market nor government can make optimum provision for certain (social) needs. A public-private partnership is useful only when the partners recognise that they cannot leave the production to one party (Klijn and Teisman, 2000). The (former) Netherlands' Minister of Finance, Mr Zalm (1998), emphasised that the economic motive for public-private partnership is not cheaper financing (nobody lends cheaper than the government!) but efficiency and the creation of added value by letting parties do what they are good at. Added value can be created only when both parties take risks upon themselves. Grant (1996) mentions some economic fundamental conditions for public-private partnership: shared authority and responsibility, joint investments, shared risks and accountability, and mutual advantages.

Return Requirements

The assumption that corporate community involvement (whether or not achieved by partnership) is a matter of self-interest does not imply that companies will automatically agree to any proposal to participate in a social project. The expectation is rather that companies – in particular for large investments – will make demands on the return. Whether a company is willing to take part in a project depends on a minimum of two – closely related – factors. First, the way the return is calculated, and second, the degree to which the company is prepared to accept a lower return than that typical of a purely commercial investment.

There are several methods to calculate the return on an investment. To treat them in detail would be beyond the scope of this book. The observation is warranted, however, that the method used and the assumptions made affect the results. Think, for instance, of the difference between short- and long-term results, of the way to deal with non-financial consequences of investments, which in the long term may indeed have financial effects. The balanced score card method, for example, does take into account that value added to non-financial assets may ultimately – through a chain of cause and effect relations – raise the financial value (Huselid, 1995; Becker and Huselid, 1998). Investments that aim at an attractive, accessible and socially balanced city can in our view generate chain reactions that are profitable to all those involved, including private enterprise. From that philosophy, companies should be concerned not only about the commercial return on their investment, but first and foremost about the social return (the measure to which problems are successfully solved or opportunities seized). However, convincing businesses that in the long run they will reap the fruits of their investment is not always easy. Uncertainty about the future effects (and the development of the economy) and the need at the same time to meet the short-term profitability demands of shareholders, can in certain cases persuade companies not to invest in certain social projects.

The investment decision is furthermore affected by the willingness to accept lower profits (even in the long term) than can be made from normal commercial investments. The corporate culture and the personal convictions of the people (norms and values) play in that respect an undeniable role. More about that in the section on cultural, psychological, political and social factors.

Legal Framework

Naturally, social public-private partnerships, like the more traditional forms of PPP, need to observe the rules which national and supranational authorities (such as those of the European Union) impose. The Dutch Board for Domestic Administration (Raad voor het Binnenlands Bestuur, 1987) ruled that public-private partnership must operate within the law and that the rights of third parties (for instance non-participating companies) must be protected. The report 'Meer Waarde door Samenwerken' (added value through collaboration) of the Project Bureau for Public-Private Partnership (Projectbureau Publiek-Private Samenwerking, 1998), states that the government must play fair: 'That implies that the government must terminate participation as soon as the activity developed means the threat of competition with other private parties'. Fair play is also the key word for the selection of partners. Projects of certain dimensions are bound to the European rules for tender. These rules may hamper public-private cooperation because they offer insufficient protection when it comes to proposing innovative and creative solutions.

Cultural, Psychological, Political and Social Factors in the Coalition-forming Process

The financial-economic conditions for a public-private partnership are necessary but not sufficient for success. No less important are the cultural, psychological, political and social factors, which derive their weight from the fact that organisations after all consist of people. In the analysis to follow below, we assume that the success and failure factors of traditional public-private partnerships are to a certain extent valid for the social variant as well. The case studies reveal how far that assumption is correct. We also point out some factors that are specifically applicable to the social form of public-private cooperation.

Awareness

People are by no means always aware of their own interests or those of others. According to Austin (2000), the participating parties need to expand their horizons. They must not suffer from 'gratefulness and charity syndromes'. One problem that may arise is that some company managers do not have the right idea about the (local) social interests of their company. They regard corporate community involvement as a form of ethics and not as a matter of self-interest. That vision results mostly in a reactionary or defensive strategy. Another point is that there may be diverging opinions on the interests within the organisations, as a result of which there is too little support for participation in social projects.

The next point to keep in mind is that the parties involved need to recognise a certain situation as a problem (or an obvious opportunity). Parties would be well advised to have the point high on their list of priorities. A shared opportunity or threat can increase the propensity to cooperate significantly (Van den Berg, Braun and Van der Meer, 1997). Of course, the parties may try to convince one another of particular interests. The efforts of common-interest groups to get certain themes higher on the (political) agenda may be crucial in that respect.

Trust

Owing to cultural differences among organisations and the possible ensuing lack of mutual trust, common interests sometimes do not result in cooperation. A primary condition for the birth of public-private partnerships is mutual trust and a good relationship between government and private enterprise (Raad voor het Binnenlands Bestuur, 1987; Borys and Jamison, 1989; Kouwenhoven, 1991). Trust is indispensable because of the long-term character of partnerships and the risks involved (Klijn and Teisman, 2000). Grant (1996) suggests that government officers and the people of the private sector must 'hit it off'. Some primary conditions for the formation and progress of coalitions are informal networks, solidarity, loyalty, trust and support (Miller, 1998).

Because the actors are different organisations with divergent cultures, mutual trust is often questionable. Companies tend to have little trust in government because of its lack of experience with business-wise partnerships. Kanter (1999) points out that the institutional infrastructure of the social sector is underdeveloped by private standards. He compares state or municipal schools and inner cities with 'emerging markets'. Companies are also naturally afraid of changes that can be brought about by political shifts. As defender of the general welfare, the government has to make continuous trade-offs between a multitude of interests, and therefore cannot readily commit itself (Bartelsman et al., 1998). Many companies complain about the bureaucracy of government. Sometimes their criticism is justified when the government is indeed unnecessarily slow on account of too much fragmentation and a surfeit of procedures. Sometimes, however, the criticism is due to lack of understanding on the part of the companies for the complex political trade-offs the authorities inevitably have to make.

Commitment

Kanter (1999) emphasises the importance of commitment as one of the factors for successful public-private partnerships One case study shows that IBM made demands on the commitment of the government in the selection of test areas for the so-called Reinventing Education Initiative. The company set much store by the personal support of the mayor, and went in search of school districts where those involved were willing to think along creative and modern lines. Commitment implies not only a show of goodwill, but also willingness to invest human resources as well as money. Moreover organisations should preferably display 'sustainable commitment', in other words, willingness to anticipate changes and accept risks (Kanter, 1999). Municipal authorities have to convince business that the commitment of the municipality will survive any political shift. Companies on their part have to explain to the authorities that a cut in their profits does not instantly mean the end of the partnership.

According to Austin (2000), commitment can be stimulated by explicitly evaluating the (social) effects, giving partners an incentive to put additional energy into enhancing the impact. However, the expectations of the partners must be realistic, or else disappointing results may invoke mutual distrust. Organisations also need to be aware of their collaboration capacity, that is, their ability to manage partnerships.

The importance of mutual trust is notably manifest at the contract stage. The factors then at work with traditional forms of PPP must not be underestimated either with the social forms. Brooks et al. (1984) pleaded for laying down clear rules for the relationship (a traditional PPP) that cannot be manipulated by one of the parties. That calls for a fair measure of trust in the agreements, between the parties as well as among third parties who are likely to feel the effects of the programme. The contract should moreover be clear about the desired return on investment (in commercial and social respects) and about its measurement. Gribbling, Van Vliet and Go (1999) recommend agreement about responsibilities, allocation of tasks, risks and returns in (traditional) PPPs for the sake of metropolitan area development. According to Klijn and Teisman (2000), the objectives of partnerships are integrated ambitions, rules for interaction, the creation of commitment, and reward for collaboration. For the proper observance of the contract agreements and to prevent skewed information, the exchange of data is indispensable (Bartelsman et al., 1998). Relational transparency is required not only with a view to mutual trust (the willingness to share knowledge and expertise), but also to gain the confidence from politicians and society. Lack of transparency can undermine confidence in the government and the principles of the free market (Klijn and Teisman, 2000). Thus, the Dutch State Planning Department (1993) recommended attention to good communication with the municipal council. In practice the municipal grassroots are inadequately regarded as a separate target group for communication. All too often the communication is limited to a small circle of direct initiators. The department stresses the importance of obtaining commitment from the grassroots (and in particular the council) right from the initiating stage by conscious interaction and positive image building.

The complexity of public-private collaboration (whether or not in the framework of corporate social responsibility) is an obstacle to obtaining commitment. There are many who have given thought to the unravelling of that complexity (notably with respect to traditional forms of PPP) (see Klijn and Teisman, 2000). One way is to specify the content of the project at an early stage, to create transparency for all parties. In that way, risks become easier to identify and thus control. However, since many projects run for a long time, early registration of the content tends to be more difficult and less meaningful than might be hoped. Another possible instrument, that of laying down procedures, has the disadvantage of making the public sector seem dominant, which may scare off private parties. A third option, split responsibilities, indeed makes for simplification, but often also reduces the sharing of knowledge, which is precisely a great advantage of public-private partnership. The primary object of PPP should be to remove obstacles and abolish the strict separation of the public and private sectors, but unfortunately many such partnerships end up raising new barriers. Klijn and Teisman (2000) argue that project management often pins down lots of things and lays down many rules, thus seriously constraining the very flexibility and expansion of responsibilities that are the prime object of the enterprise. The same authors argue for combining the good features of project management with a form of process management. The same line of thought is followed by Austin (2000), who regards a partnership as an ongoing learning process.

Communication

An important condition for mutual trust is that participants communicate well with one another. Local governments must not invite the impression of only approaching private enterprise for money. Common-interest organisations tend to address companies reminding them of their moral duties, while to point at their self-interest would probably be more effective. Sometimes, it is wiser to speak of opportunities than of problems, since business companies dislike being associated with unpleasant matters. The communication between partners must be honest, direct, frequent and meaningful (Austin, 2000). The Dutch State Planning Department (1986) pointed out the importance of partners knowing and understanding their mutual objectives, interests and risk profiles. Mutual respect is according to Zaat (1986) a must for a successful public-private partnership. From case studies, many (Dutch) municipalities seem to have a stereotyped idea of the private sector. Many civil servants and politicians seem wary of the business motive, which is frankly to make profit. Government, non-profit organisations and non-governmental organisations are apt to mistrust commercial motives (Kanter, 1999).

In practice, there are ethical limits to the local involvement of business companies. These limits depend on culture. Especially in Europe, society as well as the government are wary of too much intervention of private enterprise. In the Netherlands, sponsoring of schools and hospitals is hardly if at all accepted, while in the USA it is very common. Governments would do well to take account of such ethical and political limits, since broad social and political support is a condition for a successful project. Moreover it is advisable for the governments to communicate these limits clearly to companies, so that they, too, know what is and what is not feasible.

Leadership

To obtain support from organisations, and to remove barriers between them, leadership is indispensable. Leadership is one of the crucial elements in organising capacity. We have defined organising capacity as the talent to get actors together for the sake of exchanging ideas, and developing and implementing policy (Van den Berg, Braun and Van der Meer, 1997). Bennett and Krebs (1991) agree that to get the actors 'in line' makes high demands on the effectiveness of leadership. In their view, leaders have to exert themselves to animate the development process. That process consists of the following steps: to identify problems, to identify objectives and action domains, to develop activities and projects, and the evaluation. The animation comprises the following elements (see Figure 2.3): 1) identification of the actors and organisations that influence a given development (in other words, carrying out a stakeholder analysis); 2) bringing actors together; 3) allocating suitable roles for the actors; 4) specification of performance targets for each actor (matching targets to roles leads to an audit of best practices); 5) effective leadership. Partnerships often combine top-down and bottom-up approaches. A successful collaboration calls for sensible animation at all stages of the development process. At every stage, the relevant actors should be involved, by means of effective relationships and clearly formulated roles and performance targets.

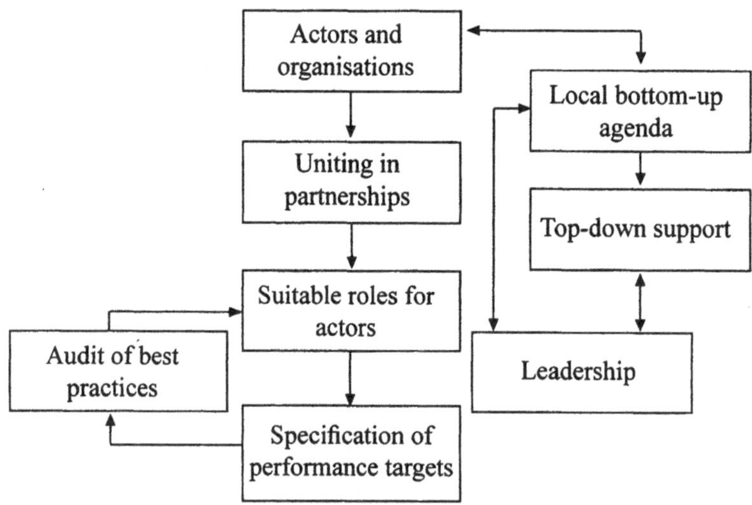

Figure 2.4 The animation of the development process

Source: Bennett and Krebs, 1991.

Austin (2000, p. 174) accentuates the importance of leadership for the 'connection with purpose and people', in other words, to make people feel connected to the social objective and to one another: 'The engagement of and relationships between top leaders of the corporation and the nonprofit largely determine the acceptance and vigor of the collaboration.' Leadership is necessary to activate and coordinate networks and to inspire people; it is also a necessary condition for obtaining social and political support (Van den Berg, Braun and Van der Meer, 1997). There is a real danger that common interests do not result in a joint project merely because none of the actors believes it is up to him to take the initiative, the excuse being 'if you do nothing, then neither will we'. In fact what we have here is a kind of prisoner's dilemma, whose resolution requires good leadership. From investigating a great number of Dutch partnerships arising from corporate community involvement, B&A-Groep (2001) found that companies take the initiative more frequently (88 per cent) than municipalities (8 per cent) and municipal agencies (11 per cent). Sometimes the initiative is taken jointly (11 per cent). Before approaching a municipality, companies mostly already have a fair idea of what the project should be. Naturally, they prefer projects that are directly relevant to their own continuity. The investigation of B&A-Groep shows that by far the most initiatives are oriented to labour-market entry (for specific groups). So municipalities would do well to adopt a more active attitude, inducing companies to participate also in other types of project concerned with care, education and safety. Municipalities should make themselves more familiar with the social and commercial interests of business companies. From that familiarity, local government can effectively take the initiative and put a certain theme on the agenda, and then set out to gather the relevant actors around it.

Vision Development

One task which leaders must undertake is to develop a joint vision. Austin (2000) mentions 'clarity of purpose' as a success factor of a strategic partnership. The partners need to set forth clearly what they expect from the partnership. The ambition levels of the parties involved must not be too divergent. For the congruence of mission, strategy and values it is vital that the partners share a future vision of the partnership. The more the objective of the partnership is in harmony with the missions and strategies of the partners, the more sustainable the alliance will be even if one or more partners get into trouble.

A requirement for drawing up a joint vision is that either party has a vision of its own. For local government's vision, Van den Berg, Braun and Van der Meer (1997) considered integrality of the essence, since the different aspects of sustainable development (economic growth, accessibility, and living environment) cannot be separated. Ideally, the vision should be based on the strong points of the city in comparison to other locations (the relative position); it should reflect the ambitions and objectives of the city, constitute a source of inspiration for other actors in the urban region, and be the basis for municipal policy. Moreover, the vision should preferably have been developed in consultation with other parties (investors, companies, residents, interest groups, etc.), to secure sufficient support for the municipal policy. Because companies increasingly want to deal strategically with their social investments – for instance by making demands on the social return – we assume that urban governments with clear and well-founded plans have the best chances of a successful appeal to the private sector's local involvement. A good vision distinguishes itself not only by an integral approach, but also by a regional approach, since many problems transcend the municipal border (think of housing, infrastructure and employment).

Summary

Fundamental developments are causing a change in corporate interests. Companies are being stimulated by external incentives to conduct their business in a socially responsible manner. Increasingly, companies are waking up to the fact that the care for people and environment must not be separated from the drive for profit and continuity. A balanced approach to the triple-p bottom line (people, planet, profit) implies a shift from traditional, ad hoc philanthropy to strategic and structural forms of social involvement, with a wakeful eye for the social as well as commercial profitability, in a broad sense. Corporate community involvement can put companies with a proactive approach at a competitive advantage.

Activities that come under the flag of corporate community involvement can be related to certain stakeholders (customers, employees, suppliers, financiers), to certain themes (education, employment, infrastructure, environment), and to certain geographical regions (neighbourhood, city, country). The way companies commit themselves socially depends strongly on the qualitative and quantitative characteristics of the companies and the markets (labour market, customer market) in which they operate.

These characteristics determine also to what degree a company has an interest in an attractive city and region, with a good spatial and social balance between economic growth, accessibility and quality of the living environment. Companies that have and recognise a (partial) interest of that kind, should in theory feel driven to cooperate with other organisations standing up for an appealing city and region, or an element of it. Such organisations are not only local governments, but also social organisations dedicated to a certain geographical area or theme, or providing certain social services.

In the process towards cross-sector collaboration, several phases can be distinguished. Our attention goes out first and foremost to the phases related to the process of coalition forming, of which the central elements are 'awareness building' (parties recognise a problem and the need for cooperation); 'initiation', 'bringing together' (people and organisations), 'negotiation' (about the form of partnership) and 'activation' (actually give form and content to the partnership). This process is presented schematically in Figure 2.5.

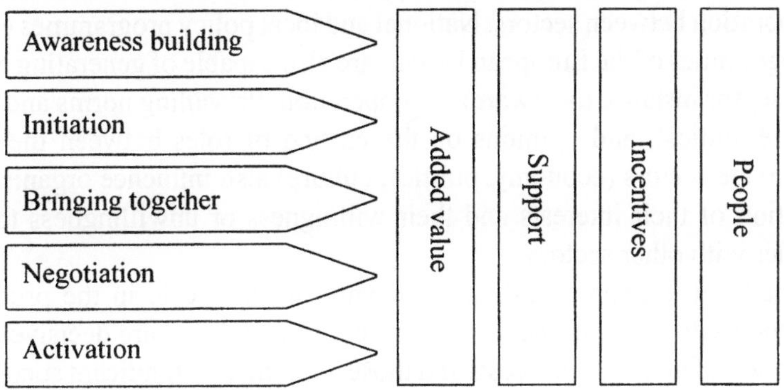

Figure 2.5 The process of coalition forming

Every element in this process has its own success and failure factors. Some factors have a prominent part in the entire process. From the literature, we can identify a whole range of financial, organisational, legal, cultural, social, ethical, psychological and political success and failure factors in the process of coalition building. In our view, however, four factors are the most important: added value, support, incentives and people.

First, collaboration must be in the interests of all organisations involved. Value added (synergy) can develop from scale advantages and the exchange of knowledge and expertise. The social interests, notably of business companies, are related to the relevant stakeholders and communities, which vary by company and sector. Participants make demands on the return to be gained from the initiatives and projects. The parties' estimates of the returns is a factor of great weight.

Second, collaboration can take off only when within the organisations there is a broad support for the plans and when most of them are conscious of the interests involved. Another condition is that the projects and initiatives can count on social support, notably among the stakeholders who will be affected. Negative image building around the collaboration can put its continuity in jeopardy.

Third, the creation of partnerships cannot be separated from local economic, political, legal and cultural circumstances. Legal regulations (taxes, subsidies, restrictions, etc.) can on the one hand inspire parties to a broader definition of their interests and to enter into partnership with other parties, and on the other hand hamper collaboration for instance as a result of red tape and restrictions. The term 'local' can refer to different geographical scales (European Union, country, state, region, city). Local opportunities and threats often stimulate collaboration between sectors. National and local policy programmes (as well as programmes of the European Union) are also capable of generating such an impulse, for instance by rewarding cooperation. Prevailing norms and values (culture, ethics), and opinions on the casting of roles between the public and private sectors (economy, politics, culture) also influence organisations' definition of their interests and their willingness or unwillingness to work together with other sectors.

Finally, it is people (individuals) who turn the scale in the process of coalition building. Their personal convictions and views are decisive for the perception of their own interests and those of partners. Significant success and failure factors in that connection are trust in the partner organisations, long-term commitment, the ability to communicate with coalition partners (mutual respect and understanding), leadership (taking the initiative, bringing people together), and the capacity to put an effective vision and strategy on the table.

Notes

1 For some companies (for instance Boeing; see Chapter 9) the government is at the same time a customer (as buyer of services and products), so that it exerts its influence through the market as well.

2 The seven Cs are: connection with purpose and people; clarity of purpose; congruency of mission; strategy and values; creation of value; communication between partners; central learning; and commitment to the partnership.

References

Austin, J.E. (2000), *The Collaboration Challenge; How Non-Profits and Businesses Succeed Through Strategic Alliances*, The Drucker Foundation, Jossey-Bass Publishers, San Francisco.

B&A-Groep (2001), *Maatschappelijk verantwoord ondernemen, een onderzoek naar praktijkervaringen,* Vereniging van Nederlandse Gemeenten (VNG).

Bartelsman, E.J., M. Canoy, C. van Ewijk and B.A. van Vollaard (1998), 'Economie van publiek-private samenwerking', EBS-Dossier PPS.

Baumol, W. (1965), *Welfare Economics and the Theory of the State*, rev. 2nd edn, Harvard University Press, Cambridge, MA.

Becker, B. and M.A. Huselid (1998), 'High Performance Work Systems and Firm Performance: A Synthesis of Research and Managerial Implications', *Research in Personnel and Human Resources Management*, Vol. 16, pp. 53–10.

Bennet, R.J. and G. Krebs (1991), *Local Economic Development: Public-private Partnership Initiatives in Britain and Germany*, Belhaven Press, London.

Berg, L. van den (1987), *Urban Systems in a Dynamic Society*, Gower Publishing Company, Aldershot.

Berg, L. van den, E. Braun and J. van der Meer (1997), *Metropolitan Organising Capacity: Experiences with Organising Major Projects in European Cities*, Ashgate, Aldershot.

Berg, L. van den, E. Braun, J. van der Meer and A.H.J. Otgaar (1999), *De binnenstadseconomie in de eenentwintigste eeuw*, EURICUR, Rotterdam, NL.

Berg, L. van den, J. van der Meer and A.H.J. Otgaar (2000), *The Attractive City: Catalyst for Economic Development and Social Revitalisation*, EURICUR, Rotterdam.

Berg, L. van den, L.H. Klaassen and J. van der Meer (1990), *Strategische City-Marketing*, Bedrijfskundige signalementen 90/3, Academic Service, Schoonhoven.

Borys, B. and D.B. Jemison (1989), Hybrid Arrangements as Strategic Alliances: Theoretical Issues in Organizational Combinations, *Academy of Management Review*, Vol. 14, No. 2, pp. 234–49.

Boudhan, B., I. Vonk and F. Nelissen (1996), *Maatschappelijk Ondernemen; Dienen en verdienen,* Stichting Maatschappij en Onderneming, Informatief, SMO-96-5.

Bowen, H.R. (1953), *Social Responsibilities of the Businessman*, Harper & Row, New York.

Bramezza, I. (1996), *The Competitiveness of the European City and the Role of Urban Management in Improving the City's Performance: The Cases of the Central Veneto and Rotterdam Regions*, Proefschrift, Erasmus Universiteit Rotterdam, Thesis Publishers, Amsterdam.

Brooks, H., L. Liebman and C.S. Schelling (1984), *Public-private Partnership: New Opportunities for Meeting Social Needs*, American Academy of Arts and Sciences, Ballinger, Cambridge, MA.

Bryson, J. en B. Crosby (1992), *Leadership for the Common Good: Tackling Public Problems in a Shared Power World*, Jossey-Bass, San Francisco.

Burke, E.M. (1999), *Corporate Community Relations; The Principle of the Neighbor of Choice*, Quorum Books, Westport.

Cahn, A. (1999), *PPPs Risk Management for Big Transport Projects*, Spanish Ministry of Civil Works and The Spanish Railway Foundation.

Carroll, A.B. (1979), 'A Three Dimensional Conceptual Model of Corporate Social Performance',

Academy of Management Review, Vol. 4, pp. 497–505.
Carroll, A.B. (1999), 'Corporate Social Responsibility; Evolution of a Definitional Construct', *Business and Society*, Vol. 38, pp. 268–93.
Chatham House Forum Report (1996), 'Unsettled Times', p. 9.
Clarkson, M.B.E. (1995), 'A Stakeholder Framework for Analysing and Evaluating Corporate Social Performance', in M.B.E. Clarkson (ed.), *The Corporation and its Stakeholders: Classic and Contemporary Reading*, University of Toronto Press, Toronto, pp. 243–74.
Davis, K. (1960), 'Can Business afford to Ignore Social Responsibilities?', *California Management Review*, Vol. 2, pp. 70–76.
Davis, K. and R.L. Blomstrom (1966), *Business and its Environment*, McGrawHill, New York.
Douma, S. and J. Eppink (1996), *Ondernemingsstrategie*, Kluwer, Deventer.
European Foundation for Management Development (1981), 'Facing Realities', p. 14.
Eilbert, H. and I.R. Parket (1973), 'The Current Status of Corporate Social Responsibility', *Business Horizons*, Vol. 16, pp. 5–14.
Elkington, J. (1997), *Cannibals With Forks; The Triple Bottom Line of 21st Century Business*, Capstone, Oxford.
Fosler, R.S. and R.A. Berger (1982), *Public-private Partnership in American Cities: Seven Case Studies*, Lexington Books, Lexington, MA.
Friedman, M. (1970), 'The Social Responsibility of Business is to Increase Its Profits', *New York Times Magazine*, 13 September, pp. 122–6.
Funck, R.H. (1995), 'Competition among Locations', in E. Giersch (ed.), *Urban Agglomeration and Economic Growth*, Springer Verlag, Berlin, pp. 227–56.
Goyder, M. (1998), *Living Tomorrow's Company*, Gower, Aldershot.
Grant, T. (1996), 'Keys to Successful Public-private Partnerships', *Canadian Business Review*, Vol. 3, pp. 27–8.
Gribling, M., M. van Vliet and F. Go (1999), 'Ondernemend besturen: Publiek-private samenwerking bij toeristische flagship projecten', Management Report No. 26-1999, Erasmus University Rotterdam.
Hall, P. (1995), 'Towards a General Urban Theory', in J. Brotchie, M. Batty, E. Blakely, P. Hall and P. Newton (eds), *Cities in Competition: Productive and Sustainable Cities for the 21st Century*, Longman Australia, Melbourne.
Huselid, M.A. (1995), 'The Impact of Human Resources Management Practices on Turnover, Productivity, and Corporate Financial Performance', *Academy of Management Journal*, pp. 635–72.
Kanter, R.M. (1999), 'From Spare Change to Real Change', *Harvard Business Review*, 1 May, pp. 122–32.
Karake-Shalhoub, Z.A. (1999), *Organizational Downsizing, Discrimination, and Corporate Social Responsibility*, Quorum Books, Westport.
Klijn, E-H. and G.R. Teisman (2000), 'Appearances of Public Private Partnerships; PPP as Governance Arrangement and the Management Problems', paper for the International Research Seminar on Public Management in Rotterdam.
Kouwenhoven, V.P. (1991), *Publiek-private samenwerking: Mode of Model?*, Eburon, Delft.
Krikke, H.R., E.J. Kooi and P.C. Schuur (1999), *Network Design in Reverse Logistics: OR-model Building in View of Practical Developments*, Springer Verlag, Berlin.
Logan, D. and M. Tuffrey (1999), *Companies in Communities; Valuing the Contribution*, The Corporate Citizenship Company, Charities Aid Foundation, Kent.
Miller, C. (1998), 'Partners in Regeneration: Constructing a Local Regime for Urban

Management?', *Policy and Politics*, Vol. 27, No. 3, pp. 343–58.

Porter, M.E. (1985), *Competitive Advantage: Creating and Sustaining Superior Performance*, The Free Press, New York.

Post, J.E., A.T. Lawrence and J. Weber (1999), *Business and Society; Corporate Strategy, Public Policy, Ethics*, Irwin/McGraw-Hill.

Projectbureau Publiek-Private Samenwerking (Project Bureau for Public-Private Partnership) (1999), 'Meer Waarde door Samen Werken' ('More Value Through Collaboration'), Final Report, Ministry of Finance, NL.

Raad voor het Binnenlands Bestuur (Board for Domestic Administration) (1987), *Partners voor vernieuwing: advies over public-private partnership*, The Hague.

Reich, R.B. (1998), 'The New Meaning of Corporate Social Responsibility', *California Management Review*, Vol. 40, No. 2, pp. 8–17.

Rijksplanologische Dienst (The State Planning Department) (1993), 'Communicatie bij stedelijke vernieuwing; de toren van Babel', De Lijn, The Hague.

Sanders, G. (2000), *Spelen met doelen en kansen; Over het creëren van partnerships en de lessen die hieruit zijn te trekken*, Rijksuniversiteit Groningen, NL.

Smith Ring, P. and A.H. van de Ven (1994), 'Developmental Processes of Cooperative Interorganizational Relationships', *The Academy of Management Review*, Vol. 19, No. 1, pp. 90–118.

Stegman, M.A. and M.A. Turner (1996) 'The Future of Urban America in the Global Economy', *Journal of the American Planning Assocation*, Vol. 62, No. 2, Spring, pp. 157–64.

Stone, C. (1989), *Regime Politics: Governing Atlanta, 1946–88*, University of Kansas Press, Lawrence, KA.

Waal, S.P.M. de (2000), 'Nieuwe strategieën voor het publieke domein; maatschappelijk ondernemen in de praktijk', Samson, Alphen aan den Rijn.

Waal, S.P.M. de, Th.N.M. Schuyt and P.A. Verveen (eds) (1994), *Handboek Maatschappelijk Ondernemerschap*, Bohn Stafleu Van Loghum, Houten/Zaventem.

Wempe. J. and M. Kaptein (2000), *Ondernemen met het oog op de toekomst; integratie van economische, sociale en ecologische verantwoordelijkheden*, Stichting Maatschappij en Onderneming, The Hague, NL.

Zaat, L.M.S. (1986), 'Private View on Public Private Partnerships', note.

Zalm, G. (1998), *Publiek-private samenwerking: meer waarde door samenwerking.* Ministerie van Financien, Centrale Directie Voorlichting, The Hague.

Discussion Partners

S. Bleker, Deloitte & Touche

R. Boelen, Regional Managing Partner, Deloitte & Touche

C.F.W.J. van der Born, Executive Vice President, Human Resources Management, ABN-AMRO Bank

A.M. Daane, Director of the ASN Bank

L.J. van den Dries, Deloitte & Touche

J. Feijtel, WoonPlus Foundation, Schiedam

F.H. Fiechter, Head Marketing and Advise, ASN Bank

J.E. Jansen, Manager Social Strategy, SNS Reaal Groep
P. Klop, Accountant, Deloitte & Touche
T. Mallenberg, Netherlands Ministry of Health, Welfare and Sport
M.N.A. van Marrewijk, Centrum voor Kwaliteit, Duurzaamheid en Innovatie (Centre for Quality, Sustainability and Innovation)
J. Mes, Director Corporate Strategy, Nuon
E. Post, Deloitte & Touche Bakkenist
C. de Reuver, Deloitte & Touche, ICS
R.J. Rubenstein, Rotterdam School of Management
W.E.C. Scheepens, Corporate Communications / Brand & Reputation Management, ABN-AMRO Bank
W.J. Scheper, Management & ICT Consultant, Deloitte & Touche
R. Slot, Deloitte & Touche Bakkenist
A.L.C. Smit, Social Investment, Shell Nederland
K.M. van Steensel, Stichting Maatschappij en Onderneming (Foundation Community and Enterprise)
C.C.L.M. Stevens, Alderman City of Amstelveen
J.B. Ventevogel, Chairman, OmslagGroep
T. van der Vondervoort, Deloitte & Touche
R.R. de Vos, Project Leader Social Return, Department of Social Affairs and Employment Projects, City of The Hague

Chapter 3

The Netherlands

Introduction

In the Netherlands, the attention to corporate community involvement[1] is undeniably growing, as is evident from the increasing number of publications, conventions, reports and news articles on this topic. Furthermore, various networks and platforms have been erected to facilitate the exchange of knowledge and experience concerning corporate responsibilities and interests.[2]

This chapter presents a selection of community projects and active companies in the field of corporate social responsibility in the Netherlands. First, we analyse the policies and initiatives of four large firms in the Netherlands. Next, we discuss the neighbourhood development projects initiated by the consultation platform for urban renewal, in which several companies participate. The next section introduces the ArenA Initiative which is considered one of the most successful Dutch examples of public-private collaboration ensuing from corporate community involvement. The final section concludes.

Policies and Initiatives of Dutch Firms

This section analyses the corporate community involvement of the following companies: electronics concern Philips, financial services provider Rabobank, employment organisation Randstad and oil concern Shell.

Philips

That corporate community involvement is not something new, can be clearly illustrated by the history of electronics concern Philips. Since its foundation at the end of the nineteenth century, the company has put its stamp on the development of Eindhoven (at the time no more than a village) into the fifth city of the Netherlands. The nickname 'city of lights' refers directly to the original incandescent lamps factory. At present, Eindhoven puts itself forward as the high-tech centre of the Netherlands, thanks not only to Philips but also to its extensive cluster of suppliers, customers and knowledge institutions. The Philips Sportvereniging (PSV, Philips Sports Association) and the Philips Stadium prove that in terms of sports, too, Philips determines life in Eindhoven.

At the end of the 1990s, the decision of the management to move the head office to Amsterdam seemed to indicate a breach between city and company. But so far, there has been no question of that. In terms of research and development, Eindhoven is still 'the place to be'. Headquarters were moved to Amsterdam to be near the stock exchange and the creative industry (Philips having become aware that consumers do not just look at techniques but also at design). The decision confirms the trend of business units to follow their own location process. As a matter of fact, Philips has some 30 factories throughout the Netherlands. Prominent ones are the units in Nijmegen (production of semi-conductors, the greatest chips factory in Europe), Drachten (electric shavers), Roosendaal (fluorescent lamps) and Best (medical systems).[3]

The Philips Employment Scheme

One of the more recent activities of Philips that can be related to corporate community involvement is the Philips employment scheme (Philips, 2000). With this project the company creates employment with other businesses in the regions where its units are established. The initiative was taken in the 1980s after government, employers and employees had agreed to keep a restraint on wages and redistribute the available employment (for instance, by shortening working hours).

Originally, the plan (which started as a youth employment scheme) aimed at fighting unemployment among school-leavers by guiding them to paid jobs (not at Philips) through work experience and schooling. The scheme appeared quite successful, with an inflow of 700 school-leavers in the first year. In 1986 the target groups of the project were redefined as long-term unemployed, women re-entering the workforce, persons of foreign extraction, handicapped persons and the higher-skilled jobseekers with a weak position on the labour market. The objective became to enable long-term unemployed to gain the knowledge, skills and experience that are in demand on the labour market.

Collaboration is an essential element of the scheme. Philips initiates and stimulates municipalities, employment services ('Arbeidsvoorziening') and/or private organisations such as employment organisations to create preliminary trajectories which can prepare people in a way suited to their individual disadvantages for a work-experience place within the employment scheme. This approach is based on the conviction that a high-quality preliminary trajectory can raise the employability of persons who have a long time been out of work.

Rabobank

Financial services provider Rabobank is also counted among the more active companies in the Netherlands as far as community involvement is concerned. The bank participates in several community investment projects. The local involvement of Rabobank is closely related to its organisational structure. Founded as an agricultural cooperative bank in the nineteenth century, it is still an unquoted cooperative society, focusing on clients and the community. Furthermore, the organisation is very decentralised, giving regional offices much elbow room for their own (social) policy.

The bank wants to contribute to economically and socially desirable developments at home and abroad (Rabobank Group, 2000). In its annual report, the bank pays attention to social and ecological indicators. Besides, the company publishes a so-called sustainability report. Although traditionally bound to the country, in recent years the company has developed strong links with the (major) cities. The involvement is not restricted to donations, subsidies and sponsoring, but in many cases encompasses the input of knowledge and people and the provision of facilities.

The Rabobank is now expanding its implicit local social engagement to become explicit and nationwide. The bottom-up approach will then be complemented by a top-down approach. To that end, the bank has developed a model composed around four (common) values related to the various stakeholders: clients' value, members' value, social value, and employees' value. These values are communicated through internal media. Local branch offices are left free to place their own special accents. Rabobank looks upon its community involvement not only as a responsibility, but also as a matter of self-interest. By investing in communities, the bank may benefit from the reduction of crime and the relief from fraud and hold-ups. Moreover, social projects give access to municipal and other local networks.

Activities in Rotterdam

In 1997, the Rotterdam branch office of Rabobank appointed a special manager to organise and communicate its community involvement. The bank decided to concentrate its activities on one specific urban problem: unemployment. The initiatives address two target groups: the long-term unemployed, and starters. For the latter target group, the Rabobank, together with the regional Chamber of Commerce, has founded a year society where entrepreneurs can exchange experiences. That network approach appeared to be a success. After one year a second club was started, followed by a third club in 2000. To help starting businesses (the second target group), the bank has established a so-called entrepreneurs' salon in a recently regenerated neighbourhood which had been threatened by degeneration.

Rabobank acknowledges that urban renewal and the revitalisation of low-income neighbourhoods demand cross-sector collaboration. Therefore, the bank has taken a share in a Neighbourhood Development Company in which the Rotterdam City Development Company and four business companies are the other partners. Such development organisations try to raise the status of backward neighbourhoods by renovating streets and giving drugs premises a new function.

Randstad

Employment organisation Randstad is a very active company in terms of corporate community involvement. This firm – founded in 1960 and the world's third largest employment organisation, with establishments in 12 countries in Europe as well as North America – looks upon community involvement as an element of its corporate culture, on the assumption that every citizen is a potential client or employee.

The social activities of Randstad are very much related to the core business of the company. Since the early 1980s, the firm has been involved in special employment programmes, aimed at specific (hard to employ) target groups. To achieve success in these programmes, Randstad cooperates with other organisations, including (local) governments. In most cases these special programmes have not been initiated by Randstad, but by one of the other organisations. Of course, the company is aware of its self-interest in the social projects, which are regarded as pilots for new markets. The strategic value of the activities became even greater after 1997, with the foundation of a separate business unit for special employment schemes. Through this unit, Randstad is also very much involved in the ArenA Initiative (see below).

Shell

The British-Dutch oil concern of Shell is frequently presented as a company that has had to learn the painful way that to survive, a company needs to spare the environment (Brent Spar) and respect humanity (Nigeria) (see Chapter 2).

Today, Shell is very much aware of its accountability to all stakeholders. Shell's annual report (Shell, 2000) pays attention not only to financial but also to social and ecological indicators, according to the principles of the triple-p bottom line. Shell recognises that the company is part of society, sharing the same agenda, and that corporate community involvement is a matter of self-interest, since a strong image and acceptance by the community make for long-term continuity. The principle of corporate responsibility helps Shell to achieve competitive advantages by costs reduction (eco-efficiency), the development of new markets, the recruitment of employees and risk reduction.

The Shell Report deals with many responsibilities that are hardly related to (European) cities, such as observing the laws of the countries in which they operate, expressing support for fundamental human rights in line with the legitimate role of business and giving proper regard to health, safety and the environment consistent with the commitment to contribute to the sustainable development of nations. Hence, the community is mostly understood as a country rather than a city. However, in its report Shell does show willingness to take a constructive interest in social problems that may not be immediately related to corporate management:

> Opportunities for involvement – for example through community, educational or donations programmes – will vary depending upon the size of the company concerned, the nature of the local society and the scope for useful private initiatives (Shell, 2000, p. 53).

This passage from the report confirms that the local context and the properties of the company affect the number of social initiatives that ensue from community involvement.

The company uses a strategic approach to its community investments. Since 2000, a separate foundation – the Shell Foundation – is responsible for the selection of social investment programmes. Moreover, the company has evolved proceedings to define social objectives and evaluate results.

Projects and Initiatives

Some people believe that it was the Brent Spar events that induced Shell to become involved in communities. The fact is, however, that for years the company has developed and supported social projects and initiatives. Some initiatives have made a perceptible contribution to the solution of social problems, whether or not in an urban context. In that connection come to mind the sponsoring of events, the stimulation of innovations through knowledge transfer, and the support given to former employees, foreign nationals and young people eager to set up their own business.

Shell started to stimulate entrepreneurship back in the 1980s, when the unemployment rate was soaring. Because employment with a major company such as Shell tends to shrink rather than expand, the company has helped to create employment in small and medium-size enterprise. Through the Small Business Unit, Shell stimulates entrepreneurship in the Netherlands by making knowledge and expertise available. Furthermore, Shell supports a fund for foreign-born starting entrepreneurs.

As a multinational that provides services to consumers through petrol stations spread across the country, Shell has little incentive to build up strong relations with cities. However, the company does have a natural affiliation with the three major cities that house establishments and staff: Amsterdam (laboratory research), Rotterdam (Pernis – production and storage), and The Hague (headquarters). In Rotterdam, for instance, Shell is involved in at least two projects: Pension Maaszicht and the City Team Project.

Pension Maaszicht is an institution that gives shelter to homeless youngsters and guides their efforts to build up a new life. For instance, a restaurant has been purchased where young people can gain experience in hotel and catering work. The project is an interesting example of cross-sector collaboration. Other participants are Rabobank (for financial advice and guidance towards creating a communication department), the municipality, and a school that provides hotel and catering courses. Thanks to this project, underprivileged youngsters who have not been able to profit from economic growth, find entrance to the labour market.

The City Team Project enables multicultural teams of young people to perform full-time and paid work for their city, with a view to promoting the participation of youngsters in the multicultural community and raising the quality of life in the cities. Together with many other participating companies, Shell offers traineeships and training courses. Through such participation, the firm gets an opportunity to recruit and motivate manpower and to distinguish themselves from their competitors (Boudhan et al., 1996). The concept of the City Team Project is based on the American City Year, a public-private initiative promoting the cooperation of young people, business companies, citizens and authorities.

The Consultation Platform for Urban Renewal

In the Netherlands, the Consultation Platform for Urban Renewal[4] is one of the business platforms that show willingness to set up partnerships with local governments. The platform was set up in 1998 on the initiative of Ahold (Real Estate), the owner of supermarket chains in the USA, Europe, Latin America and Asia. The Dutch supermarkets, which bear the name of their founder Albert Heijn, work with relatively high prices, thus addressing the medium and higher income groups.

The property leg of Ahold is responsible for the location policy. In consideration of certain factors (such as a minimum number of potential customers), the company opens and closes the doors of its supermarkets. Latterly the supermarket chain has displayed a renewed interest in (inner-)city locations. The firm is convinced that low and moderate income neighbourhoods have the potential to develop into interesting market areas. The present situation is, however, that many city neighbourhoods are marked by a high concentration of social problems and a poor stock of shops. On the one hand, Ahold believes that its supermarkets can act as motor of a shopping centre. On the other hand, the firm takes the view that it has a stake in the quality of the whole centre and its surroundings, since the quality of the living environment (in terms of green areas, services, housing supply, etc.) affects the income profile of the population. That is why the company is very much aware of the need to cooperate with other relevant stakeholders, including housing corporations and municipalities.

The Platform's Principles[5]

Because Ahold has found it far from simple, as an individual company, to negotiate with municipalities and housing corporations about joint neighbourhood development, the company decided to create the Consultation Platform for Urban Renewal together with some other organisations. Among the participating organisations are an association of housing corporations, three property developers, a bank (Rabobank), an employment organisation

(Randstad), a chain of stores selling household goods (Blokker) and a chain of fast food restaurants (McDonald's). These organisations complement one another nicely (the developers serving each their own market segment) and together can have a considerable share in urban renewal.

The platform takes a businesslike attitude: the objective is to contribute to urban renewal because it will be profitable to the partners in the (short and) long term. The profit is quite direct since the participating companies are able to strengthen their core business. Image-building motives are secondary. The coalition aims at structural improvement of the investment climate and the employment situation in the neighbourhood. To that end it wants to work closely with other public and private parties. The platform relies on the development potential of a neighbourhood and supports an integral approach, by which economic, physical and social reinforcement of the structure go hand in hand. In that frame of thought, the partners are willing to compensate plan elements promising little, if any, profit with more rewarding elements. The platform stimulates urban renewal notably at the stages of initiative and vision development. The concrete implementation of projects is left to the individual partners (not all partners are involved in each and every project) and to other parties who are willing to take on risks. The platform itself is not involved in the implementation of projects.

The principles guiding the platform's actions at the stages of initiative and vision development confirm the importance of organising capacity in urban development. Strategic networks are formed at the stage of initiative. Participants are to probe the feasibility of cooperation and to formulate corresponding rules for the game. The willingness to cooperate is the key notion. Parties will have to determine their position on the basis of their responsibility for, and/or interests in, a certain neighbourhood. They must, moreover: 1) have trust in the future of the neighbourhood; and 2) agree in outlines on the approach. The platform prefers 'loose' partnerships, based on mutual attraction. The focus should be first on the contents and the confidence, to extend later to the organisation structure and the legal aspects. The involvement of the municipality and the housing corporations is considered essential.

Once the rules of the game have been laid down, a collective vision should be forthcoming. Probings and discussions should result in a commonly sustained vision of development and jointly formulated principles, a shared level of ambition, tentative planning and a work schedule for the continuation of the process.

Barriers to the Coalition-forming Process

Although the platform gets much political support on the national level, many municipalities are not all that keen to share their control of urban development with private companies. Most Dutch cities feel little inducement to involve private enterprise in urban projects because they have sufficient (financial) resources of their own. They derive their funds mostly from national budgets, such as that of the Major Cities Policy and the Investment Budget for Urban Renewal. The conditions for the allocation of the latter budget do state that local partners such as housing corporations, market parties and citizens' organisations have to be involved. The impression is, however, that the effective involvement of private enterprise in the urban renewal projects is minimum; whether that is due to the private sector, the local authorities or both is not clear.

Because the cooperation between the local government and the private sector (in this case the platform) is sub-optimum, some interesting initiatives have been slow to take off. Since its foundation, the platform has presented several renewal plans for shopping centres. The effective realisation of these projects has been cumbersome, however. In some cities the local government is a weak counterpartner lacking in decisiveness, leadership, willingness to cooperate and/or ambition. Many officials do not have the knowledge and skill to give shape to such integral projects of urban renewal. Besides, political processes can be a heavy drag on decision making. Some projects are held up by the unwillingness of property owners to cooperate towards neighbourhood improvement (by adjusting or selling their premises). Sometimes that attitude is understandable in view of the owner's risk profile (think of pension funds); sometimes the owners have a preference for 'free-riding' (yes to profit, no to commitment).

The ArenA Initiative

The ArenA Initiative is considered one of the most successful Dutch examples of public-private partnership ensuing from corporate community involvement. The initiative is named after the Amsterdam ArenA, a multifunctional venue located in the borough of Amsterdam Southeast.

The Borough of Amsterdam Southeast

With over 730,000 inhabitants, Amsterdam is the largest city of the Netherlands. It is not only the capital, but also the country's unchallenged financial-economic, cultural and tourist centre. The city is part of the so-called Randstad, a conurbation that stretches into three provinces (Noord-Holland, Zuid-Holland, and Utrecht). It has no separate administration, but counts as a prominent economic centre, comparable to London, Paris, and the Rhine-Ruhr region. The four major cities in the Randstad each have a distinct economic profile. The Hague is the seat of government, while Rotterdam is the greatest port and industrial town. Utrecht, in the very heart of the Netherlands, is generally considered the centre of trade and traffic.

Since the Middle Ages, Amsterdam has been a major merchant city. Its economic success reached a climax in the seventeenth century, when the impressive network of canals was constructed. The position of Amsterdam declined somewhat in the eighteenth century. In the nineteenth century, the age of industrialisation, the manufacturing and financial sectors flourished. Amsterdam became the domain of diamond dealers. From 1970 onwards, the city's development has been strongly influenced by the tertiarisation of the economy and notably the rise of tourism. Nowadays the city is one of the principal destinations of mass tourism in Europe. The rising service society, changing housing preferences and increasing mobility have led to a (partly planned) deconcentration of people and activities. In the 1970s many people left the inner city in quest of more space and easier access. One prominent expansion area was Amsterdam Zuidoost (Amsterdam Southeast), of which more below. Other important economic centres in the Amsterdam region are the zone around the international airport Schiphol, and the Zuidas (Southern Axis), situated just south of the inner city. The Amsterdam region is becoming more and more a polycentric urban region (Van den Berg, Braun, Van der Meer and Otgaar, 1999).

From Bijlmer to Zuidoost

Amsterdam Zuidoost, originally called Bijlmer, was built in the 1970s, mainly to supply housing for the suburbanising Amsterdam population. At first, the high-rise apartment buildings – with fairly spacious apartments – were much sought after and counted as a paragon of modern architecture. That was not to last, however. People changed their ideas of good housing, and Zuidoost became the domain of low-income groups, in particular immigrants (from

Surinam and the Netherlands Antilles, among others). At the same time (the 1980s) firms began to settle in this town quarter, mostly on the west side of the railway which crosses the area. The arrival of business was due not only to positive developments on the office market, but also to an adventurous city-marketing campaign, which proclaimed Amsterdam Zuidoost as a no-nonsense, high-tech business centre.

The campaign had been started because the pension fund PGGM had been unsuccessful in selling or renting out its office properties in the area. An investigation conducted by an advertising agency showed that potential tenants appeared to know very little about the office accommodation available in Amsterdam Zuidoost. The agency rapidly concluded that the area had to be promoted, and the campaign was given a wider reach than the traditional ones, which were content with simply pointing out the number of available square metres. Because the name Bijlmer had by that time acquired a negative connotation among entrepreneurs, the new unblemished name Amsterdam Zuidoost was used in all further communication. The campaign addressed not only the management of companies (those who make the decisions), but explicitly also the people who were going to work there (Van den Berg, Klaassen and Van der Meer, 1990).

The advertising agency advised to combine advertising with public relations (PR) initiatives. After a short period of aggressive advertising, the agency had to exert very little pressure to achieve a flood of press publicity. For the approach to be successful, the companies already established in the area had to respond instantly to developments and be prepared to give interviews and to function as a sounding board for the advertising and PR agency. To that end the Interest Association Amsterdam Zuidoost was founded, in which all companies were represented. This association proved immensely useful in the campaign.

The campaign was sponsored by the municipality, the Amsterdam Medical Centre (AMC), and some companies, among which the insurance company Nationale Nederlanden, the ING-bank and computer giant IBM. The partners recognised their common interest in the effective communication of the qualities of the area. The public-privately financed organisation succeeded in giving Amsterdam Zuidoost a position among other centres in the Amsterdam region (such as the inner city and Schiphol).

Strong solidarity is a characteristic of private enterprise in Zuidoost, inspired in part by such common problems as the neighbourhood's unfortunate image of the 1980s and 1990s (now being slowly but surely sloughed off). The Amsterdam Zuidoost Business Association[6] (arisen from Interest Association Amsterdam Zuidoost), counts some 500 members, is very active and enjoys a good reputation. The association defends the social interests of the companies, namely, their common interest in an attractive, easily accessible and socially balanced city neighbourhood with a good supply of employment. The association takes an active stand in discussions about the spatial layout of the area. Much thought has been given, for instance, to the question of whether the ArenA would indeed fit in with the Zuidoost concept.

The Development of a New Entertainment Cluster

In 1996 the ArenA – the new stadium of football club Ajax Amsterdam – was completed. The municipality expected the stadium, with its futuristic architecture, to be a catalyst for the economy of Amsterdam Southeast. Thanks to its sliding roof – unique in Europe at the time – the ArenA could not only be a multifunctional sports and entertainment venue, but also function as the driving force of an envisaged urban centre, one of the cores in a polycentric urban region, on a level with the historical inner city, Schiphol and the Zuidas (which many consider the very top location for companies in the Netherlands). The realisation of the ArenA Boulevard (a multifunctional area around the venue with space for offices, houses and entertainment provisions) is regarded as having been a tremendous boost for employment in Amsterdam Zuidoost, with a forecast employment of 15,000.

The Initiative

Public indignation is regarded as the main driving force behind the ArenA Initiative. After the opening of the venue, residents of Amsterdam Southeast were indignant about the fact that job opportunities generated by the venue were being almost entirely filled by people from outside, while the unemployment rates in the borough itself, especially among those of foreign extraction, were many times higher than elsewhere in the Amsterdam region. Individual residents and associations of residents protested in many ways, and sought support from the local and national media. Not only private enterprise, but also the borough council were put under heavy pressure.

Neither the authorities nor the private sector could afford a passive attitude any longer. The municipality decided to organise a conference to discuss possible solutions with residents and companies. The companies began to see that in their own interest they must do something, or pay a heavy price later on. Not only the image of the companies was at stake, but also that of the Zuidoost area. Moreover, the companies also began to understand the advantages of a harmonious development of the borough in terms of the labour market (admittedly relatively easy at the time), the consumer market, and overall security. The outcome of the deliberations and considerations was the birth of the ArenA Initiative, a joint undertaking of the municipality (Municipal Social Department, the Borough), private companies (among which employment agencies), and social organisations.

Organisational Structure

Characteristic of the initiative is the lack of formal structures and the great number of stakeholders. Activities are coordinated by the project leader who is also the director of the local business association. In the first two years, the project leader's main task was to gain support from companies in the context of their social responsibilities and interests. As a kind of ambassador, he conducted interviews with companies, pointing out to them their common interests. That was necessary to make the initiative clearly and widely known.

The informal executive committee consists of representatives of all actors involved. They meet on a regular basis to discuss the state of affairs and ideas for new projects in an informal atmosphere. Breakfast and luncheon meetings are organised regularly to talk about social themes. At these meetings, which function as a kind of general assembly, many ideas for new projects have been presented and discussed. Naturally, the initiative cannot proceed without the assistance of some civil servants to take care of the formal proceedings, such as applying for municipal budgets.

Employment Projects

One of the first projects that resulted from the ArenA Initiative is a as a shared establishment of the commercial employment agency Randstad and the regional non-profit Employment Services ('Arbeidsvoorziening') on the ArenA Boulevard. This example of cross-sector collaboration shows what type of synergies can be created by partnership. Because the two organisations are complementary – Employment Services registers, selects and screens candidates, and Randstad takes on the schooling and placement of the candidates – the target group (job-seekers) is better served. Furthermore, the joint establishment helped to gain support for other projects, because it visualised the 'virtual' and informal ArenA Initiative.

Within the framework of the Initiative, the public and private partners also try to improve the use made of the labour potential present in the local community. First, the business association exerts pressure on its members to give priority to jobseekers from Southeast. Second, companies and suppliers of employees (employment organisations) have signed a supply and demand contract. The companies specify their demand for labour, coinvest in jobseekers and guarantee them a job. The suppliers guarantee a sufficient supply of suitable jobseekers, if necessary by reschooling them to the desired qualification level for starters (supply guarantee). In close cooperation with private enterprise, commercial employment agencies appointed sector committees to ensure a target-oriented, branch-based approach to the supply of labour. They work on the principle of 'barefoot recruitment', enlisting informal neighbourhood leaders to approach potential (often long-time unemployed) workers. There are, for instance, sector committees for cleaning work, the automobile sector, care, hotels and catering, and the retail trade. Third, the Social Department of the municipality and the regional Employment Services together set up Recruitment East, a shared desk maintaining intensive contacts with those registered. The contact is not broken until a proper solution has been found for each single client. The Social Affairs Department offers reschooling programmes for clients who qualify.

The Arena Academy

Another initiative is the founding of the Arena Academy, where school-age vmbo[7]-students are trained to become skilled workers. Once the trainees have successfully passed through the heavy two-year after-school programme, the business companies (through employment agency Randstad) guarantee them a job. Twelve companies (the so-called 'founders') located in Amsterdam Southeast – among which are a cleaning company, a furniture business, an employment agency (Randstad), retail and catering establishments, and the ArenA venue itself – finance one-fifth of the Academy and supply study material. Praxis building market has set up a complete shop for the youngsters to practise what they have learnt. The government finances the greater part (four-fifths) of the four-year project, from European subsidies and other sources.

At the Academy, much attention is given to learning about the Netherlands' corporate culture. Naturally, companies expect their employees to have certain social skills. The Academy works closely with regular schools to adapt programmes as well as possible. In the final year, the trainees (as the students are called) follow a trainee and career orientation course. Companies are not allowed to put the trainees to work as cheap stockboys or girls, but have to take trouble to acquaint them with the business.

Results

The cooperation has produced the envisaged effects: many people have been helped to a job and the acceptance of ethnic minorities among employers has improved. The reduction of unemployment in Amsterdam Zuidoost is three times the Amsterdam average (Samenleving en Bedrijf, 2000). Table 3.1 shows that unemployment has been cut by almost half.

Table 3.1 Development of non-working jobseekers

	Amsterdam Zuidoost		Rest of Amsterdam	
	Number	Decrease/increase	Number	Decrease/increase
1 January 1996	14,940		68,416	
1 January 1997	14,779	-1.4%	69,172	+1.1%
1 January 1998	12,511	-15.5%	62,749	-9.3%
1 January 1999	10,023	-19.9%	56,577	-9.8%
1 January 2000	8,349	-16.7%	51,029	-9.8%
1 January 2001	7,505	-10.6%	45,535	-6.0%

Source: Bedrijvenvereniging Amsterdam Zuidoost (2001).

Naturally, the causes of the reduction are various. The decrease was due in part to the favourable economic climate and the poor starting position of the area which made improvement easier to realise. Nevertheless, we can state with reasonable objectivity that employment in Zuidoost developed better than elsewhere in Amsterdam, even in comparison with other backward regions (which shared the 'advantage' of a poor starting position).

Success Factors

The success of the ArenA Initiative can be ascribed to several factors. For one thing, the relaxed, informal organisation structure ensures broad support, since the initiative was nobody's, and therefore everybody's. For another, the various stakeholders respected the motives of others. Some companies participate from a kind of social awareness, others frankly confess to commercial motives. In the third place, most stakeholders operated on the same geographical scale, which prevented conflicts between similar organisations. Amsterdam Zuidoost is a clearly delimited area, which means no bother with different borough councils or different common-interest organisations of the same ethnic minorities. In the fourth place success was due to the input and enthusiasm of a few key figures who persuaded others of their self-interest in participation. Prominent drivers of the project were (as they still are) the project leader who is also the director of the business association, one of the borough's aldermen, the director of Employment Services, and the director of the Amsterdam Medical Centre (AMC).

Conclusions

More and more companies in the Netherlands are widening their scope beyond the purely economic interests. The triple-p bottom line principle is gaining credibility, as witness, for example, Shell's annual report. Companies mostly oriented to the local market appear to have a strong incentive to initiate or join social projects in cities. In some cases, such initiatives can in time contribute to the expansion of their core business. Good cases in point are the projects of Rabobank in Rotterdam and the participation of Randstad employment agency in the ArenA Initiative.

In the Netherlands, many initiatives ensuing from corporate community involvement deal with employment. Obviously, companies are aware of their self-interest related to this aspect of urban development. The willingness to participate and invest in special employment projects seems to grow as the labour market becomes tight, as happened in the late 1990s.

There are relatively few examples of positive experiences with investment in accessibility and the quality of the living environment. The principles of the Consultation Platform for Urban Renewal look promising, but the number of concrete initiatives is disappointing. Most initiatives are still at the stage of discussion. Possible explanatory factors are the lack of (financial) incentives to cooperate, and the clash between the administrative culture and the corporate culture. There is also a lack of financial and organisational instruments to give shape to the partnership.

From the ArenA Initiative we can learn that the creation of cross-sector partnerships cannot be separated from the location. For one thing, the gravity of the problems incited companies to assume a more social attitude. Local threats functioned as incentives for cooperation. For another, the private sector in Amsterdam Zuidoost is strongly represented by a business association that in the 1980s sprung from a joint city-marketing initiative. This association is very much aware of the interests that businesses have in a pleasant, accessible and well appointed environment. Moreover, on the occasion of the opening of the Amsterdam ArenA the companies in the area experienced – under pressure from residents and the media – that indifference to the environment can damage their image. Thirdly, the cooperation of parties has been smoothed by the relative autonomy of Amsterdam Zuidoost, where many municipal and social organisations have the same geographical focus.

Other success factors refer to the individual qualities of the persons involved, such as enthusiasm, commitment (support) and mutual respect. The organisation form chosen, in this case a loose informal structure, is also thought a reason of success. Finally, the case has revealed that a visible project – here the joint establishment of Randstad and Employment Services – works as a stimulus.

Notes

1 In Dutch: 'maatschappelijk verantwoord ondernemen' (socially responsible enterprise).
2 Examples of such networks: Partnership for Social Integration (Community and Business), Social Venture Network Nederland (SVN), Netwerk Bedrijfsethiek Nederland (NBN, Network for Business Ethics, the Netherlands), Business In The Community The Hague (BITC), Consultation platform for Urban Renewal (OPS), Association of Investors for Sustainable Development (VBDO), Amnesty International Round Table, and Young Executives for Responsible Business (YERB).
3 See www.philips.nl.
4 In Dutch: 'Overlegplatform Stedelijke Vernieuwing (OPS)'.
5 See 'Ondernemen in Stedelijke Vernieuwing' (Enterprise in Urban Renewal) (Stichting OPS, 2000).
6 In Dutch: 'Bedrijvenvereniging Amsterdam Zuidoost'.
7 'Voorbereidend Middelbaar Beroepsonderwjs' (Preparatory Secondary Vocational Education).

References

Berg, L. van den, E. Braun, J. van der Meer and A.H.J. Otgaar (1999), *De binnenstadseconomie in de eenentwintigste eeuw* [*The Inner-city Economy in the 21st Century*], EURICUR, Rotterdam, NL.

Berg, L. van den, L.H. Klaassen and J. van der Meer (1990), *Strategische City-Marketing*, Bedrijfskundige signalementen 90/3, Academic Service, Schoonhoven, NL.

Boudhan, B., I. Vonk and F. Nelissen (1996), *Maatschappelijk Ondernemen; Dienen en verdienen*, Stichting Maatschappij en Onderneming, Informatief, SMO-96-5.

Philips (2000), 'Jaarverslag Philips Werkgelegenheidsplan 2000'.

Rabobank Group (2000), 'Jaarverslag 1999'.

Samenleving & Bedrijf (2000), 'Samen', No. 4, May, p. 8.
Shell (2000), *The Shell Report.*
Stichting OPS (2000), 'Ondernemen in Stedelijke Vernieuwing'.

Discussion Partners

D. van den Akker, Public Relations, McDonald's Nederland
M.D.P. Broks, McDonald's Haaglanden
A.L.C. van der Bruggen, Manager Philips Employment Plan, Philips Electronics Nederland
H. Blaauw, Director Human Resources, McDonald's Nederland
R.E.F.A. Crassee, OverlegPlatform Stedelijke Vernieuwing (Consultation Platform for Urban Renewal), Ahold Vastgoed (Real Estate)
M. van der Horst, Vice President, City of Amsterdam, Borough Zuidoost
B. van Kanten, Rabobank Nederland
P.M. Kroon, Head ING Bank Public Affairs
W. Lageweg, Rabobank Nederland, Adviescentrum Coöperatie-Ontwikkeling (Advice Centre Cooperation Development)
M. La Rose, Project Leader Arena Initiative
A. Larouz, Project Coordinator West Werkt/Go 4 West
M.J.M. Smulders, General Director, Rabobank Rotterdam
M.H.J.J. Vissers, Director External Relations, Randstad Nederland
F.A. Voermans, Director Amsterdams Medisch Centrum (AMC) – Operations

Chapter 4

Chicago

Introduction

This chapter is about corporate community involvement in Chicago. As in many other US cities, the business sector in Chicago has a long tradition of community involvement, not only in terms of philanthropy but also through organisations that defend the social and commercial interests of companies. Furthermore, Chicago is the home town of fast food restaurant McDonald's and foodstuff producer Sara Lee: two companies with a strategic approach to community involvement.

After a profile of Chicago, we consider the role of privately funded intermediary agencies active on the interface of public and private sectors, and the urban themes to which companies have committed themselves. The next section analyses the activities of two prominent companies with headquarters in the region, and the vision of a local project developer. The final section concludes.

Profile

Chicago is among the North American cities that appeal most to the imagination of Europeans. In films, the city often serves as background to gangster conflicts inspired by the years of Prohibition, when alcoholic beverages were banned from the USA. The renowned Al Capone often features in these films. Some of that underworld image still attaches to the city. But Chicago also stands for other things, and has for quite some time been a well-known city in and outside the USA. Its strategic situation on the south side of the gigantic Lake Michigan (one of the Great Lakes), connecting it with the east coast, gave rise to the development of an important harbour in the nineteenth century. The Chicago River which flows through the city connects it with places farther inland, strengthening its position. The 'Windy City'[1] is also known for the first 'modern' skyscraper (Home Insurance Building, 1885), which fitted the new enthusiasm with which the city was rebuilt after a devastating fire in 1871. Nor did it remain the only building of that type. Chicago boasts many extraordinary edifices and figures in many books of architecture, proudly displaying, among other things, the highest office building of the USA (Sears Tower), dating from the 1970s. Since 1984 Chicago has been the city of Michael Jordan and the home base of the plural NBA champion, the Chicago Bulls.

Table 4.1 Population Chicago 1890–1999 (x1000)

1890	**1900**	**1910**	**1920**	**1930**	**1940**
1,100	1,698	2,185	2,702	3,376	3,397
1950	**1960**	**1970**	**1980**	**1990**	**1999**
3,621	3,550	3,369	3,005	2,784	2,800

Source: Chicago Library, <http://www.chipublib.org/>.

From the last decade of the nineteenth century until World War II the city went through a period of boisterous growth. After the Great Fire of 1971 there were many who expected the city to be swept off the map for good, but Chicago was rebuilt at a fast pace. Nowadays Chicago is one of the major cities in the USA, with more than 2.8 million inhabitants, the beating heart of a functional urban region with some eight million inhabitants. The Chicago metropolis lies in the northeastern part of the State of Illinois and comprises nine 'counties'. Chicago and its adjoining suburbs together make up Cook County, counting more than five million residents. The other eight counties[2] can be reckoned to fall under Chicago's sphere of influence. Despite the typical American skyline in the downtown area, it is also a pleasant city where people still like to live in the centre and where they actually walk the streets (except in winter). On the borders of Lake Michigan, which are free of buildings, there is an extensive city park as well as a marina and several other leisure provisions, for instance on Navy Pier, a former base of the American Navy. Interestingly, the open waterfront, the strips of garden and the city park on the water's edge are elements of the first ever American architectural plan (1909), which is still the guideline for the further development of the city (see below).

The fast population growth from the end of the nineteenth century onward reflects the strong industrial development which the city went through at the time. Easy access across the water spurred the city's development in the second half of the nineteenth and the first half of the twentieth century into an industrial centre. Even today, industry offers employment to Chicago residents (see Table 4.2), but the city is known first and foremost as a service city, the excellent accessibility by air being one of the trump cards (World Business Chicago, 1997). O'Hare Airport is among the busiest of the world and has excellent national and international connections, making Chicago an attractive location for such professionals as consultants and register accountants. All major players in those markets are well anchored in Chicago, even when their headquarters are elsewhere.

Table 4.2 Employment in Chicago by sector of activity

Sector	Active population (%)
Construction	2.9
Manufacturing industry	17.6
Transport, energy and communication	5.2
Commerce	15.2
Banks and insurance companies	9.2
Business services	28.8
Public sector	15.4

Source: Bureau of Labor Statistics, 1998.

The administrative structure of metropolitan Chicago is among the most fragmented in the USA. The region counts 273 municipalities, and for good measure, 1,030 tax-levying bodies. In comparison to the Dutch regime, the city council and the associated civil service have fewer means at their disposal. In practice, however, municipal services like the planning and development department are inadequately equipped for any proactive and directive action. The government is mostly reactive. Within the administrative structure of Chicago, the mayor can tip the scales. There is no doubt that a mayor exerting strong political leadership can be very effective. On the whole, the initiative is often left to the private sector. That is the background against which active companies in Chicago operate.

Public and Private Interests

It is no exaggeration to say that Chicago's private sector has from of old been exceptionally committed to its place of location. One of the oldest and undoubtedly the best known organisation is the Commercial Club of Chicago, founded in 1877.

The Commercial Club of Chicago

The Commercial Club of Chicago is a meeting platform primarily for prominent personalities from the private sector, and to a lesser extent from the cultural and educational sectors. But besides fulfilling a social function for its members, the club supports several community development projects and new initiatives in the realm of education.

Among the principal projects supported by (members of) the Commercial Club at the beginning of the twentieth century, was the elaboration of an inspiring urban development vision for Chicago and its surroundings. Its original title was 'Plan of Chicago', but it is also frequently referred to as 'the Burnham Plan' after its inventor and architect, Daniel H. Burnham. It was the first of its kind in the USA, and most adventurous even by present standards. The banks of Lake Michigan were central to the plan; they had to be kept as much as possible free from building and be open to the public at large, so that on Sundays Chicago families could have the pleasure of ambling along the water's edge. To that vision Chicago owes its generously laid-out Grant Park at the kind of top location that in many other cities would have been ruthlessly given over to industry, offices, or housing. The various museums, the marina and other leisure provisions fit in the concept of the plan, which furthermore provided for many parks and gardens spread throughout the town, and protection of the nearby woodlands as a kind of natural buffer. Even the main stretches of the present road infrastructure can be found in the old plan.

The Civic Committee

In the first half of the 1980s, the commitment of private enterprise to the development of Chicago took a new direction. The city was struggling under the transition from a traditional industrial city to a modern service city. Chicago's share in national employment had steadily declined since the 1950s. Employment was the challenge in those days, and the Commercial Club issued a report on 'Jobs for Metropolitan Chicago', a title that needs no comment. The Commercial Club felt the need for a smaller, decisive organisation, the 'Civic Committee'. This non-profit organisation was founded in 1983 and unites some 65 chief executive officers (CEOs for short) of Chicago's prominent companies and schools. These CEOs help to pay for the activities and have a moral obligation to attend the regular meetings in person. To send a deputy is considered 'not done' and does not fit the culture.

The new organisation responds to the need of the more progressive, visionary companies that want not only to discuss problems of urban developments but also to be more explicitly involved in the metropolitan economy. Besides the contributions from the businesses, the Civic Committee receives support from several (charitable) foundations. The appointment of the Civic Committee is a distinct sign of a change in attitude: it has taken on the proactive role that was hardly feasible for the much larger and more traditional Commercial Club (with over 500 CEOs).

The Civic Committee aims at stimulating the growth of the metropolitan economy by improving the overall location climate for business, in the widest sense. It is concerned with the decisiveness of the municipal council, the regional transport and communication system, education, health care, and of course local taxes and legislation. The committee is not at all a large body, and has a relatively small staff. The commitment of the entrepreneurs and other public and private actors in the various subcommittees[3] is therefore of the essence.

Link between the Public and the Private

The Civic Committee functions as defender and intermediary, and is sometimes co-responsible for project and programme management. Its members promote improvements that they consider of strategic importance for the region. In that function they have, for instance, lobbied to get education or the expansion of O'Hare higher on the political agenda. Most of the work is done behind the scenes; the organisation will rarely make a forceful statement in the media.

One key function is that of intermediary (broker) between the public and the private sector. The committee unites in fact companies that want to do something for their city and region, and translates their ideas into an agenda with subjects of strategic general interest. At the same time, the organisation is a fully fledged discussion partner with the local governments and a likely partner for projects and programmes. It can be a pivot between the public and private spheres of action. Besides acting as a defender and intermediary, the committee (on its own or with partners) also takes responsibility for concrete projects and/or programmes.

The task description of the Civic Committee may be wide, but in practice, public education takes up 70 per cent of its attention. That is not surprising, since from research in the early 1980s the quality of the public schools, especially in the western and southern parts of the city, was among the lowest in the USA. The members of the committee took the view that stimulation of the metropolitan economy should begin with excellent and, in particular, widely accessible education. Therefore, unlike the more traditional (regional) Chamber of Commerce, the members are in favour of channelling more public money to education.

The Civic Committee supports schemes aimed at improved school administrations, smaller classes, better teachers in public schools, and integration of ICT. A lobby has been conducted for more flexible and stimulating legislation, and money has been collected and intervention offered for some Charter Schools. Charter Schools have become possible since the law was amended to provide for new public schools to be created on private initiative. The government allots to such schools the same financial means per student as the existing schools, to spend at their own discretion, as long as the education satisfies the quality requirements.

Private enterprise heartily supports that commitment to flexibility and has adopted some of the Charter Schools, contributing considerably to their budgets. That intermediary role has been the special responsibility of an organisation affiliated to the Civic Committee, Leadership for Quality Education (LQE), which cooperates closely with education authorities. LQE is partly financed by the Civic Committee, but has an administration of its own and undertakes supplementary fund raising among the various foundations. Thanks to LQE, the 550 public schools now have their own chosen council (a clear example of a successful lobby for legal amendment). Furthermore, parental involvement, for instance through membership of the school council, is considered highly important. Much remains to be done in public education. In the past few years the first (modest) improvements have become visible.

Another organisation associated with the committee is World Business Chicago (WBC). It was founded in response to a study comparing the region of Chicago to other urban regions in the world. One suggestion was for WBC to attract foreign investors ('foreign direct investment'). Before 1997, there existed no regional organisation to take up this matter,[4] nor a regional information system (integrated database). WBC is financed by the Civic Committee and several corporate foundations, among which Sara Lee. In October 2000 WBC merged with the largely publicly-funded Chicago Partnership, a relatively new organisation, created by the mayor to improve the marketing of Chicago. WBC is now the foreign direct-investment branch of the Chicago Partnership.

Chicago Metropolis 2020

Since the Burnham Plan and the creation of the Civic Committee, the Commercial Club has substantiated its involvement with the region by elaborating a new metropolitan vision entitled Chicago Metropolis 2020, and associating it with a new body of the same name. What does a liveable and dynamic Chicago need for the future? The report 'Preparing Metropolitan Chicago for the 21st Century' discusses frankly the main challenges of the metropolitan region of Chicago, such as racial and economic segregation, deficient public education, dependency on the motorcar, the worsening congestion, the shortage of affordable housing, intraregional competition among the counties, etc.

The non-profit organisation Chicago Metropolis 2020 continues the tradition of the Commercial Club, but in a more regional perspective.[5] More than 200 members of the Commercial Club of Chicago are involved in the development of the plan, and many meetings have been held with experts and other stakeholders. The report discusses the following strategic themes: 1) to invest in young people, especially in matters of public education, health care and children's day nurseries; 2) to improve transport of people and goods, and indeed everything to do with internal and external accessibility; 3) planned use of space and housing, with the emphasis on checking unbridled suburbanisation and stimulating 'smart growth'; 4) a regional approach to matters exceeding the local interest, including harmonisation of corresponding local tax systems, without pleading a full-fledged metropolitan administration; and 5) to control, and invest in, the economic competitive position, with as spearheads educating the active population (motivating the unemployed as well as investing in the education of the average employee); anticipating developments in the modern information economy, and coordinating regional marketing.

A fact to point out is that those involved in CM2020 promote regionalism, in other words, strive for the sustainable long-term development of the metropolitan region of Chicago. Another is that the report's suggestions to improve the situation emphasise the interconnection of the challenges. Chicago Metropolis 2020 proposes an integrated approach to spatial planning, public transport and private transport and protection of the environment. The proposals encompass improvement of public transport, road pricing and toll gates, a check on urban sprawl, harmonious zoning plans, and planned transport infrastructure.

In the realm of education, raising the quality of the public school system is mentioned along with adequate affordable day nurseries and the debate on accessible health care for children from underprivileged families. The plan suggests building houses with the fight against economic and racial segregation in mind. Another serious problem is the lengthening distances between work and residence, in particular for the lower salaried. An appeal is made to employers to help their lower salaried workers finding suitable accommodation and if necessary to invest in affordable rented dwellings for their own employees.

Chicago Metropolis 2020 recommends the appointment of a Regional Coordinating Council, and makes a plea for switching the accent of the economic policy to investment in human resources and improved services. With reference to World Business Chicago, mentioned above, a plea is made for national as well as international marketing of the region. This comprehensive Plan covers a range of subjects, which seem to be progressively removed from traditional direct corporate interests. In sum, the prominent business leaders behind the vision have fully recognised their own interest in a well-organised and flourishing region (Johnson, 1999).

The key question is how Chicago Metropolis 2020 can realise its ambitions. During the first stage much energy was spent on getting the discussion about the regional future under way, and creating more support for the plan. Besides, the organisation took an active part in a lobby which succeeded in obtaining an extra 12 billion dollar (an investment programme named 'Illinois First') for transport infrastructure and the direct financial needs of public education. Practical efforts are being made to organise support among regional businesses for better and affordable day nurseries.

Appeals are made to induce regional entrepreneurs to subscribe to the Metropolis Principles, implying their commitment to take into account, for decisions of (re)location or expansion, such aspects as accessibility by public transport, municipal zoning policies, and affordable housing for workers. Chicago Metropolis 2020 often suggests solving problems either by using government means in a different way or by reforming the government. In 2000, the organisation was busy implementing its plans for the region of Chicago with the help of the means from investment programme Illinois First. The next step would be to come up with concrete statements about what private enterprise can contribute in terms of knowledge, human resources and financial means. The plan has made some ambitious suggestions and created expectations as to the role of private enterprise.

Metropolitan Planning Council

The regionalism propagated by Chicago Metropolis 2020 is by no means a new idea. The Metropolitan Planning Council (MPC), active since 1935, is also in favour of a regional perspective. This council is a public-private consultation platform in which government, the private sector, the universities and the non-profit sector are represented. In conjunction with project developers (!) and the municipality the Metropolitan Planning Council conducts a campaign for smart growth, denouncing the urban sprawl and pointing a finger at the inferior architecture of the suburbs in particular. The quality of the living environment is another subject dear to the council. The organisation is financially supported by the John McCarther Foundation[6] and other agencies. It has a wider scope but less ambitious objectives than Chicago Metropolis 2020. The council was the founder of Business Leaders for Quality Transport, a group that stages hearings about plans for regional transport services.

Brokers and Democracy

In Chicago, the brokers (the Civic Committee, Metropolis 2020, and the Metropolitan Planning Council) can be said to fulfil a crucial role towards linking the broad social interest of companies with the general public interest. On the one hand these American-style non-profit organisations are highly democratic in that many agencies are involved or get heard, on the other they are not, since the proceedings are for the most part hidden from democratic inspection by the municipal council. The mayor appreciates the input of private enterprise and takes 'political possession' of good plans and projects, as far as the political situation permits. In that way he can guard the cohesion of the mishmash of initiatives in a politically-administratively fragmented region.

Highly Involved Companies

In this section we review three Chicago-based companies and their activities related to corporate community involvement: Sara Lee (producer of foods, household products and clothing), McDonald's (fast-food restaurant) and the Shaw Company (a local project developer).

Sara Lee

For many years, Sara Lee has had a strong bond with Chicago as the location of its headquarters. Sara Lee produces and markets consumer goods in the categories of food and beverages, household products and (under)clothing, achieving a yearly turnover of over US$ 20 billion (Sara Lee Corporation, 2000). In the product lines mentioned, Sara Lee has several A-brands in its range. It is truly a global company, with establishments in more than 40 countries and customers in over 140. In total, the company employs about 138,000 people. It is one of the largest companies in Chicago in terms of turnover, though not of manpower.

In this decentralised concern, only a limited number of the employees live in Chicago. Nevertheless, Sara Lee has a special relationship with Chicago. More than 40 years ago, the then president of the Consolidated Foods Corporation (the predecessor of Sara Lee Corporation) took the initiative to make donations to local charities and non-profit organisations. In 1981 that tradition was institutionalised in an autonomous organisation, the Sara Lee Foundation.

It is a private foundation and can be regarded as the concern's philanthropic arm. Through the medium of the Sara Lee Foundation, the Sara Lee Corporation tries to set aside 2 per cent of its profit before tax annually for non-profit organisations. The Foundation has its own administration and responsibility, in contrast to the philanthropic activities of some other companies in the USA. The Foundation, too, has its headquarters in Chicago, and many of the gifts find their way to initiatives of Chicago institutions. The objective of the Foundation is to contribute positively to the communities where Sara Lee's employees live and work, but most of the Sara Lee benefits end up in Chicago. Outside of Chicago, giving is decentralised: the division is free to determine how to address the needs of the communities where the company operates.

The Sara Lee Foundation does not itself start up projects, but is mainly engaged in giving financial support to initiatives of others, outside or occasionally within the Sara Lee Foundation. As far as direct subsidies are concerned, two programmes of the Foundation put a face on its policy: the disadvantaged programme and the cultural programme. The former gives attention to: 1) hunger, food and homelessness; and 2) efforts to strengthen the position and development of women in society. The choice of the first theme is bound up with the core business of the company: to produce and sell food. Chicago counts many homeless people who have become scattered as old living quarters were revitalised and rehabilitated. Many foundations offer one-room apartments for the lowest incomes, but regrettably the number of those with minimum income is rising while that of small apartments diminishes. In the inner city, Chicago pursues an ambivalent policy: on the one hand it favours single-room occupancy, on the other it promotes the building of new offices, thus causing a further reduction of the number of small dwellings. With regard to the second theme, Sara Lee spends much thought on women both within and outside its own organisation. Women are strongly represented in the concern, on all levels (over three-fifths of the Sara Lee employees are women). Moreover, women are still the most important customers; they still do most of the shopping. The programmes refer to education and schooling, day nurseries, legal assistance and initiatives smoothing the way for women to ascend to top positions in business companies. Other objectives are to support the black community, promote equal opportunities in general, and create jobs in neighbourhoods with a low average income. Moreover, the foundation supports research activities of the Metropolitan Planning Council.

The foundation's cultural programme focuses on investment in art and culture, a prominent location factor for Sara Lee. Initiatives that may count on support from Sara Lee are those concerned with museums, professional aid to artists, stage performances, the accessibility of art to a broad public, etc. Besides direct financial support, every year the Foundation grants several awards to commendable initiatives that make a sizeable contribution to the quality of life in Chicago. An example is the Leadership Award for non-profit organisations that are a source of inspiration to others. There is also a scheme for matching contributions from employees to non-profit organisations.

As well as the Sara Lee Foundation, the Sara Lee Corporation itself pays attention to good corporate citizenship, among other things through its employment policy and a charter of global business standards. The president (CEO) of Sara Lee talks about local involvement as 'enlightened self-interest', a notion that goes beyond that of 'obvious self-interest'. A generous interest in the community is thus suggested, one that cannot be directly translated into profit. Clearly, Sara Lee's policy has changed: the concern now treats corporate philanthropy more strategically than in the past, putting concrete objectives and result-oriented work first.

McDonald's

The main office of McDonald's is in the suburb Oak Brook, outside the city itself. McDonald's is regarded by many as a global company, but the company prefers to call itself multilocal rather than multinational. Although the brand is global, the organisation is in fact an extensive collection of small entrepreneurs, spread across 119 countries. The fast food chain is represented in some 28,000 communities (cities, localities) the world over. The headquarters at Oak Brook has relatively little control over franchise holders and licensees. Naturally, McDonald's entrepreneurs are bound by certain conditions as to the appointment and design of the shop, marketing, hygiene, products, etc., but outside those umbrella agreements the McDonald's Corporation has no direct control of the franchise holders.

The concern is known for its 'good relations with the neighbourhood community'. As is generally known, during the large-scale disturbances in Los Angeles, the McDonald's restaurants were hardly if at all attacked by the rioters. Right from the creation of the business, the local involvement has been integrated in the corporate culture, as befitting the vision of founder Ray Kroc. That the headquarters of the McDonald's Corporation has initiated several (inter)national programmes is not surprising, since on the level of the Corporation, 'giving back to the community' is considered an implicit element of the strategic policy adopted to protect and improve the McDonald's brand. Preferably, the social activities are chosen in line with the core business, with the support of shareholders in mind.

Within that strategic policy, attention is given to strategic philanthropy (Ronald McDonald House Charities, see below), environmentally-friendly management, scholarships and educational programmes, social responsibility and community involvement, animal welfare, and safety. A case in point is the strategic cooperation with the Environmental Defence Fund (EDF) with respect to environmental programmes. Several people within the concern are occupied with those aspects. Another example – in the realm of education – is the granting of scholarships not only to employees but also to others (neighbourhood residents). The initiative comes either from the local establishment or from central offices. In the USA as well as many other countries there is a national scholarship scheme.

There is a scheme specifically oriented to Hispanics and a scholarship sponsored by the Ronald McDonald House Charities. McDonald's takes a flexible attitude towards employees who want to combine study and work. And, not to be forgotten, there is the 'Hamburger University', where McDonald's managers are trained and taught the principles of local involvement (including voluntary activities). A certificate from the Hamburger University gives credits towards a business degree. There are 10 training facilities of McDonald's in the world. The fast food chain is probably one of the world's greatest providers of training and education.

McDonald's has the ambition to be an all-round good citizen with respect for the law, a decent human resources policy, and a responsible purchasing policy. Besides, McDonald's keeps a vigilant eye on social developments: what trends could be important to the company in the coming years? McDonald's policy is inspired by the philosophy of the founder, which puts good corporate citizenship in the centre, but keeps the long-term commercial interest in mind. The brand reputation is gaining importance, with the ever-fiercer competition and the abundance of choices for the consumer. The brand is one way to keep customers' attention. Actually, McDonald's has paid for missed opportunities in the past, when its response was too late or inadequate. McDonald's as a global brand is instantly confronted with changing social preferences, which compels the management to anti-cyclical and anticipatory thinking. As one symbol of globalisation, the company also encounters a lot of opposition, and cannot afford to confine itself to mere window dressing.

The approach of McDonald's combines the activities of the umbrella organisations (worldwide or national) with local initiative. Within the loose McDonald's structure, the responsibility for community involvement is largely on the level of the restaurants. McDonald's regards itself not as a product on the shelves of a shop but as an association of people who together make up the McDonald's identity. McDonald's cannot possibly communicate with all those people and does not try to. Many of its (inter)national schemes are an incentive to local initiatives (often through promises of matching the amount put in). McDonald's aims for a local image and that is one reason for requiring that franchise holders have their roots in the community in which the restaurant stands. In that sense McDonald's franchise concept differs from many others. McDonald's has a natural bond with the American community, for one out of every seven Americans at one time had a job (often 'on the side') with McDonald's and acquired there the basic skills that proved useful later on. A large proportion of the management started their career in McDonald's kitchens.

The local involvement of McDonald's in Chicago is not significantly different from or greater than elsewhere. The company is represented in some intermediary organisations, but probably not as actively as some others. The 115 establishments in Chicago are, of course, involved in their communities. In special cases the main office does something out of the ordinary, such as financing a great dinosaur exhibition.

Ronald McDonald House Charities Among the best-known philanthropic activities associated with the McDonald's Corporation are Ronald McDonald

House Charities, a separate body coordinating McDonald's charitable actions. It started with the first Ronald McDonald House in Philadelphia. The philosophy behind the houses is that the parents of very sick children can be accommodated close to the hospital. By now there are 206 of such houses worldwide, of which 144 are in the USA and 11 in the Netherlands. Most of the funds for them come from the franchise holders, gifts from restaurant clients and other sponsors (large companies among them). The Ronald McDonald House Charities is not only involved in these accommodations but also stages other activities for children.

One recent development is Ronald McDonald Care Mobile; a medical clinic on wheels which provides basic medical care to uninsured children in deprived neighbourhoods. It was originally a Chicago initiative, taken over by the McDonald organisation, which now plans to equip 14 such mobile clinics.

The Shaw Company

An interesting enterprise, far less known than Sara Lee and McDonald's, is the Shaw Company, a firm of project developers who have a strong representation in the Chicago region. They have courageously undertaken to stage a new project at a former Sears location in one of the less prosperous neighbourhoods of Chicago. Admittedly, Sears has put in the land for free. That was to their own advantage: they need no longer pay maintenance expenses while making a nice gesture towards their long-time community. Moreover, there was nobody much interested in the grounds, which were used for storage and distribution and on which some storehouses are still intact. The market value was obviously very low at the time.

Shaw has decided to go ahead with the project despite the state of decay and deprivation of both the area to be developed and the immediate surroundings. An advantage was that no houses need to be demolished to make way for new building. The purpose of the project is to give the neighbouring residents access to facilities. The 55-hectare area lies west of the central business district. The plans envisage houses, shops, offices and a community centre of 70,000 square feet. The centre will house a sports hall, a health clinic (private property but open to all), and a training centre (among other things for remote learning) and other facilities for children.

The project is public-privately financed. Shaw is the orchestrator of the project which was started seven years ago. Shaw can be said to operate from a long-term vision that is not too sensitive to market fluctuations and short-term profit. Shaw has opted for 'leaving money on the table' rather than short-term profit maximisation. Nevertheless the firm is compensated for its services and rewarded with a good image. Such a challenging project is considered a once-in-a-lifetime opportunity, a development to be proud of. Moreover, through this project Shaw earns credibility with the municipality and other parties, which in the event may lead to commercially interesting propositions.

Conclusions

The private sector in Chicago has long been interested in the development of the city, both individually and in an organised fashion. The Civic Committee and Chicago Metropolis 2020 are among the agencies that have speeded up the local involvement of private enterprise and given it a more strategic character. These non-profit organisations fulfil an important intermediary function between the public and the private sector, and give direction to the efforts of private enterprise. The businesses behind Chicago Metropolis 2020 recognise that a well-organised and harmonious region is in their own interest. They present plans with regard to education, urban sprawl, public transport and general accessibility.

The private sector has ambitious visions and objectives and expects the public administration to take a new course. The key question is whether private enterprise itself is also prepared to invest more generously in the future of the region. The good cooperation between organised private enterprise and the politically strong mayor is considered a prominent basis for many new developments in the city. Nevertheless the fragmented administrative structure of the region may frustrate the strategic decision-making about questions that transcend the municipal border.

The overall globalisation of private enterprise and the trend of mergers and take-overs, especially in the financial sector, are regarded as a threat to the commitment of private enterprise. Nevertheless, Sara Lee has a very strong bond with Chicago, and a major portion of its philanthropic dollars benefits the Chicago community. Sara Lee's philanthropic policy has been subject to change in the sense that the Sara Lee Foundation is no longer just a passive provider of subsidy, but explicitly chooses themes that are in line with the core business of the corporation. McDonald's headquarters does not have a special bond with the Chicago region (apart from incidental initiatives). Local involvement is intrinsic in the corporate philosophy; the managers and franchise holders are implicitly expected to associate themselves with the neighbourhood. Chicago counts more than 115 McDonald's establishments which are active in the community. McDonald's looks upon corporate social responsibility as a matter of pure self-interest in view of the relation with the customers (in the neighbourhood), and certainly also as a means to protect and consolidate the McDonald's brand.

Notes

1 The nickname 'Windy City' has nothing to do with the local climate. A reporter on the *New York Sun* wrote about the 'Windy City' because of Chicago politicians continuous boastings about the World Exhibition held in Chicago in 1893.
2 Dupage, Kane, Lake, McHenry, Will, DeKalb, Kendall, and Iroquois.
3 Namely: Aviation Task Force, Education Sub-Committee, High Tech Marketing Advisory Committee, and Inner-City Business Development CEO Committee.
4 On the level of the state, the Illinois Trade Office had been active for a long time, but was abolished by the previous governor.
5 Chicago Metropolis 2020 is concerned with six counties: Cook (including Chicago), Dupage, Will, Kane, McHenry and Lake.
6 John McCarther was the founder of a successful insurance company who at his death left more than US$ 1 billion. Under the administration of the Foundation this amount has at the time of writing risen to about US$ 4 billion.

References

Bureau of Labor Statistics (1998), *Geographic Profile of Employment and Unemployment*, Chicago.
Johnson, E.W. (1999), 'Chicago Metropolis 2020: Preparing Metropolitan Chicago for the 21st Century,' The Commercial Club of Chicago.
Ronald McDonald House Charities (2000), 'Ronald McDonald House Charities 1999 Annual Report', McDonald's Corporation.
Sara Lee Corporation (2000), '1999 Annual Report', Sara Lee Corporation.
World Business Chicago (1997), 'Advancing An International Metropolis,' The Civic Committee of The Commercial Club of Chicago.

Discussion Partners

M.A. Angelini, Vice President of The Shaw Company
J.S. Ayers, Executive Director, Leadership for Quality Education
T.W. Bartkoski, Project Manager, World Business Chicago
M. Bush, President of the Woodstock Institute

A. Gini, Professor Business Ethics, Loyola University Chicago
D.R. Judd, Professor of Political Science, University of Illinois at Chicago
J. Kossy, Council of Adult Experiential Learning Chicago
C.C. Meyer, Vice President, Civic Committee of The Commercial Club of Chicago
D. Perry, Professor of Urban Planning and Policy, Director of the Great Cities Institute at University of Illinois at Chicago
W. Riker, Senior Director Corporate Communications, McDonald's Corporation
J. Schaefer, Senior Manager Public and Community Affairs, McDonald's Corporation
S.C. Schnell, Senior Manager Economic Development, Civic Committee of The Commercial Club of Chicago
C.A. Selcke, Director International Field Relations, Ronald McDonald House Charities
S.R. Slaughter, Program Director, Chicago Metropolis 2020
H. Steans, Director of Economic Development, Civic Committee of The Commercial Club of Chicago
B. Trask, Director Corporate Communications, McDonald's Corporation
R.S. Tryloff, Executive Director of the Sara Lee Foundation
W. Wiewel, Dean of the College of Business Administration, University of Illinois at Chicago

Chapter 5

Leeds

Introduction

In comparison with cities like Chicago, London, New York and Seattle, the English city of Leeds is less known. This former industrial city is the capital of the region of Yorkshire and Humber. In discussions about business involvement in urban development, Leeds is often quoted as a successful example. Observers within and outside the UK refer to Leeds as a city where the private sector plays an active part in the development of city and region.

The structure of this chapter is as follows. After a brief profile of Leeds and its surroundings there follows an analysis of three interesting initiatives and projects. The next section contemplates the active role of Business in the Community Yorkshire and Humber (BITCYH), a regional branch of the national organisation 'Business in the Community'. The following section is concerned with the social activities of football club Leeds United, in particular its catalysing role in that respect. Next we discuss the Leeds Initiative, a joint initiative of government, non-profit organisations and organised private enterprise. Finally, we will sum up the chapter's main conclusions.

Profile

In the urban system of the UK, London is the absolute centre. No other city can measure up to this 'global city'. Besides London, the UK counts some places that are looked upon as 'second cities'. Leeds belongs to that category, along with such cities as Manchester and Birmingham. These cities are important regional centres. The city of Leeds has nearly 740,000 inhabitants and is the economic motor of the Yorkshire and Humber region. The latest estimate (City of Leeds, 2001) shows that Leeds boasts some 440,000 job opportunities. Every day, many commuters travel to (the centre of) Leeds. The number of commuters is still rising and they seem prepared to cover increasing distances. The expanding functional economic region reinforces the economic relation between city and surroundings.

Economically, the city of Leeds has been on the map since the seventeenth century. The local economy used to be dominated by the production and processing of clothing, but commerce and other activities were important as well. Leeds was one of the leaders in the Industrial Revolution; at the beginning of the twentieth century the city housed 450,000 people, and 45 per cent of employment was related to clothing, machine building, and textile. Nevertheless Leeds had an edge on other industrial cities whose dependence on one or two sectors was even more pronounced.

Thanks to that more diversified economic basis, Leeds suffered less than other 'second cities' from the effects of the industrial reorganisation and restructuring that started in the 1950s and went on into the 1980s. Nevertheless, employment in manufacturing industry fell considerably. While in the early 1950s half the active population was still employed in industry, by the time of writing, the proportion has fallen to less than 15 per cent (about 51,000 jobs in 1999). To turn the economic tide (in the 1980s) Leeds began to concentrate its attention on the financial sector. At the time, the governors glimpsed the opportunities provided by the good London connections. London was becoming too expensive or losing its appeal for lack of space for certain activities. Leeds thus advertised itself as a centre of financial services, and with success. By now, the city ranks third in financial and business services (London obviously remaining the unchallenged number one). The employment structure of Leeds illustrates the importance of this sector for the city (see Table 5.1).

Table 5.1 Employment in Leeds

Sector	1996	Relative (%)	1999	Relative (%)
Energy and water	3,700	1.06	2,700	0.69
Manufacturing industry	56,100	16.03	51,600	13.27
Building trade	14,100	4.03	21,400	5.50
Hotels, catering and distribution	83,600	23.89	83,400	21.45
Transport and communication	19,200	5.49	22,500	5.79
Financial and business services	73,000	20.86	91,600	23.55
Government	81,400	23.26	98,400	25.30
Other services	17,700	5.06	17,000	4.37
Total	348,800	100.00	388,600	100.00

Source: City of Leeds, 2001.

The majority of employers in Leeds belong to small and medium-size enterprise. Nearly four-fifths of the registered companies employ 10 or fewer people; their employees account together for 17 per cent of employment in Leeds. Only 1 per cent of the companies employ more than 200, generating no less than 37 per cent of total employment (see Table 5.2).

Table 5.2 Size of business companies in Leeds[1]

Company size	1–10	11–99	100–199	>200	Total
Companies	19,991	4,655	327	272	25,245
Number of employees	66,900	131,850	44,450	145,800	389,950

Source: City of Leeds, 2001.

Business in the Community Yorkshire and Humber

Business in the Community Yorkshire and Humber (BITCYH) is a regional department of the nationally operating Business in the Community (BITC). BITC is a not-for-profit organisation that tries to persuade companies to raise the quality and quantity of their contribution to social and economic revitalisation by promoting corporate social responsibility as an essential element of good entrepreneurship (BITC West Midlands, 2000). BITC refers to the Business Excellence Model of the European Foundation for Quality Management, in which 'impact on society' is considered one of the advantages ensuing from the conduct of businesses. The members of BITC recognise that a sustainable development of the community contributes to the continuity of the business company: 'Business excellence and community excellence are interdependent' (BITC, 1999). The organisation is convinced that more companies ought to be prepared to contribute to the solution of structural problems in certain neighbourhoods. Companies should be more aware of their self-interest in a sustainable development of the community, in view of the relations with their stakeholders: customers, employees, communities, suppliers, the government, the media, and investors. Some 650 companies participate in the national organisation, which counts eleven regional offices,[2] among which one in Yorkshire and Humber.

Historical Background

BITC was founded in the early 1980s at a time of high unemployment rates, great social problems, and social disturbances in many English inner cities. The founding was one of the first signals that British private enterprise had a part to play in the drive for sustainable community development. In the first instance, BITC set up local organisations which gave free advice to starter entrepreneurs (local enterprise agencies), activities that by now have been transferred to the organisation Business Link.

After the founding, many nationally respected companies became members of BITC, of which the Prince of Wales has been president since 1985. Its attention has shifted towards such themes as equal opportunities, the environment, education and related matters. At first, the members were mostly from London and the southeast, and many activities were addressed to just those areas. There were few regional initiatives. At the end of the 1980s the decision was made to reinforce the regional structure of BITC by appointing paid regional directors.

That decision was one reason for BITC to merge in 1995 with the organisation Action – Employees in the Community. That merger put BITC in the public eye, and enabled it to make use of Action's regional network.

Activities in Yorkshire and Humber

In the region Yorkshire and Humber the organisation has been quite active, despite a small financial base. By now BITCYH has grown considerably: its present turnover amounts to some £1.3 million. Within BITC the department is well thought of as one of the most active and enterprising regional agents. That is confirmed by the list of campaigns under the auspices of BITCYH. For one thing, the platform stimulates diversity in company staffs to make them a better reflection of the community. The Bradford riots in the summer of 2001 have strengthened the attention of private enterprise for young ethnic minorities. Another programme is Opportunity Now, which aims at the improvement of development opportunities for women in business. BITCYH has also adopted the American '… Cares' (Leeds Cares, Bradford Cares, etc.) concept by which employees invest time in the improvement of the living quality in the neighbourhood (BITCYH, 2000). The programme is applied across many places in the region, including Leeds and Bradford.

Furthermore, the organisation assists companies in their efforts to prevent environmental pollution, in a campaign entitled Business in the Environment.

In the framework of Pro Help, professionals give free advice to voluntary organisations and charity institutions, while Partners in Leadership stimulates experienced managers of regional private companies to help directors of elementary schools in matters of management. The campaign 'Right to Read' recruits volunteers from private enterprise to help children between the ages of seven and 11 to improve their reading proficiency. The national 'Seeing is Believing' programme is successful in Leeds as in other places; decision makers from private enterprise come to see with their own eyes what problems they can help solve and what can be the results.

Principles of Business in the Community Yorkshire and Humber

BITCYH's actions rest on a number of principles. Firstly, the power of the programme is vested in the companies rather than in the supporting organisation. Without the active involvement of individual companies, success is unthinkable. Every one of the projects mentioned above – 'Right to Read', for example – has its own leadership team, in which decision makers from private enterprise direct the project (BITCYH, 2001b). The BITCYH organisation also has its own leadership team to direct the activities.

Secondly, the organisation stimulates its grassroots support to take a more strategic look at corporate social responsibility. An extra challenge is that the great majority of private companies are small or medium-sized. For lack of time and people, such companies are not the most likely leaders of corporate social responsibility. BITCYH operates a step-by-step approach, encouraging positive initiatives instead of emphasising what companies should or should not do. In the setting of Business in the Environment, for instance, a ranking is drawn up to display which companies in the region are performing well on environmental-friendly behaviour (BITCYH, 2001a). A good position on that ranking may help a company recruiting suitable staff. No extensive attention is given, however, to companies performing badly. The organisation indeed acts from the conviction that strategic corporate social responsibility cannot be forced, but that companies need to grow into it.

Thirdly, BITCYH is actively trying for cooperation with other stakeholders in the region. Since the strategic shift of its course towards a more regional approach, collaboration with other organisations, and with companies that have already done much for the region, has been growing. Several initiatives have been the result, among which the above-mentioned 'Cares' model. BITCYH has contributed to the formation of several partnerships with representatives of all relevant organisations. What is lacking, however, is adequate mutual adjustment of the different partnerships, of which some are now even in competition with each other.

Fourthly, BITCYH wants to improve the support inside the companies by building a bridge between the often highly active community-affairs department and other departments such as human resources (staffing policy). To that end the organisation wants to clarify, among other things, how the relation among departments should ideally be. Hopefully, better relations can be stimulated through the CEOs, who on the whole are strongly committed to community activities.

Finally, the organisation acts as spokesman for private enterprise, working together with the recently founded regional-economic development company Yorkshire Forward (Yorkshire Forward, undated).

Leeds United

In general, professional football clubs are not leaders in corporate social responsibility. On the whole, professional football clubs – whether or not quoted on the Stock Exchange – are directed in a highly traditionally and perhaps even 'old-fashioned' way. Frequently, they are introspective organisations where at best a glimpse of modern ideas of management can be seen. Mostly, the relation with their direct environment has no place in their corporate strategy. The successful Premier League football club Leeds United is an exception to that rule. In 1998, the exchange-quoted company mounted a programme entitled Community United, with the primary aim of optimising the relation between the club and (local) community. Community United is an element of the strategic corporate plan and fits in with the management's determination to invest in the future of young people: within but also outside the club, keeping the interest of the club in mind. The club interest reaches beyond 'training young talents within the club for the first team'. Leeds United defines the relevant community as 'all people who have a stake in or a tie with Leeds United'.

Topics

The programme has gained general applause by its innovative and unorthodox approach. The projects in the framework of Community United address specific target groups. There are three zones of attention (see also Leeds United PLC, 2002): 1) Football in the Community; 2) Education; and 3) Corporate Affairs.

For Football in the Community, football coaches visit schools to give football training courses. Such visits of grassroots football coaches to schools help the club to find talent (talented youngsters may qualify for a place at the football school Leeds United Academy), but also serve the broader social purpose of encouraging young people to take up sports. To date, Football in the Community has reached over 50,000 young boys and girls at 350 schools.

Education ranks high among the interests of Community United. The educational projects 'Playing for Success' and 'Learning Through Football' are carried out in the Learning Centre, situated underneath the southern stands of the stadium. It is a well-appointed mini-school with a library, computers, discussion tables, etc. The lessons are given by qualified teachers and about 100 volunteers, among whom are students and managers from the private sector. Children are taught here in a relaxed fashion. Football and the football idols of Leeds United appear to be a strong stimulus to the participants. School subjects such as mathematics and literacy are given more glamour by the use of computers, as well as through the association with football. The programme utilises the entire stadium in a creative manner to exercise all subjects in practice. For example, the children may be instructed to calculate the square area of the field. Although younger children are taken on as well, the emphasis is on youngsters between the ages of nine and 13. Besides, there are personal development programmes for 14- to 25-year-olds, oriented to the labour market. At the end of a programme, the participants appear to score considerably better than before in arithmetic, language and computer skills.

In the third place, Leeds United, under the heading of Community United, takes in hand the more traditional corporate affairs related to football, such as anti-racism initiatives and a reading campaign by which photographs of top footballers inspire children to read.

Strategic Approach

In all, 30 people are involved full-time and 35 part-time in the projects, among whom are many football coaches. Even before 1998 the club had been socially active, but there was then no direct relation with the corporate strategy ('to guard the reputation and the status of Leeds United as a robust brand of football'), and the social activities were not vested in a coherent vision. The proactive approach of Leeds United to corporate social responsibility has by now been copied by some other football clubs playing in the Premier League. The budget made available by Leeds United is not exceptionally high, but because the club always works together with authorities and sponsors, a lot more money flows into the projects. The collaboration with authorities and the strong commitment of business companies to the club, has yielded a leverage effect. The football club functions as a catalyst for additional investment. The club's policy is to ensure that every pound the club invests generates at least one more pound. The club cooperates with, among others, clothing sponsor Nike and home banker HSBC.

Collaboration with public parties is not always easy for the club. The municipality is on the whole an awkward partner: subsidy procedures are complicated and call for a lot of patience. Moreover, entrepreneurs and civil servants speak different languages. Finally, it is important for the Club not to get implicated in political questions. Leeds United is for all, is the motto.

Lessons from Leeds United

What we can learn from the experiences of Leeds United is that the sector in which this company operates offers many opportunities for an additional impulse to social activities. Football in general, and top class football in particular, has – at any rate in Europe – great natural appeal ('football is sexy'). Football can connect and inspire people, and serve as a means to get to grips with social problems in an unorthodox fashion. Thanks in part to the product 'football', the club acts as a catalyst for investments from other parties that for several reasons like to join the 'flagship' Leeds United (a strong sports brand). Moreover, Leeds United possesses a strong organisation with deep roots in the city: football clubs indeed tend to have a natural bond with their immediate environment, if only because many football players come from the less prosperous families. In the future, Community United will remain eager to intensify and expand its collaboration with the local government, club sponsors and other social organisations.

A final important observation is that the club managers themselves believe in and are committed to the social programmes. They believe that ultimately the club's social activities will redeem themselves. At presentations to commercial partners, the social activities are brought to their attention. Sponsors like to associate with such initiatives. The projects moreover generate a lot of free publicity. The media come to the projects unbidden, and such free publicity is worth money to the club. In the long run the projects even add to the supporting crowds. Those are the arguments used by the club to demonstrate the value of investments. Up till now Leeds United has succeeded in convincing the shareholders of the relevancy of such programmes. In the club's annual reports the state of affairs with respect to these programmes is (briefly) mentioned.

Leeds Initiative

Leeds initiative was founded in 1990 by Leeds City Council and seven other partners. The initiative has developed into an extensive partnership of 20 major organisations (including the Chamber of Commerce, the Leeds Training and Education Centre, the two universities, the Leeds Health Authority, regional television, and the airport authority). In all, no fewer than 500 organisations are directly or indirectly involved in activities coming under the flag of the Leeds Initiative. The value added of the initiative springs from the joint planning, joint ventures, coordinated lobbying, and the networking to exchange knowledge and ideas and create confidence.

Right from the start, the partners have sought to act decisively and purposefully and to prevent the initiative being cluttered up by red tape. The parties agreed jointly to take the city centre in hand, the Chamber of Commerce stimulating companies to invest in the centre, and the government taking responsibility for the necessary infrastructure. The revitalisation of the city's heart had a plural objective: to attract more residents, companies and visitors, and, by the joint undertaking and the investment in the town centre, to improve the image of the city of Leeds. Owing to economic problems in the 1970s and 1980s, Leeds had regularly been in the news in a negative sense, and there was a risk that the perception of investors and other prominent parties would be an obstacle to economic recovery. The image of an industrial city in distress conflicted with the vision of some eminent personalities within the partnership, who on the contrary could see development potentialities. The option chosen was to put Leeds on the map as a financial centre, with the accent on financial services.

Vision and Strategy

There are those who believe that the Leeds partnership has acted as a model for the British government's present national urban policy. In the setting of the City-Challenge programme, public-private partnerships are stimulated, collaboration being one condition for financial support. In the second half of the 1990s, the principal cities were requested to develop an integral vision of the future of city and region. They were more or less obliged to draw up such a long-term vision, as it would be taken into account for the allocation of funds. The vision-development process started in 1997 and lasted about 18 months, efforts being made to involve as many parties as possible. The vision for Leeds identifies six strategic work fields, the efforts being expected ultimately to ensure the sustainable development of Leeds. These six themes were formulated and approved at workshops, seminars and participation hearings (Leeds Initiative, undated).

The first theme is 'Competing in a Global Economy'. Leeds wants to be recognised internationally as a dynamic and cosmopolitan centre for the world of business, education and art. Secondly, the city aims at 'Making the Most of People'. Leeds should be a town where all residents have an opportunity for maximum self-development. The third issue is 'Integrated Transport'. Leeds is to be an accessible city with a high-grade transport system that supports the urban economy and its social life with the least possible damage to the environment. Fourthly, Leeds wants to be a large, clean and attractive city where the environment is constantly improved ('Looking after the Environment'). Fitfthly, Leeds is to become a city where people would like to live in any of the neighbourhoods ('Creating Better Neighbourhoods and Confident Communities'). Finally, the city prefers 'A Planned Approach to Technology': a well-considered input of communication and information technology for a better economic performance and a higher quality of life in Leeds.

For each of the six themes a strategy group has been appointed to work out the relevant partial vision. The strategy group translates the vision into an unequivocal and well-founded strategy including a plan of action which lays down the details of contributions and actions of the different partners. The cohesion with the regional strategy of Yorkshire and Humber is to be guarded as well. The key to success of the Vision for Leeds rests in the translation of the vision into strategies and action plans. The translation is in full swing, the special recognition for 'Excellence in Sustainable Governance' by a UN-sponsored international committee being significant encouragement.

One of the most successful partnerships is the Leeds Economic Partnership, which was started two years ago by the Leeds Development Council, the University, and regional development companies. Essentially, however, this is a public affair. In a general sense, the (regional) private sector has participated in the accomplishment of the partnership and in the development of a vision. The participants were mostly the organised companies represented by the Chamber of Commerce. Although the Leeds Initiative explicitly pretends to be a public-private partnership, the municipality is at the moment still 'leading'. The contribution of organised private enterprise has so far been mostly one of content. By far the greater part of the initiative is paid for by the public partners. In the coming years the initiative is to become a spider in the web of a great many other partnerships. The intention of Leeds Initiative is for the private sector to assume a more prominent part over time.

Conclusions

What are the main lessons to be drawn from the Leeds experiences? There is no doubt that the private sector in Leeds has been and still is actively engaged in the problems of the region. There are plenty of good intentions and quite a lot has been accomplished. But in this city, as in others, there are clearly a good many companies which still have not proceeded to a more strategic approach to corporate community involvement. Remember that the great majority of companies in Leeds and its surroundings belong to small and medium-sized enterprises. In consequence, the initiatives often keep knocking at the doors of the same major companies. Much mission work will be required to make smaller companies aware of their stakes in corporate citizenship.

It is interesting to follow the activities of BITCYH. This regional department of BITC is active and enterprising. Step by step it tries to enthuse companies in a more strategic approach to corporate community involvement, forging partnerships between companies and with other stakeholders in the region. BITCYH tries to involve companies closely in its own organisation, and fulfils a leader's role together with the 'enlightened' businesses in the so-called leadership team. This team tries to influence the agendas and priorities of member companies. BITCYH is not only a 'broker' but also a dispenser of knowledge, and to some degree a trainee's coach for companies that are waking up to their social responsibility.

Professional football club Leeds United has won much attention in the UK for the programme Community United, which puts the relationship between club and community at the centre. Leeds United has even set up a mini-school underneath the stands, where notably children between the ages of nine and 13 can improve their proficiency in reading, writing and arithmetic, and acquire computer skills (with the approval and financial support of the government). Football clubs have magic and appeal and Leeds United uses this among other things for educational and social purposes. The same fame of the football brand Leeds United serves as a catalyst for investments from other companies and organisations. The club encourages notably its sponsors and other business relations to invest in the activities of Community United, and creates a leverage effect, each pound from the club being expected to generate at least one additional pound of investment money.

The last form of partnership to be discussed in this case report is the Leeds Initiative. The partnership from which the present Leeds Initiative has sprung contributed in the 1980s to the setting of a new economic course with financial and business services as spearhead. At the time, the directors and decision makers from private enterprise joined forces. The Leeds Initiative has drawn up the vision for Leeds, together with partners. Its success depends on the translation of that vision into strategies and actions. Strikingly, the partnership is supported mainly from public resources. The explicit intention is to involve the private sector more closely in the elaboration and implementation.

Notes

1 As 'companies' this statistic counts the number of units (work locations), so that the figure is a little above reality.
2 East Midlands, Eastern London, North East, North West, Northern Ireland, South East, South West, Wales, West Midlands, Yorkshire and Humber. Moreover BITC has a sister organisation in Scotland: Scottish Business in the Community.

References

BITC (1999), 'Positive Impact, Business in the Community'.
BITCYH (2000), 'Leeds Cares for the Community by the Community', Business in the Community Yorkshire and Humber.
BITCYH (2001a) 'Regional Index of Environmental Engagement', Business in the Community Yorkshire and Humber.
BITCYH (2001b), 'Right Read Annual Review 2000–2001', Business in the Community Yorkshire & Humber.
City of Leeds (2001), 'Leeds Economy Handbook 2001',< http://www.leeds.gov.uk/bus_info/economy/handbook.html>.
Leeds Initiative (undated), 'Vision for Leeds – A Strategy for Sustainable Development 1999–2009'.
Leeds United PLC (2002), 'Leeds United PLC Annual Report 2001: Marching on Together'.
Yorkshire Forward (undated), 'A World Class Approach to a World Class Region', Yorkshire and Humber Regional Development Agency.

Discussion partners

J. Booth, Not For Profit Ltd
J. Bird, Area Manager, South Yorkshire Business Community Partnership
R. Gregory, Managing Director, Yorkshire Television
N. Harold, Corporate Development Manager, Westfield Health Scheme
K. Kudelnitzky, Director of Leeds Initiative
P. Lee, Regional Director, Business in the Community Yorkshire and Humber

S. Robinson, Deputy Regional Director, Business in the Community Yorkshire and Humber
D. Spencer, Director Operations, Leeds United Football Club
E. Stanford, Head of Community Affairs, Leeds United Football Club
J. Unsworth, Business in the Community Yorkshire and Humber
L.M. Walker, Assistant Area Manager, Leeds, HSBC

Chapter 6

London

Introduction

For several reasons London is an interesting case to be studied in the context of corporate community involvement. For one thing, private enterprise in the UK has been stimulated by the government's relatively passive role (notably in the 1980s and the early 1990s) in taking matters into their own hands. For another, London is beset with structural problems of accessibility, housing, education and unemployment, problems which could make companies in this metropolis aware of their social interests.

This chapter aims to analyse the possibilities for cross-sector partnerships ensuing from corporate community involvement in London. A profile of London, is followed by a section on some initiatives from government and intermediary organisation to get the private sector more involved in a sustainable development of London. Next we bring up the policies and activities of three London-based companies with a strategic approach to corporate social responsibility. Finally, conclusions are drawn.

Profile

London, with New York, Tokyo and Paris, belongs at the top level of the urban hierarchy. Within the UK, London is not only the capital, but also by far the largest metropolis, with a population of about 7.4 million. The city is considered the financial centre of Europe, as is reflected among other things by the presence of 108 main offices of the 500 greatest concerns of the world (Department of the Environment, Transport and the Regions (DETR), 1998). Moreover, more than 500 foreign banks have an establishment in the British capital. No wonder then that business and financial services generate a lot of employment, as is clear from Table 6.1. However, London has qualities in other areas as well, such as international communication, creative and cultural activity (media, internet), (higher) education and tourism.

Since 1980, the number of persons working and/or living in London has been on the increase. Population and employment are expected to go on growing in the coming years. Unfortunately, investment in infrastructure and public services has not kept up with growth. London has serious problems (both quantitative and qualitative) with respect to transportation, education (skills), housing and business location. These problems raise costs and slow down economic growth, jeopardising in the long run the status of London as a metropolis (London Development Agency (LDA), 2001). One of the greatest problems is the aggravating polarisation, some neighbourhoods suffering from extreme poverty (14 of the 20 poorest neighbourhoods in England are situated in London), whereas others are known as the richest in Europe.

In particular, the Londoners of foreign origin, notably on the east side of Central London, are hardly if at all socially integrated and feel no affinity with the 'other' London. The number of homeless persons is rising, one-fifth of the population lives on a benefit, and unemployment at 10 per cent is above the national average of 8 per cent. Housing is another serious problem: 800,000 residents are confronted with a form of housing shortage. For more and more people London has become a place to work but not to live in. The city is quite simply getting too expensive.

Table 6.1 Employment structure in Greater London (1999)

Sector	Number of employees	%
Industry	296,405	7
Construction	133,333	3
Trade	639,114	16
Hotel and catering industry	276,161	7
Transport, storage and communication	303,759	8
Financial services	340,505	9
Business services	912,331	23
Government, social security	227,900	6
Education	251,234	6
Health care and social work	307,127	8
Other social services	256,362	6
Other	15,425	0
Total	3,959,656	100

Sources: Office for National Statistics (ONS), 1999; LDA, 2001, p. 26.

There are striking differences among the London residential areas in social-economic status, ethnic origin, language, culture, etc. Highly divergent communities have developed which have hardly any affinity with other parts of London. The lack of mutual social-economic ties, due in part to deep-rooted social-cultural divergences, is characteristic of the kind of town that London is (Llewelyn Davies et al., 1997). The contrasts seem to consolidate rather than level off. Many inhabitants are hard put to it to benefit from the favourable economic developments. There seem to be imaginary walls separating the various parts of the town. Llewelyn Davies et al. (1997) have pointed out how remarkably few East Enders (from the social-economically weakest part of London) work in the City, while they do commute to the West End or other parts. Canary Wharf (in the Docklands) draws many commuters from Essex, whereas in the immediately surrounding boroughs there is much unemployment. The proximity of that new business centre has hardly opened any new prospects to these underprivileged boroughs.

Besides the social troubles, which are much more massive and poignant in London than in other UK cities, plenty of other problems are threatening its functioning as a metropolis. There are many who feel concerned that London has become so dependent on the highly cycle-sensitive financial sector; they believe that economic diversity should be stimulated. The state of the transport system is another reason for anxiety. The backbone of London Transport, the Underground, suffers from acute over-occupation and unreliability as a result of years of neglected maintenance and delayed replacement investment. The over-occupation of the tube system is in part the result of the housing problem, for many people who work in the inner city of London ('Inner London') have their homes far outside it. The air pollution due to the traffic is another great worry. Only lately have voices been raised to give more attention to the sustainability aspect.

Administration

The administration of London is most complicated. London consists of 33 boroughs (districts), which can operate fairly independently. These boroughs had long been the only democratically chosen local government bodies in the town of London, when in the late 1990s the British government agreed to proposals to create an elected urban government: the Greater London Authority (GLA). That Authority has a directly chosen mayor and a chosen municipal council: the London Assembly.

Within the Greater London Authority four separate organisations can be distinguished: the London Development Agency (LDA), Transport for London (TfL), the Metropolitan Police Authority (MPA), and the London Fire and

Emergency Planning Authority (LFEPA). The London Development Agency was founded in July 2000 to assist the mayor in drawing up an economic development and revitalisation strategy. Its competencies are similar to those of the eight other Regional Development Agencies, as laid down in the national Act of that name.

The London Development Agency's objective and responsibility is to promote sustainable urban development. Instruments to that effect are increasing the competitive power of the private sector, stimulating employment, and raising the quality of the labour supply. To accomplish all that, the Agency works in close harmony with boroughs, private enterprise (mostly through its representative organisations: London First/the Chamber of Commerce and the Confederation of Business Industry), organisations of volunteers, and educational institutions. The strategy that the Agency is working on takes into account that, while London is unquestioningly the motor of economic growth, many of its residents fail to enjoy the fruits. London strives for economic growth that is balanced with social and ecological aspects. That is not always easy, because environmental interests and economic interests tend to be at loggerheads. But many companies are in favour of sustainable development because they recognise their own stake in it. Especially in transport, education and housing the problems are so grave that they seem impossible to solve without a (financial) contribution of the private sector. So, the question now arises how and where private enterprise can help. Arguably, some problems are more susceptible to private intervention than others.

How to Involve the Private Sector?

Government and intermediary organisations have taken several initiatives aimed at involve the private sector in a sustainable development of London. On the side of the government, the London Development Agency has worked out an economic development strategy for London in consultation with business companies, and laid it down in a report entitled 'Success Through Diversity' (LDA, 2001). Four principles constitute the guideline for the strategy: 1) economic growth; 2) knowledge and learning; 3) diversity, inclusion and innovation; and 4) sustainable development. These principles also form the foundation of the so-called 'Charter for London', a declaration of intent of all relevant stakeholders, including London First as representative of private enterprise. Together with seven other strategies (concerned with spatial development, transport, culture, noise nuisance, air quality, waste management, and biodiversity), the economic development strategy serves as a blueprint for the future development of the town.

The agency has taken three roles upon itself: 1) to develop a framework of ideas to direct the development and revitalising of the London economy; 2) to make available its own funds to give shape to that framework; and 3) to stimulate the maximum leverage of other private and public funds jointly setting the priorities (LDA, 2001, p. 15). The last task is particularly interesting from our point of view. The government could stimulate companies to invest in community development. The agency's tasks are given substance in the components of the strategy by the formulation of 'actions'. However, whether the ensuing investments would be purely commercial (project developers creating a shopping precinct or laying out a new stretch of underground railway), or have social aspects as well (companies contributing to the new stretch of underground railway because they set store by good accessibility in the town), remains the question.

One component of the drive for economic growth is the upgrading of the infrastructure. The agency seeks collaboration with the Greater London Authority, Transport for London, the boroughs and possibly others to try, in partnership with the private sector, to achieve a leverage effect for the financing of new transport projects (ibid., p. 42). Actually, such partnerships are essentially traditional public-private partnerships, private partners making their investment decisions by purely commercial criteria. Evidently, the government is still considered primarily responsible for the solution of transport problems.

Local Strategic Partnerships

In its drive for social inclusion, the London Development Agency wants to join forces with Local Strategic Partnerships (LSPs) to stimulate the economic development of backward regions by integral revitalising programmes (such collaboration is encouraged by the national government). The Agency wants to contribute to the coordination of LSPs and provide them with a regional context in which they can operate effectively. It also intends to communicate best practices, and, most interesting of all: to orchestrate an effective contribution to LSPs from the private sector (ibid., p. 73).

The formation of Local Strategic Partnerships is a component of the national urban policy in the UK. A Local Strategic Partnership is a separate organisation which binds together on the local level public authorities, business companies and social organisations, for the purpose of mutual adjustment of activities.

The partnership approach is in line with other policy programmes (DETR, 2001). LSPs that submit good plans, can count on support from the national government. Collaboration between government and private enterprise will undoubtedly be a significant factor for the allocation of budgets. From the description of the ideal functioning of a Local Strategic Partnership, organising capacity appears to be crucial. A primary requirement for the formation of such a partnership is leadership – there must be somebody who: 1) takes the initiative; 2) expresses and inspires vision and commitment from other partners; and 3) ensures that all partners have an opportunity to play a full and active part in its work. Partnerships already active (such as Business in the Community, and London First) could assume the leadership role (ibid., p. 12).

The Role of Private Enterprise in Local Strategic Partnerships

Involvement of the private sector is a necessary condition for success, since business companies are the principal buyers and suppliers of local activities and services. They play a crucial part in the prosperity and welfare of neighbourhoods. The private sector moreover possesses the necessary knowledge and expertise (ibid., p. 68). The involvement of the private sector can take shape through the representatives of the principal employers, the Chamber of Commerce, or other intermediary organisations which defend the (commercial and social) interests of private enterprise. Companies will notably be interested in LSP-participation when they recognise its value added and the plans meet their own needs and priorities.

From British research, four approaches appear to contribute to success (ibid., p. 69). Firstly, early involvement means that businesses can help to design the projects (strategy building) and feel more committed (support). Secondly, employers who are already active in the community can inspire others, using their networks and credibility as instruments. Thirdly, employers who understand local matters, or have experience in supporting local projects, are obvious candidate-partners. And fourthly, incentives like 'staff training and development' (participation of employees), 'business opportunities' (product and market development), and 'raised profile' (reputation, image) can intensify the involvement and participation of businesses.

These approaches confirm the thesis that there must be a distinct self-interest at stake, whether or not 'enlightened'. Participation in a LSP that tries to find integral and coordinated solutions for matters of metropolitan scope, can help companies reach their own more limited goals. Moreover, participating businesses can exert influence on the government and the social organisations, as well as profit from any scale advantages and cost reductions. Furthermore, companies welcome a reduction of red tape and government regulation. LSPs offer companies access to a great network offering the most diverse knowledge and skills, and can be helpful in innovation and learning processes. Despite all these benefits, the national government sometimes considers additional incentives needed, for instance on behalf of backward regions where the problems tend to be more complex than elsewhere. The national government stimulates the creation of LSPs in such areas by additional financing from the Neighbourhood Renewal Fund.

The formation of LSPs is still in full swing. London is exceptional in that the partnerships are formed not on the level of the town but on that of the boroughs. The London Development Agency has undertaken to coordinate all these LSPs. It is still too early for final conclusions, but evidently the dimensions of the town and the involved administrative structure do not make for smooth cooperation between the public and private sectors through LSPs.

London First

One of the organisations that defend the (social) interests of London's private enterprise, is London First. This organisation was founded in the early 1990s as an instrument for mobilising business leaders to make London more attractive and promote it more effectively. Direct reasons for its foundation were the economic recession (the first white-collar recession to hit London as well as the rest of the UK), the regrettable state of the transport infrastructure, and the lack of a central strategic unit to take such matters firmly in hand. More and more people in private enterprise became convinced of the need for action. It was Stephen O'Brian, chairman of Business in the Community (see Chapter 5), who together with some others, took the initiative to found London First.

Until 2001, the scope of London First was limited to defending the interests of large companies in London. In 2001, its scope was widened by the merger with the London Chamber of Commerce and Industry, which from of old has oriented itself more to small and medium-sized enterprise. The third prominent defender of interests is the Confederation of Business Industry (CBI), which represents mostly industrial companies.

Objectives and Activities

London First is funded through the membership subscriptions of private companies and institutions of higher education. The organisation tries to involve companies in the decision making about London's future. Companies can make use of their membership for PR purposes. The organisation envisages improving the accessibility and liveability as well as raising the quality of the labour supply. To that end it works together with companies, the local government, voluntary organisations and other stakeholders.

Right from the moment of founding, transport has been a spearhead of London First's policy. Although some improvements in the transport system have already been accomplished (among which the completion of the Jubilee Line extension), the members consider further investment in the safety, reliability and quality of the transport system highly advisable. The costs of improving the system and preparing for growth are estimated at £25 billion. London First pleads an active role for private enterprise in the drive for better accessibility.

In the course of the years London First has taken up some other matters in which private enterprise has a stake, namely, the quality of the active population and that of the living environment. A well-educated and motivated workforce is considered a condition *sine qua non* if London is to keep its status as a metropolis (London First, 1999). In that line of thought, the organisation intends to unite educational institutions and companies (members of the organisation) in an endeavour towards more business-oriented education. Moreover the organisation is involved in developing a marketing strategy for the education sector.

London is so large, so diverse and so complex, that in the eyes of London First its economic development has to be taken on in a decentralised way. To that end the town has been divided into five regions: north, south, east, west, and central London. The organisation stimulates and supports the founding of partnerships of private companies with local stakeholders in these regions. To that end London First unites the relevant parties around common objectives, especially those concerned with transport, the attraction and retaining of business companies, and the promotion of demand-oriented education.

London First and the New London Government

From the start, London First has applauded the advent of a new central administration and a mayor for London. The many and manifold authorities in London are an obstacle to the smooth and decisive settlement of important matters, and were even more so while there was no central administration. London First was therefore highly pleased when the Greater London Authority Bill was published in December 1998. In broad outlines, this Bill was in accordance with the proposals submitted by London First in 1996 in a document entitled 'A Governor for London'. Moreover the Bill confirmed the need to involve private enterprise in the new decision-making structures. In 1999, London First published a task description for the new mayor which drew attention to the skills that are more essential for the job than the candidate's public persuasion.

Once the Bill had been passed by parliament, London First and the two other representatives of private enterprise (the Chamber of Commerce and the Confederation of Business Industry) drew up a so-called 'Business Manifesto for the Mayor'. This manifesto presents the private sector's vision on the future development of London and is London First's attempt to involve its members in debates on the urban administration, and to set its stamp on the way the new London Authority operates.

The Greater London Authority has an interest in good collaboration with London First; for one thing to create support (acceptance) among companies, and for another to open the way for effective (financial) support from private enterprise. The relatively small budget assigned to the Greater London Authority by the British government makes financial support of private enterprise indispensable if it is to perform the ambitious plans. London First does not supply that financial contribution directly but serves as an intermediary, identifying win-win situations for the public and private sectors and smoothing the road to cooperation. To enhance the cooperativeness, London First tries to bring the idea of corporate social responsibility to the notice companies as well as government and politicians. The assumption is that corporate self-interest cannot by itself cope with all social needs. There is indeed need for a government to direct the process, notably because business interests are subject to change.

Business in the Community London

The London branch of Business in the Community (BITC) pleads more strategic involvement of London private business, using several programmes as described in Chapter 5. BITC attaches more and more value to the urban dimension of corporate social responsibility. Consequently, BITC, like other organisations, is encouraged by the formation of Local Strategic Partnerships to consider collaboration with local governments a real option. However, to convince companies (the members of BITC) of the usefulness of collaboration with the public sector is not an easy proposition, since many companies are very distrustful of anything to do with the government.

In the view of BITC, the relations between the private and the public sector on the one hand, and between private enterprise and social organisations on the other, should be improved. The relation between social organisations (the voluntary sector) and private enterprise is marked by mutual distrust. Many of London's very active voluntary organisations are loath to collaborate with business companies which are venturing into corporate community involvement for the sake of (long-term) profit. And yet, for the very sake of a sustainable development of London social organisations may have to accept the capitalist motives of the private sector.

The Strategic Approach of London-based Companies

Now that it is clear that the government seems willing to cooperate with the private sector, the question of how far the private sector is responsive arises. In this section we analyse the strategic approach with regard to community involvement of three London-based companies: energy supplier Centrica, manufacturer of foods and beverages Diageo, and network and infrastructure manager Lattice.

Centrica

Centrica is a prominent energy supplier in the United Kingdom. The company was born in 1997 when the former state-owned company British Gas was split up with a view to the liberalisation of the energy market. The split up was an organisational measure to separate the management of the infrastructure from the distribution of energy.

To be able to stand up to new competitors on the energy market in 1998, Centrica adopted a wider definition of its core business. The company now presents itself as a supplier of essential services, not only at home, but after the recent take-over of the AA, an association of car drivers, also on the road. Under the brand names of British Gas, Nwy Prydain and Scottish Gas, Centrica supplies gas and electricity to private persons and companies in Great Britain. The company is also active in North America, under the names of 'Direct Energy' and 'Energy America'. Besides, the company is developing as a provider of financial services, with the Goldfish credit card as its main weapon. Centrica also offers telephone services under the name of One.Tel.

Social responsibilities Centrica's first 'social' responsibility as a commercial organisation is to provide its customers with the services they want in and around the home. In that way the company creates welfare for its employees, taxes for the government, jobs with suppliers and, for the investors, a return on their money. But besides all that, Centrica is very aware of its social responsibility towards the community in general. That feeling of responsibility is indeed an element of its corporate culture. The company translates that social involvement into support for good causes and contributions to the communities in which the company is active, reduction of noxious effects on the environment and the provision of a safe and healthy workplace for the employees.

Centrica's approach to its social responsibilities is a strategic one, as is evident at once from the thematic set-up. Present priorities are support to elderly and handicapped customers, energy saving, support to good causes and local voluntary organisations, and education. These themes are related to the company's core business. The choice of senior citizens as a target group is exceptional, because most companies prefer to associate with young people. The company works together with specialised organisations who well informed about the problems of the elderly target group. Special bus services have been made available to render elderly people more mobile. Donations have been given to shelters lacking essential facilities. Knowing that the problems of many elderly persons are related to energy – indeed, every year tens of thousands of senior citizens die of cold in the UK! – the company has set up a scheme which addresses 500,000 senior citizens.

That Centrica regards corporate community involvement as an integral element of its policy is evident from the decision made in 1999 to intensify the collaboration between the department concerned with corporate community involvement and the marketing department. The order was to develop a policy that would benefit the company as well as the community. Until that time, the company's social activities were not based on any clear vision or strategy. Budgets were spent in an ad hoc manner, a large number of cheques written out haphazardly for small amounts. The social activities were hardly profitable for the company and its brands. In the new approach, Centrica looks upon its social activities as instruments to enhance its image and make its brands better and wider known.

To assess whether the investments made indeed benefit the company as well as the community, their impact is extensively evaluated, by panels and questionnaires and other means. To that end, Centrica uses the model of the London Benchmarking Group. Some results are easy to quantify, such as the number of persons who were helped by the 'Help-the-Aged' project. Other results lend themselves less readily to quantification and become visible only in the long run. What has already transpired is that the social projects clearly enhance the fame and reputation of Centrica's brands. In 1999, of every 10 positive media communications about Centrica, seven were about the social projects (see www.centrica.co.uk). The company is often quoted as an example of corporate social responsibility, for instance in the 'seeing is believing' programme of Business in the Community, and has won a series of awards, among which a marketing award for the community involvement programme. Centrica has found that its strategy gives the company a better image among jobseekers. Graduates show an increasing interest in the organisation's culture, on the argument that a company that is good for the community is probably good for its employees.

Urban revitalisation Although Centrica is conscious of its own stake in attractive cities, the company is not effectively involved in projects of urban revitalisation. That is undoubtedly due to the character of the company (market, product, organisation). The possibilities have been investigated, but the conclusion is that participation in such projects would be a form of philanthropy, of which the returns (even if defined broadly and for the long term) would not weigh up against the costs.

Centrica is in principle willing to cooperate with other companies, social organisations and authorities, as long as a clear self-interest can be identified. The difficulty with large-scale (urban) projects involving a multitude of parties is to bring all their interests in line.

Diageo

Diageo is one of the world's greatest producers of beverages. The company developed from a merger between GrandMet and Guinness in 1997, and sells such well-known brands as Smirnoff, Johnnie Walker, Malibu and Bailey's. It operates the world over, and has its head office in London. Diageo is known for its highly proactive policy towards social responsibilities.

On the internet, Diageo presents itself as a company that 'wants to make a positive contribution to the welfare of the stakeholders and the economic, social and ecological sustainability of the world'. Thus, as a producer of alcoholic beverages the company has undertaken to stimulate consumers and employees to a 'responsible consumption of our products'. Diageo also proclaims its commitment to all local communities where the company is active. One per cent of the profit before tax (£18.1 million in the year to 30 June 2000 (Diageo, 2001)) is spent on social targets. A portion of that amount is destined to the Diageo Foundation, which has a yearly budget of some £3.5 million. Diageo's approach is strategic: its principle is that its social investments (made through the Foundation and otherwise) should in the event contribute to the long-term continuity of the company. For that reason, Diageo insists on measuring the effects of such investments. To that end it has, together with other companies, developed measuring instruments to assess the impact of social investments (notably on the national level).

Tomorrow's People One of the most successful social projects – and the most relevant to sustainable urban development – is Tomorrow's People. This foundation (a trust) was created in 1981 in response to the discontent among unemployed young people in British cities, and in line with the company's ambition to help solve structural unemployment problems. The firm was indeed becoming concerned about the (future) availability of skilled staff. Halfway through the 1990s the project's definition was widened somewhat, the accent shifting to the provision of a broad package of services to employers and unemployed persons. The objective has remained the same, however, namely, to help the jobless to a job! The complexity of the unemployment problem makes high demands on the management of the foundation, which has to work together with other organisations, among which local governments (including Training and Enterprise Councils), schools and employers. Collaboration is necessary to reach the target group and meet their requirements.

Tomorrow's People provides vocational training courses, advises and coaches unemployed people, and supports employers. One sub-project is New Steps: a community task force for 16- to 18-year-olds who are working on schemes that are of direct benefit to the local community. This project can be compared with the American City-Year programmes and the City Teams in Rotterdam. Participants receive training, a financial compensation and help in finding a job.

The projects of Tomorrow's People have proved successful. Since its inception, 350,000 people have been helped to a job. The national government has even adopted some sub-projects and elevated them to the status of national initiatives within the Welfare-to-Work Programme. Tomorrow's People has helped to set up other non-profit organisations, such as the Foyer Foundation which opens hostels for young people to save them from the negative cycle of unemployment and homelessness. Tomorrow's People is useful not only for the community but also for the company. Thanks to this initiative, Diageo has acquired for itself a social image while building up a close relation with the national government. The initiative has also helped towards the development of the London Benchmarking Group model (see Chapter 2).

Social strategy The social strategy of the Diageo Foundation is based on the experiences with Tomorrow's People. The Foundation initiates the formation of foundations and funds, makes people aware of a problem, unites individuals and organisations, finances a kick-start, and tries to find financial support from other companies and authorities. The Foundation thus serves as a catalyst and connector. Once a project is running smoothly, Diageo (that is, the Foundation) withdraws to become just one of the private sponsors. The projects are mostly managed by local people and organisations that are familiar with local needs. The Foundation tries to generate, with a relatively limited financial impulse, as much more money as possible: the leverage effect. With an investment of £20 million in Tomorrow's People – spread over 20 years – the company has managed to being in a total contribution of £160 million from other sponsors. The Foundation sets much store by a clear relation between the expenditure and the envisaged effects, and for that reason would rather keep aloof from 'tokenism', that is, from donating a relatively small amount (as a token of good will) to a common project initiated by others.

The social commitment of Diageo is based on the so-called LIFE-blood principle, LIFE standing for Leadership (the company wants to take the lead in the sector), Integration (the social activities need to be integrated in all departments of the company), Focus (the activities are focused on a limited number of themes that are connected with the core business of the company) and Engagement (involvement of the employees is of great importance, because it contributes to their personal development and feeling of pride).

On the level of urban development, Diageo is mainly interested in projects of education and employment (one of the focal points is Skills for Life). Besides, through the Foundation the company tries to give substance to the notion of 'local citizen'. While the company does not have a special bond with any specific city, not even with London, it is co-founder of London First and through that organisation involved in the town's ups and downs. Precisely because of its strategic approach (and the avoidance of tokenism), Diageo does not pretend to a prominent part in solving London's great problems such as the worsening accessibility (the number of employees in London is only 600). Initiatives on that score are left to other companies with a greater stake in the solution of such problems. Diageo agrees with others that the complex administrative structure of London – and the clutter of intermediary organisations – makes collaboration with authorities very difficult. An important condition for collaboration is in Diageo's view long-term commitment (for the sake of long-term advantages!), which tends to be hard to realise on account of the democratic proceedings that are inevitable in the public sector.

Measuring the impact Diageo attaches much worth to measuring the effects of social investments. To that end input-output analyses are carried out according the London Benchmarking Group Model. One per cent of profit before tax is spent on projects under the headings of philanthropy, social investments and commercial initiatives, the upper three levels of the pyramid. Because commercial initiatives (such as cause-related marketing) have clearly identifiable marketing effects, such initiatives may count on complementary support from marketing budgets.

Three examples may serve to explain the input-output analysis operated by Diageo. Under the heading 'philanthropy', the company donated £5,000 after a cyclone in India (disaster relief). On top of that amount come £1,000 from local employees of Guinness UDV India. These sums are used to build houses for the victims of the catastrophe (social usefulness). The company profits from an enhanced reputation with the government and the local population (business benefit). An example of social investment is Tomorrow's People (related to the Skills for Life scheme). The contribution of £400,000 a year has so far drawn in £150 million in additional funds. The project has helped 350,000 persons to a job, saving the national government between £6 and £20 million a year on benefits and such. This project has yielded the company a better reputation and direct support for its Welfare to Work and Plant Closure Programmes. The Tangueray Bike Rides in the USA are commercial initiatives in the framework of the focal object Global Brands (reinforcement of the brands). This form of cause-related marketing has cost Diageo £900,000 in cash and £700,000 in marketing and advertising support. The bike rides have yielded US$160 million, which sum has been remitted to good causes working for HIV/AIDS patients, to give support to 1,000 sufferers from AIDS. The benefits for the company are 280,000 instances of media attention, a rise in turnover and an improved relationship with business partners and employees (Diageo, 2001).

Although the impact of social activities on the community is undoubtedly positive, the fact should be kept in mind that Diageo, and business companies in general, achieve their greatest contribution through 'normal' corporate activity (business basics). The value added which businesses generate, indeed profits suppliers, governments (through tax), employees and investors. Diageo's distribution of the value added (after deduction of the cost of products and services supplied) is represented in Table 6.2. The table also shows that part of that value is invested back into the company on the argument that this is necessary for the continuity of the company and in the interest of (future) stakeholders. The picture further shows that the contributions to local communities account for only 0.3 per cent.

Table 6.2 Diageo's distribution of value added

Governments	43.3%
Employees	25.6%
Payments to investors	19.8%
Investments in the company	11.0%
Local communities	0.3%

Source: Diageo, 2001.

All this implies that strategic corporate decisions, such as openings, closures and moves of establishments, have a much greater impact on the community (and cities in particular) than decisions with respect to the distribution of contributions to local communities. Diageo is aware of this and for that reason involves the Foundation in corporate decisions with a social impact. When a factory in Scotland was closed down, the Foundation, together with local authorities, set up a Regenerating Task Force to breathe new life into the local economy. In Diageo's eyes that intervention was important to secure the reputation of the company and the relation with governments and consumers, notably as a producer of scotch whisky.

Lattice

Like Centrica, the Lattice Group emerged from the split-up of British Gas into several parts. Lattice – since 23 October 2000, a quoted company – is engaged in the construction and maintenance of infrastructure and networks. The principal business unit is Transco, the owner, operator and developer of a large portion of the gas transportation system in the UK. As in many other utility companies, certain departments of Lattice are under the supervision of the government, because of the general interest in good and affordable infrastructure. Thus, Transco is regulated by the Gas and Electricity Markets

Authority (OFGEM). The Lattice Group is also active on the telephone market. The company is constructing a national fibreglass network to meet the demand for broadband transmission and related services.

Lattice is another company that can be regarded as highly active in community development. The Lattice Foundation operates as a business unit of the company, carrying on social activities in line with the long-term strategy of the company. The Foundation is not engaged in philanthropy but responds to clear business needs, such as the need for a good workforce not only for Lattice itself (a fairly large concern with 12,000 employees), but also for other companies in the supply chain (production costs): suppliers and consumers together account for some 100,000 employees. All these companies have difficulty recruiting suitable staff. The labour market is tight and the unemployment rate low, especially among engineers.

Target groups The Foundation addresses three problem groups: young people not following education (truants), youngsters in prison and young structurally unemployed (see Lattice Foundation, 2001; www.lattice-foundation.com). The Lattice Foundation makes use of the leverage effect and with limited means (a budget of £2 million in 2001, a mere 0.3 per cent of the profit after tax,[1] tries to tap additional sources. The projects are relatively cheap instruments to recruit employees. Besides, the projects contribute to a good relation with local schools (including universities), local authorities and other companies in the production chain. They are, in short, instruments for establishing relations.

Every year, one million children in Great Britain play truant. Of these children, 100,000 are suspended from school, with 13,000 of the total number being permanently excluded (Lattice, 2001). These problem children have difficulties with the traditional forms of education. In Reading, at one of its establishments, Lattice has opened a Learning Centre which offers to 50 youngsters between the ages of 14 and 16 a creative, alternative form of education. This new type of education combines three schooldays (in small classes and with much personal attention for the students) with two days of work with an employer they can choose themselves.

The work experience places are offered by the local private sector, and vary from hairdressers and day nurseries to hotels and offices. The statistics show an average attendance of 89 per cent, considerably more than the average of 40 per cent they reached in their previous schools. The success is attributed to the client-oriented approach and the combination of school and work. The participants like to be looked upon as scarce resources. That makes them more eager to learn. Some of the youngsters even continue their education in regular schools. The three-year project is supported by the local and national authorities. At the request of the national government, Lattice, together with other companies in the production chain, has helped to set up a second Learning Centre in Peterborough, near Cambridge, which is to be fully subsidised by the government.

The Lattice Foundation has joined forces with a prison in Reading to set up a programme of training young prisoners as forklift drivers, who are in great demand for the transportation of goods ordered through internet. The Foundation has promised £50,000 for the training of 50 young people. The results are overwhelming. More than seven out of 10 have found a job and only 6 per cent have fallen back into their old ways, against the normal 70 per cent. That saves the community £25,000 a year per prisoner (Lattice, 2001). There are few companies that wish to associate with crime. Nevertheless it is in the interest of private enterprise that young people on being discharged from prison should not fall back into crime. Moreover, they are potential employees.

Furthermore, the Lattice Foundation has undertaken to help reduce structural unemployment among young people. Through the so-called Transco Green Futures Initiative, youngsters between 18 and 24 are offered a combined scheme of work and education. This initiative is in line with the New Deal Environmental Task Force Programme of the national government, and has in part been responsible for hauling in an extra subsidy of £14 million from the European Union, as well as other government subsidies and private sponsor moneys (Lattice, 2001).

The initiative is oriented to areas marked by a combination of much unemployment and environmental decline (a declining quality of life). Such areas are inner cities, rural zones and mining and industrial zones (in Leeds and Manchester among other places). The establishments of Transco are actively involved as suppliers of work and trainee places. Moreover they have access to suppliers and can provide material, advice and expertise. Almost half of all the participants succeed in landing a job, which is double the national average. The training subjects and traineeships are geared to the environment: lessons in house insulation, advice on the conscious consumption of energy, and research techniques. The project is a joint effort of Lattice and Groundwork, a voluntary organisation for environmental improvement.

Cooperation The Lattice Foundation evidently likes to work together with other parties, local and national governments included. Cooperation proves necessary to effectuate employment projects. The company does not exclude participation in projects directed to other themes. As a utility company, Lattice has a natural relation with the community. The company is not particularly active in London, but does feel committed to the town. However, Lattice considers the complex administrative structure of London an obstacle to cooperation between the public and the private sector.

Conclusions

London is beset with serious problems which put the attractiveness of the residential and location climate in jeopardy. The spatial-economic conditions are raising the social awareness of companies and serve in principle as a stimulus to join forces with other sectors. Urban policy on the national level may stimulate the cooperation between governments and companies. Local governments experience an encourage to evolve Local Strategic Partnerships with private enterprise because the national government takes cooperativeness into account when allocating budgets for social-economic revitalising. In certain underprivileged zones additional financial incentives are required to bring the parties together. The implication is that the need for incentives grows as the value added for the partners is less clear, for instance when the risks are great and the envisaged period of recuperation long.

The complex administrative structure of London is generally regarded as an obstacle to public-private partnership on the level of the town. Cooperation between the public and private sectors could lift off faster and easier on the level of the borough (the district), the same level on which in London Strategic Local Partnerships are being developed. The Greater London Authority is confronted with the challenge to put forward integral solutions for problems that transcend the borders of boroughs. That requires not only coordination between the Local Strategic Partnerships, but also a clear vision of the possible contribution of the private sector to investments in a sustainable development of London.

The experiences of Centrica, Diageo and Lattice confirm that companies are occupying themselves more and more strategically with social projects. With Centrica that is evident, for instance, from the intensive collaboration between two of its departments, Corporate Community Involvement and Marketing. The Foundations of Diageo and Lattice try with relatively little financial resource to attract as much additional money as possible (the leverage construction). Moreover, the three companies set much store by measuring the value added (impact) generated by the projects. None of the three companies has a special bond with the town of London. The relevant communities (customers, employees) of these companies operating on the national and international markets, are considerably larger than the town.

Note

1 The budget of the Foundation is not fixed, however. The Foundation is financed by the 'we-take-what-we-need' principle.

References

Business in the Community (1999), 'Positive Impact'.

Business in the Community West Midlands (2000), 'Thanks!; Annual Review 2000'.

Department of the Environment, Transport and the Regions (1998), 'London Governance', <www.detr.gov.uk>.

Department of the Environment, Transport and the Regions (2001), 'Local Strategic Partnerships; Government Guidance'.

Diageo (2001), 'Corporate Citizenship 2001 Guide'.

Lattice Foundation (2001), *Linking People ... Linking Lives.*

Llewelyn Davies and UCL The Bartlett School of Reading University of Essex (1997), *The London Study: A Socio-economic Assessment of London*, Association of London Government, London.

Logan, D. and M. Tuffrey (1999), *Companies in Communities: Valuing the Contribution*, The Corporate Citizenship Company, Charities Aid Foundation, Kent.

London Development Agency (2001), 'Success Through Diversity; London's Economic Development Strategy'.

London First (1999), 'London First Group Agenda 1999/2000'.

Office for National Statistics (1999), 'Annual Business Inquiry'.

Discussion partners

G. Bush, Director of Corporate Citizenship, Diageo

C. Carruthers, Director – National Membership, Business in the Community

P. Davies, Managing Director, Business in the Community

D. Fell, Director Sustainability Unit, London First

D. Halley, Head of European Development, Business in the Community

M. Harris, Director, Lattice Foundation

S. Henderson, Community Affairs Manager, Centrica

M. John, Social Policy Adviser, Lattice Foundation
P. Lambert, Director – Regeneration, Business in the Community
S. Scott Parker, Chief Executive, Employers Forum for Disability
P. Shepherd, Executive Director, UK Social Investment Forum
R. Souter, Research analyst, Employers Forum for Disability
R. Stone, Director Community Investment, Deloitte & Touche
M. Ward, Chief Executive, London Development Agency
S. Waugh, Group Director Marketing, Centrica

Chapter 7

Munich

Introduction

In Germany, forms of corporate social responsibility are developing reluctantly (notably in comparison with North America). As in the Netherlands, various symposiums, conventions and workshops on the theme are being organised, which could be a sign of growing response. German companies primarily resort to traditional channels to safeguard their (social) image, such as sponsoring of sports and culture. To that end, separate foundations are often created. Many companies are wary of active participation in social projects because they fear an undesired association with social problems. The political climate is another factor of importance. Because the government in Germany, like many other West European governments, offers an extensive package of social services, companies do not feel a strong urge towards community involvement.

This chapter analyses the current state of affairs with regard to corporate community involvement in Munich and tries to identify barriers to cross-sector collaboration. After a profile of Munich, we focus on two projects that are more or less related to corporate community involvement. Subsequently, the community involvement of three relatively active companies will be successively examined. The chapter rounds off with some conclusions.

Profile[1]

Munich is situated in the south of Germany. It is the capital of the free state of Bavaria and, with a population of 1.3 million, the third-largest city of Germany, after Berlin and Hamburg. The city is the centre of an urban region with about 2.4 million inhabitants. Besides the city of Munich the urban region comprises eight Landkreise with populations varying from 97,000 to 278,000. These Landkreise encompass some relatively small but influential municipalities. Because the 'Umland' – the suburban area – has grown rapidly in number of population in the past decades, home-to-work traffic has risen by 140 per cent since 1970. The heavy commuter flows are due to the concentration of jobs in the centre of Munich and the dispersal of the population across a very extensive area. Two out of every three jobs are in the city of Munich, which houses only half the regional population.

The economy of the city of Munich as well as that of the region are well developed. The region is known for its high standard of life and sound economic performance, and is counted among the most successful regions in Europe. The unemployment rate in Munich is very low. In 1998, only 5.8 per cent of the active population were on the records as unemployed, a considerably lower percentage than in other German cities (10 per cent or more).The economic structure of the city of Munich and the urban region of Munich is highly differentiated. The spread of activities across the sectors does not show up any substantial difference between city and region, although services have a distinct preference for the city. The modern and balanced economic structure of Munich is sometimes called the 'Münchner Mischung' (the Munich mixture). Not only the distribution among sectors is well balanced, but also the size of business companies. Munich accommodates very large companies such as the headquarters of Siemens and BMW, but also numerous, very vital, small and medium-size businesses, notably in the innovative ICT branch.

The economic strength of Munich is related to the eminently educated active population. The educational level of the population is among the highest of German cities: no less than 14 per cent have a university education, against 6 per cent in Germany as a whole. The high level of education makes Munich a very attractive location for companies.

Projects and Initiatives

Munich is, by German standards, relatively active in the field of corporate community involvement. The Department of Social Affairs is the point of address for companies that want to take on their social responsibility. The municipality can act as contact to find partners for projects in which associates can express their social commitment. According to the department, none of the actors are lacking in cooperativeness. Companies as well are increasingly waking up to their co-responsibility for the social situation and the living environment in the city. They engage in various ways in social and ecological projects and are prepared to cooperate with social institutions. Such projects are in line with the drive for a sustainable development of the city. Below, two projects are discussed in more detail: Munich in Artificial Light and the Munich Business-plan Contest.

Table 7.1 Employment in Munich (1997)

Sector	Region	City	Surroundings
Agriculture	6,147	2,120	4,027
Energy and water supply	9,434	7,454	1,980
Manufacturing industry	229,436	139,843	89,593
Construction	49,396	30,058	19,338
Retail and wholesale trade	148,485	91,708	56,777
Transport and communication	58,599	36,566	22,033
Banking and insurance	72,420	63,379	9,041
Other services	331,276	221,095	110,181
Non-profit organisations	33,903	28,311	5,592
Regional public authorities	54,301	33,670	20,631
Total	993,397	654,204	339,193
Secondary sector	29.0%	22.5%	32.1%
Tertiary sector	70.4%	72.6%	66.7%

Source: Referat für Arbeit und Wirtschaft, 1997.

Munich in Artifical Light

On the whole, private enterprise in Munich is deeply involved in art and culture in the city. Most companies express that involvement through traditional channels such as sponsoring and donations, whether or not through the intermedium of specially created foundations. However, the project Munich in Artifical Light[2] – staged from December 1999 to February 2000 – was an example of social commitment that goes one step further.

This event was a joint venture of the municipality and private enterprise to highlight art in the public space. Five international artists designed lighting installations for the city. The idea for this project was conceived by the private sector, more specifically the association of retailers in Bavaria. The support of the retail trade – which counts mostly small and medium-sized companies – to a cultural project is rather unusual. To make other companies enthusiastic for the project as well, a special meeting was organised at the Town Hall. The envisaged budget amounted to DM2.5 million (about €1.3 million) and was to come from the municipality as well as the private sector.

In the event, DM1.5 million (less than €767,000) was put up for the project. The municipal contribution is, at DM150,000 (less than €77,000), on the modest side. Many local companies, among which banks (such as the Stadtsparkasse, see under that heading below), building contractors, breweries and clubs, were heartily supportive and came forward as sponsors. The contribution of national and international companies with an establishment (or even their headquarters) in Munich was a bit disappointing. The list of sponsors contains few (internationally) well-known names, with the exception of the Deutsche Bank and C&A. Remarkably, Siemens and BMW – two concerns that have their headquarters in Munich – have both refused to participate in the project. On the one hand that could be ascribed to the large number of sponsors, which could water down the marketing effects. On the other hand these concerns have their own cultural programmes, and might look upon Munich in Artificial Light as competitive to them.

The project has created a great deal of debate in Munich. The local press was very critical of the initiative, especially doubting that it was worth the expense. For one thing opinions differed about the lighting installations as such (art or kitsch?). For another, both in the media and in political debates fear for too much interfering of the private sector was expressed. Many people were (and still are) afraid that the funding of art by business will end in commercialised art and culture. In comparison with other cities in Germany the attitude towards innovations in culture financing can be called conservative. For that reason, corporate social responsibility in relation to culture seems to be a delicate subject in Munich. Such feelings were stirred the more as Munich in Artificial Light (temporarily) meant a change of the public space, indeed right in the centre of the city.

The negative attitude of the local media sowed dissatisfaction among the sponsors of the project. The fact that the international media praised the event could hardly alleviate the pain, especially because so many sponsors were oriented to the local market. The whole sequence of events has made a possible follow-up highly questionable.

The Munich Business-plan Contest

Private enterprise in Munich also participates in initiatives aimed at stimulating (young) entrepreneurship. Several large companies are actively involved in the Munich Business-plan Contest. This contest serves two purposes: 1) to strengthen the entrepreneurial climate by stimulating young people to set up in business; and 2) to develop new technologies and related services (for instance, software). The underlying thought is to match ideas and capital.

The idea of this contest was conceived in the 1980s by the Massachusetts Institute of Technology in Boston. Close cooperation between universities, business companies and investors makes it possible to create innovative businesses and thus make a significant contribution to the economic development of a region. The assumption is that economic growth depends on innovation, and that innovation is largely the result of the creation of new businesses, for which an enterprising and innovative regional network is required.

The initiative for the contest came from consultancy firm McKinsey. This company wanted to improve its image of 'job destroyer' by creating jobs as well. Moreover, starting entrepreneurs are among the potential customers of the company. In 1996, McKinsey together with institutions of higher education, the Förderkreis Neue Technologien (FNT), several business companies, investors and branch associations, mounted the first contest. McKinsey financed the project during one year, after which it was taken over by the FNT, a committee of the Bavarian state government that promotes technical advance in the region, among other objectives for the sake of the international positioning. Thanks to the contest – which is organised every year – 103 companies have been founded, which together have invested DM 160 million (€81.81 million) and generated 740 job opportunities. A large portion of these new businesses are active in the area of ICT, in conformity with the project's objectives.

The participating companies have organised themselves into three categories. Among the main sponsors are car producer BMW, Deutsche Bank and the HypoVereinsbank. Among the second category are such companies as McKinsey, Siemens and KPMG. Naturally, the main sponsors make the largest contribution, not only financially, but especially in terms of coaching. Representatives of these concerns coach the participants and deliver lectures on certain aspects of the business plan. Besides, experienced entrepreneurs exchange knowledge with starting entrepreneurs during specifically organised forums. Because the companies offer these services free of charge, the expenses of the project organisation itself are limited to the minimum.

The contest opens opportunities for the participating companies to make a financial stake (for instance, by the provision of venture capital), as well as providing them with knowledge (for instance, about the latest technological developments) and access to networks. Moreover, participation adds to their 'social image'. City and region profit from the contest through the creation of (high-grade) employment, innovative activities and the strengthening of networks, not only among companies, but also between the municipality, private enterprise and schools. The city of Munich and the state of Bavaria have an interest in the starting entrepreneurs' settling in the city or the region and remaining settled there. To that end, the municipality offers them accommodation. The marketing organisation for the region, MAI (see under Stadtsparkasse), also wishes to play a role in keeping young entrepreneurial talent in the region.

Active Companies in Munich

The social activities of the following companies will now be reviewed in succession: BMW (motorcar manufacturer), Siemens (electronics), and the Stadtsparkasse (bank).

BMW

Motorcar manufacturer BMW has for many years shown commitment to the development of the city of Munich. The company makes active efforts to solve traffic problems in and around the city. The thought behind that proactive attitude is the concern's interest in keeping cars and motors afloat now and in the future. Moreover, BMW hopes that its feats of social involvement contribute to a good image, not only among (potential) BMW drivers, but among all car drivers.

Since the 1980s BMW has worked with strategic partners on solutions for traffic problems. In the beginning the company primarily acted as financier, but the commitment has much widened in the course of time. Nowadays the company itself initiates projects and provides for intensive coaching by making knowledge and human resources available. The region of Munich, where the BMW headquarters is, represents for BMW a prominent testing place for new systems of traffic management, which later on, when proved successful, can be introduced into other cities. Since 1987 the concern has, together with schools of higher education and the municipality, started up several projects. The first multimodal project initiated by the company in 1987 was 'Kooperatives Verkehrsmanagement München' (Cooperative Traffic Management in Munich). Since then, BMW has also mounted projects in other German cities, among which Berlin, Dresden and Cologne.

Together with the municipality of Cologne, BMW has developed a system of automatic admission and payment, to which all parking garages are connected. In the future this system will be connected to navigation systems in cars. That BMW leads the way in Cologne of all places is due in the first place to that city's liberal climate. The municipality's philosophy is that in principle everybody should be able to drive into city, albeit at a certain price. In many other cities (Munich among them), such a system of controlled parking would be less simple to introduce, because of political resistance against 'a system that stimulates people to use the car'. Moreover, Cologne has the advance of an integral approach to traffic problems: planning (for the short as well as the long term) and implementation come under one single department. In that respect Cologne distinguishes itself from Munich and other German cities.

Accessibility and sustainable urban development In Munich, BMW has made important contributions to projects that strive for an accessible region, sparing the urban living environment as much as possible. Together with the municipality BMW took the initiative to organise a meeting with all relevant stakeholders to discuss the future of accesibility in the Munich region. During this meeting the participants set out to develop new (technological) concepts for the traffic policy as well as to decide how these concepts could be given shape by the joint efforts of government, private enterprise and other organisations (organisational concept). Among the participants were, as well as delegates of the City of Munich and BMW, representatives of the Chamber of Commerce, the state of Bavaria and the Munich TU (Technical University). From the meeting ensued a number of projects based on a clear strategy (MOBINET-Konsortium, 2000a).

One of the concrete projects that resulted from the meeting, is the so-called Mobinet Project, which aims at securing mobility for future generations while avoiding its undesirable side effects (in terms of environment and safety) (MOBINET-Konsortium, 2000a and b). The project is supported by the German Ministry of Education and Research. The challenge is to develop an integral and intermodal mobility system for Munich and surroundings, making use of new techniques. The consortium of Mobinet is composed of 25 partners from the public sector, science and the private sector. Among them are, besides BMW and some other companies, ADAC (the German association of motorists) and the Munich Technical University.

Social projects In the coming years, BMW will probably add social projects to its activities. The company expressly wants to prevent expensive cars from becoming a symbol of a divided community. The purchase of a car is more and more determined by emotional factors. The marketing department of BMW responds to that trend by considering not only what potential buyers expect from a car, but also what they think important in their lives.

Especially members of the higher-income groups are now paying heed to a company's behaviour in society. BMW responds to that trend by erecting a special department for social research projects. To distinguish itself from other car manufacturers, BMW sets up in each of its sales areas research projects to improve the traffic situation and/or reduce the social problems. The idea is to make a general concept applicable to the local situation. BMW can and will take the initiative in this matter, because to politicians and civil servants the presentation of innovative plans would be risky.

Siemens

The electronics concern of Siemens is undeniably a global company, with 440,000 employees spread across 190 countries. The main office of this multinational is established in Munich. The concern is somewhat centrally organised in that its policy is outlined by 'die Zentrale' (the headquarters). The head office sets certain objectives, leaving it to the separate units to work out how to attain them. The local commitment of Siemens is mainly determined from the bottom up. How far a unit feels socially involved thus depends on the local conditions (the location) and the local managers. Like many other global companies, Siemens has not a generally prevailing corporate culture. Indeed, many (technocratically minded) managers are not yet convinced of the relevancy of community involvement.

Siemens encompasses several business groups. One of them is ICN Siemens with a presence in Munich, which produces among other things mobile telephones and basic stations, develops information and communication networks and provides advice (consultancy) in this field. The establishment has for years cooperated closely with several grammar schools, delegating associates to these schools on a voluntary basis to familiarise teachers with the internet, and giving management courses for the headmasters.

Switch One of the community projects in which Siemens is involved is Switch: an innovative teaching programme for managers in the private sector, responding to the ever higher demands on their social skills. This project offers the associates of business companies an opportunity to work for some time in a social institution, a situation which demands entirely new skills from them. The experiences gained in such a different employment can be profitable in their regular work situation. Through the exchange of knowledge, managers of companies and social institutions can learn from each other.

Similar programmes have run for more than 30 years in the USA, Canada, the Netherlands and the UK, and for about a decade in Switzerland. From those programmes the Munich Institute for Social Science has, jointly with Siemens and the municipality, developed the Munich Model. This model sets out to combine different ways of spending time (work time, training time, family time, leisure time, and social time). The model is based on the assumption that the employment society is changing into an activities society, in which all socially useful activities are of equal value (Mutz, 1999). Such a society functions optimally when the different activities can interact. It requires the cooperation of all parties that directly or indirectly participate in the regional labour market: business companies, trade unions, municipalities, provinces (Länder), as well as social, ecological and cultural institutions. The model is made up of four layers: self-chosen work, stable social commitment, working hours, and social commitment as a form of training.

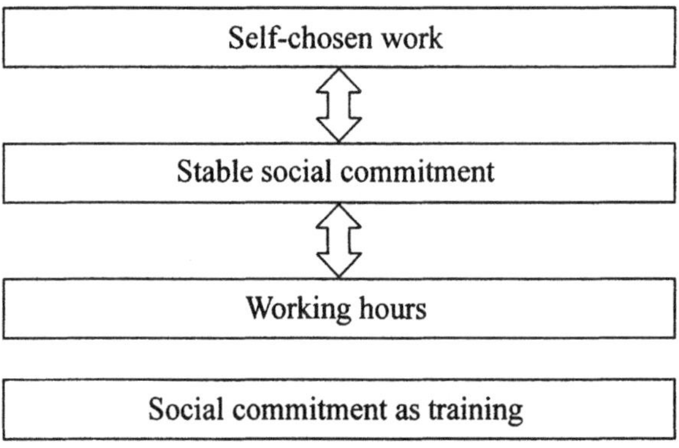

Figure 7.1 The four layers of the Munich Model

Source: Mutz, 1999.

By 'doing their own thing' in their own time (leisure time), people can pursue their personal ideas and preferences, for instance by temporarily making their hobby their work. With the participating companies the agreement is made that – taking regard to the present labour market – employees may, for at most one year, take up their own work. In that period they will receive no salary, but remain insured. Stable social commitment refers to the possibility for employees of the participating companies to spend a portion of their working hours (up to 20 hours a month) in social occupations, under professional guidance. Employees may even choose to take up cumulated 'social hours' at one go. Finally, social commitment is put in by the participating companies as a form of training. Employees are free to master social and communicative skills outside the company. For the two last-mentioned variants the rules are that during their 'social hours' the persons involved remain in the company's employ as non-working workers. For these hours they will receive 70 per cent of their net wages and remain insured. The difference in income is compensated by a foundation.

The Munich Model foresees a foundation council which encompasses all participating institutions. The foundation council establishes a dialogue centre which unites companies and employees with social, ecological and cultural agencies. The dialogue centre constitutes the heart of the Munich Model and functions as intermediary between: 1) the needs of the social, ecological and cultural institutions; 2) the needs of the entrepreneur; 3) the wishes and possibilities of the interested employees; and 4) the general interests of the region. A committee authorised by the foundation council has to guarantee the general usefulness of the activities. The independent dialogue centre offers opportunities for cooperation of new and existing civil organisations.

The Munich Model is profitable to all participating parties, as witness the experiences with Switch, the first concrete project mounted in the framework of this model. It differs from regular training courses in that the transfer of knowledge is achieved within rather than outside the normal workdays. Unlike other retraining schemes, Switch is more than just a training programme, since it also sets out to stimulate the social commitment of employees in a structural manner.

Siemens AG has had many years of experience with programmes based on emotional learning. Since 1984 a number of managers have attended, under the leadership of social workers, at least two therapeutic group sessions in clinics for the addicted. The purpose is to make them aware of alcohol problems. From the experiences gained with this preventive measure, these managers seem better able to handle such situations and to motivate people.

In September 1999, jointly with the Sozialreferat of the Landeshauptstadt München (Department of Social Affairs of State Capital Munich), Siemens AG introduced the Switch programme as a pilot project: four managers from the middle management switched for one week from their usual position to a job in a social institution. In that period they got to know a work life entirely different from their own professional environment. The choice of candidates for Switch was in the hands of the personnel department of Siemens; the Landeshauptstadt München selected the social institutions.

Switch is successful because it combines different interests. Companies want managers able to respond fast and flexibly to new situations and to evolve efficient forms of teamwork. Responsible behaviour toward the associates works positively on the latter's motivation and their identification with the company for which they work. Managers should not only know their own professional area, but also have social competencies that enable them to judge, act and communicate in their professional and social environments. With Switch, managers are given a chance to improve their social competencies and to use their active experiences of 'the other side' for daily decisions in their regular work environment.

Social institutions also benefit from Switch. The mutual exchange of knowledge makes them, too, aware of 'the other side'. Suggestions and inspiration springing from active participation are welcome. Moreover, the participants are multipliers in their own environment, since in their regular function they have opportunities to transfer their social sense to their colleagues.

The Department for Social Affairs of the municipality of Munich is pleased with the project, because it adds to the mutual solidarity in the community. The municipality has gained a new partner for its efforts to raise the quality of life, the economic capacity and the social climate in the state. Moreover, all partners stand to gain from the publicity generated by the project: companies underline their good social intentions with concrete actions, social institutions breed more appreciation for their activities by making them more transparent, and the municipal department for social affairs gains support from private enterprise for such joint projects as Switch. When the positive effects of such projects can be objectified, a change of culture in private enterprise could be accomplished, for a start within the top management of Siemens.

ICN Siemens has understood that Switch is in certain respects more effective than the somewhat artificial training in team building. Real-life experiences are appreciated more than dry runs. The city can function as a laboratory for learning such social skills as communication, teamwork, understanding of other cultures, and appreciation of self and others. Especially for young managers – who still have much to learn – real-life experiences are valuable. Newly graduated employees often lack desirable social skills. They are gifted and industrious, but have seen little of 'real life'. When Switch continues to be successful, ICN considers raising the number of participants to some 30 a year.

Stadtsparkasse

Even more than other banks, Stadtsparkasse (Municipal Savings Bank) has a natural and historical relation with the region and the city. Stadtsparkasse is socially involved for one thing because of its many clients in the region and for another because of its close relation with the municipality which is the bank's guarantor. The bank wants to know what motivates their clients and how best to respond. More latterly, with the increasing competition and the progressive homogenisation (products tending to be more and more alike), banks have been looking for ways to distinguish themselves. Hence the significance of a good (social) image is rising.

The bank feels involved in social, cultural and ecological interests. By that Stadtsparkasse understands donations and sponsorships, foundations for culture and senior citizens, environmentally friendly behaviour, the promotion of ecological plans, the participation in organisation for public welfare, and a family-friendly attitude towards the employees. By means of 'active partnerships' that contribute to the welfare of Munich the bank aims to display its relation with the regional community and in that way to distinguish itself from competitors.

Marketing the region One of the organisations that receives financial contributions from the Munich Stadtsparkasse, is a marketing organisation for the Munich region. This organisation is named MAI, after the three major cities in the region: Munich, Augsburg, and Ingelstadt.

MAI aims to put the region better and more univocally on the map, by traditional means such as a logo, brochures and fairs, but also through the internet. The organisation is financed by the participating cities as well as some large companies, among which four Municipal Savings Banks (Stadtsparkassen) and car manufacturers Audi and BMW. The activities have been divided among some thematic work groups. MAI operates at some distance from the administrative apparatus and is free to move within politically determined limits.

Other activities In the (near) future the bank hopes to market the Munich location more powerfully, through internet as well as otherwise. Together with the city and Siemens the bank strives for the creation of a virtual city with one portal. Furthermore the bank is closely involved in the Munich Business-plan Contest, and efforts are now in progress to make a connection between the contest and MAI by stimulating starting entrepreneurs to settle in the Munich region. Finally, the bank also participates in several projects initiated in the context of Agenda 21.

Conclusions

One thing we can learn from the Munich case is that corporate community involvement has its (ethical) limits which differ by region. In Munich, people and politicians appeared wary of business interfering in culture and in the dressing of public space, especially in the centre of the city. Another lesson concerns the importance of organising capacity: the Mobinet project owes its success to leadership (displayed by BMW and the mayor), informal networks, and the develoment of a strategic vision towards sustainable urban development.

The Switch project fits the assumption that the interests of city and enterprise are converging in some cases. Participating companies look upon the city as a testing ground for making their managers community-involved and socially skilful. This kind of projects may achieve a change of corporate culture, to the benefit of corporate community involvement. Finally, the experiences of Stadtsparkasse confirm the importance of strategic partnerships as instruments of corporate community involvement policies.

Notes

1 Borrowed from 'Growth Clusters in European Metropolitan Cities' (Van den Berg, Braun and Van Winden, 1999).
2 In German: 'München im Kunstlicht'.

References

Berg, L. van den, E. Braun and W. van Winden (1999), *Growth Clusters in European Metropolitan Cities: A Comparative Analysis of Cluster Dynamics in the Cities of Amsterdam, Eindhoven, Helsinki, Leipzig, Lyon, Manchester, Munich, Rotterdam and Vienna*, EURICUR, Rotterdam.

MOBINET-Konsortium (2000a), 'Verkehrsprobleme gemeinsam lösen; eine Initiative von BMW und der Landeshauptstadt München'.

MOBINET-Konsortium (2000b), 'MOBINET, Mobility in the Greater Munich Area – A Reference Project'.

Mutz, G. (1999), 'Strukturen einer neuen Arbeitsgesellschaft; Der Zwang zur Gestaltung der Zeit', in *Aus Politik und Zeitge-schichte,* Bundeszentrale für politische Bildung, B 9/99.

Referat für Arbeit und Wirtschaft (Employment and Economy Department) (1997), 'Landeshauptstadt München'.

Stadtsparkasse (1995), 'Was sind wir – was wir wollen'.

Discussion partners

W. Arndt, Manager of the Münchener Business Plan Wettbewerb (The Munich Business Plan Contest)

B. Eller, Referat für Arbeit und Wirtschaft (Department for Employment and Economy), City of Munich

P. Giloy-Hirtz, Kuratorium Munich

B. Grolik, Leiter Bereich Unternehmensentwicklung, Stadtsparkasse München, Vorstandsekretariat

C. Janowicz, Münchner Institut für Sozialforschung (Munich Institute for Social Science)

D. Kessler, Leiter Verkehrskonzepte (Director Mobility Concepts) BMW

T. Mager, City of Munich

G. Mutz, Münchner Institut für Sozialforschung (Munich Institute for Social Science)

A. Schmöller, Manager Human Resources, Siemens ICN

K. Schußmann, Referat für Arbeit und Wirtschaft (Department for Employment and Economy), City of Munich

M. Sommer, Director of the Business Department, Vereinsbank Victoria Bauspar AG

Chapter 8

New York

Introduction

New York is an interesting case with regard to corporate community involvement for several reasons. First of all, the financial institutions in this city have been, and still are very active in the field of community development, stimulated by the federal Community Reinvestment Act. Moreover, many companies and property owners pay an additional tax to make their local environment more attractive, within the framework of Business Improvement Districts (BIDs). In addition, New York is the hometown of pharmaceutical concern Pfizer: a company with a strategic approach to its social responsibilities. Finally, the terrorist attack on the World Trade Centre (11 September 2001) raises the question to what extent the private sector can help the city towards recovery and the rearrangement of Downtown Manhattan, and Ground Zero in particular.

After a profile of New York, we analyse the impact of the Community Reinvestment Act and the concept of Business Improvement Districts. The next section deals with the activities of intermediary agencies as brokers between public and private interests. The experiences of Pfizer with the creation of partnerships for the benefit of community development around the establishment in Brooklyn form the focus of the following section. Conclusions will complete this chapter.

Profile

New York is part of the select group of 'world cities' which includes London. Its modern history started in 1626, when some Dutchmen bought the island of Manhattan from the Red Indians. New Amsterdam developed quickly into a trading centre of importance. The city was renamed New York when the English took over the colony. By 1700, the city was already a multicultural community accommodating several nationalities. Large immigration flows have since then strengthened its international character.

New York consists of five districts (boroughs): Manhattan, Brooklyn, the Bronx, Queens, and Staten Island. With 8.6 million inhabitants, New York is the largest city in the USA. It is the unquestioned financial centre of the world (with a distinct concentration around Wall Street in Lower Manhattan), and prominent in the world of culture and (new) media. The Big Apple, as New York is fondly known, is the home base of many great multinationals (some 50 of the Fortune 500 companies), as well as of various international bodies, the United Nations among them.

In the past, the city has had its share of social and economic problems. Think, for instance, of the deep recession that followed the stock exchange crash in 1929. From the 1950s onward, New York has been confronted with the phenomenon of urban sprawl. The white middle classes began to leave the city, followed, after some delay, by businesses. The consequences were serious, such as a drop in employment opportunities and diminishing revenues for the municipality. Moreover, large parts of Harlem, the Bronx and Brooklyn declined into ghettos where drugs, crime and prostitution prevailed. In 1975, the crisis reached an all-time low and the municipality was balancing on the edge of bankruptcy (Fuchs, 1992). Thanks to the support of the federal government and the State of New York, the failure could be prevented.

After a slight recovery in the 1980s (a rise in employment and a cautious return of the middle classes), 1987 brought another manifestation of the New York economy's perilous dependency on the financial markets. The crash of the stock exchange plunged the economy in a deep recession which continued into 1993. The effects of employment growth and the return of the middle classes in the preceding years were completely cancelled out. After 1993 a period of economic prosperity followed, due mostly to speculations about 'the new economy' allegedly spurred by 'the new medium': internet. A part of Manhattan even received the nickname Silicon Alley because new media companies were shooting up there like mushrooms.

Employment

New York is a genuine service city. Especially important sectors are business services (consultancy, accountancy), media, financial services and tourism. The tourist sector has made a remarkable comeback from the 1980s onward. For one thing thanks to an aggressive fight against crime ('zero tolerance') the municipality has succeeded in converting New York's negative image (unsafe, unpleasant and noisy) into a positive one. Along with a sharp drop in crime, a sharp rise occurred in the occupancy rates of hotels.

Nevertheless, in the past 30 years the position of New York in relation to other North American cities has worsened owing to a relatively slow growth of employment and relatively little diversification in economic growth. High costs, a lack of infrastructure to support new growth sectors, and question marks at the productiveness of the active population, may explain the moderate economic development. Moreover, one-fifth of the residents are still structurally poor, dependent on benefit and/or structurally unemployed. They are concentrated in neighbourhoods that exist in isolation from the mainstream economy, with badly functioning schools and few opportunities for economic evolution (New York City Investment Fund, 1999).

The Impact of a Terrorist Attack

The events of 11 September 2001 have placed new challenges before New York. Here follows an impression of the situation in New York, two months after the attack, based on discussions with people on location.

The short-term impact of the terrorist attack on the World Trade Centre has been tremendous. The tourist sector suffers particularly heavily from people being afraid of flying. The number of tourists has about halved, notably because Americans prefer to stay at home. Foreign tourists seem slowly but surely to be finding their way back to New York, although the air crash in Queens (12 November 2001) no doubt delayed the recovery of confidence in air transport. Hotels suffer from rather low occupation degrees (60 instead of 90 per cent). Restaurant owners complain about low turnovers that are due not only to the non-appearance of tourists but also to the eating habits of New Yorkers, who are reported to prefer fast food these days. Restaurants in the vicinity of Ground Zero are particularly hard put to survive. The disaster has accelerated the economic recession, and the least profitable restaurants have been forced to close their doors. In other sectors as well, the attack has speeded up the process of natural selection (only the strongest survive).

But there are positive signals as well. As before, on Times Square people are queuing up for theatre tickets. The tourist boat is once more packed with visitors anxious to see the Statue of Liberty from close up and to take photographs of New York's new skyline. Analysts expect the economy to pick up in the second quarter of 2002, and the stock exchange has by now digested the shock of the attack. Meanwhile, public and private sectors do their very best to win back the confidence of consumers. In a country-wide campaign, the association of restaurant keepers, appealing to patriotism, beseech Americans to go out for their meals. Airline companies tinker with their prices to fill their planes after and before Christmas. The municipality and the tourist sector in New York (hotels, restaurants and attractions) have started a campaign to entice tourists back to the Big Apple with special, cheap package deals, something they had no need of before (tourists would come anyway!).

Many companies that were established in the World Trade Centre have resumed their normal business. Some of them have found temporary accommodation with colleague companies, while others have by now taken refuge in a location elsewhere in the city. Because the office space available in Manhattan is limited, many companies have been forced to continue their activities elsewhere – at any rate for the time being – for instance, in Brooklyn. That can be troublesome for their employees, who have to travel much further to get to work. Because the premises in neighbourhoods outside Manhattan cannot always meet the high demands of the companies concerned (which indeed were accustomed to A locations), investment in for instance the telecommunication infrastructure is inevitable.

The Reappointment of Ground Zero

What is going to happen with Ground Zero is still unknown at the time of writing. There are those who are making a case for a monument and a park, while others would prefer a new tower, even taller than the old ones. The final decision probably end up somewhere in between. Clearly, extreme high-rise buildings have lost something of their former status. Many New York residents – and perhaps other citizens as well – have become (temporarily) more aware of the risk involved in such tall office buildings. To lay out a park with a monument would display a feeling for style and respect for the victims, but will be hard to reconcile with the economic value represented by the land and the interests of the landowner. Moreover, many businesses that used to be accommodated in the World Trade Centre, would in spite of everything prefer to return to the Central Business District.

At the moment a plan is circulating to build four towers of 50 floors. At the same time the feeling is growing that the disaster of 11 September – harsh as that may sound – has created opportunities to rearrange the Central Business District according to new insights. The hitherto mono-functional office area would profit from the development of other functions, such as living and shopping. The blending of function would add to the vivacity and liveability of the district, and thus raise the quality of the environment for residents and business companies alike. The residents of apartments on Battery Park (at the top end of the island) have long complained of the lack of shops (there is no supermarket, for one thing). Moreover, the interest of businesses for accommodation in large-scale offices in the Central Business District is waning. More and more businesses decide to limit their presence in the centre to a small but high-grade and representative office. In the terminology of Van den Berg et al. (1999): 'downsizing and upgrading'.

The events of 11 September may well have reinforced the deconcentration tendency. Many companies, painfully confronted with the vulnerability of their location, are feeling the need for back-up locations and back-up systems that in the event of such catastrophes could ensure the continuity of the company. Some companies might even weigh off the relevancy of physical proximity and face-to-face contacts against the risks of a location in the vulnerable CDB (the more vulnerable when all companies depend on the same communication structure). Alternative locations elsewhere in the region (such as Brooklyn), where costs are lower and the transport infrastructure good, might greatly appeal to some businesses. New York's city railway system, not centrally planned nor oriented exclusively to the centre, but developed by five independent companies to meet market demands, is no obstacle to de-concentration. On the other hand, the reappointment of Ground Zero may have negative consequences for the suburban neighbourhoods. There are those who fear that the massive (financial) attention for the Central Business District might jeopardise plans for affordable housing.

In theory at least, property owners have a stake in the liveability brought on by function blending, since that might raise the land price (on the assumption of an increase in the demand for pleasant, dynamic office environment). However, whether the owner of Ground Zero is prepared to allow a place to functions that yield less money per square metre – the ultimate example of corporate social responsibility! – remains to be seen.

The Community Reinvestment Act

The inclination of entrepreneurs to conduct their businesses varies much among sectors. In New York as in many other American cities, banks belong without doubt to the top category in terms of corporate community involvement. In the 1960s and 1970s, however, that was still far from the case. Banks were guilty of large-scale 'red-lining', that is the advance exclusion of certain population groups and neighbourhoods from credits and other financial products. Owing to such discriminating behaviour, underprivileged neighbourhoods – such as Brooklyn, the Bronx, and Harlem – could not escape from the negative spiral of diminishing employment, decline of the living environment (with out-of-repair houses and other buildings), rising crime, and a one-sided demographic profile (non-white, badly educated, and poor).

To fight red-lining, two acts came into force in the course of the 1970s. In 1975, Congress approved the Home Mortgage Disclosure Act, which obliges certain financial bodies (among which banks, credit unions and other mortgage providers) to report to whom and in what neighbourhoods they deliver their financial products. In that way the authorities can assess how far banks fulfil the credit needs of their communities. From the data provided, the Federal Financial Institutions Examination Council (FFIEC) draws up overall reports for each metropolitan statistical area (MSA), and publishes them (see www.ffiec.gov.). In 1977 the Community Reinvestment Act (CRA) came into force. This act stimulates credit institutions – 'as long as it is consistent with safe and sound banking practices' – to meet the credit needs of the neighbourhoods in which they operate, including 'low and moderate income neighbourhoods' (LMIs). Halfway through the 1990s, the Communiy Reinvestment Act was sharpened up by shifting the accent from observation to an objective assessment of the effective performances. The periodical evaluations by federal bodies produce 'CRA-ratings', data that are weighed heavily when consent is asked for credit facilities, mergers and take-overs.

How the company is evaluated depends on its size and on the market it serves. Large retail or consumer oriented banks are subjected to several tests (*Federal Register*, 2001). The lending test charts the number of loans in a certain area and their geographical and demographic spread (including the spread across income groups). Loans in the context of community development, and the application of innovative or flexible loan formulas for 'low to moderate income individuals or geographies in a safe and sound manner' receive special attention. The investment test judges qualified investments for volume, innovativeness and complexity as well as on their fulfilment of credit needs and requirements for community development. The degree to which private investors put up their money in a non-routine manner is also assessed. The service test considers the spread of establishments across areas with different income levels, information concerning the opening and closure of branch offices notably in LMI neighbourhoods, the availability of alternative systems for bank services in LMI neighbourhoods and to LMI individuals, the number of services rendered (in all neighbourhoods), and the degree to which the services are tailored to the needs of these neighbourhoods. Services related to community development are also weighed in this test. By community development the rules understand affordable housing for LMI individuals, services directed to LMI individuals, schemes to stimulate economic development by financing small companies, and activities that revitalise or stabilise LMI neighbourhoods.

Financial institutions are always judged in relation to the specific context in which they operate. To that end, information is gathered on the institution itself (products, strategy), the relevant community (demographic data, sales opportunities), the competitors, and similar institutions. The relevant community (assessment area) is the geographical area whose credit needs an agency is supposed to meet. In that area are found branch offices and cash dispensers of the agency, and buyers of the financial products. The federal bodies naturally see to it that LMI neighbourhoods are not wrongly excluded in the delimitation of the area.

Initially, the two Acts had little effect on the banks' behaviour. However, in the course of the 1980s the media (especially newspapers) began to give increasing attention to the urban problems and the role of banks in it. Moreover, on the part of science (in the person of Michael Porter (1995)) the competitive advantages of inner cities were pointed out. Sharpened evaluation method and the inclusion of CRA ratings in the approval proceedings of take-overs and mergers have made banks highly conscious of the need for corporate social responsibility. Globalisation and the drive for scale enlargement have very probably contributed to that growing awareness. Despite the positive effects of the Acts, similar rules are highly unlikely to be issued for other sectors. Banking more than other sectors is dependent on the federal government since the insurance of banks is in its hands. Extension of the CRA to the insurance branch is the most probable. Insurance companies are now trying to prevent it by the voluntary adjustment of their social behaviour.

The banks' dealings with the Community Reinvestment Act have considerably changed in the past few years. While many banks at first regarded the Act as a kind of social tax, more and more of them now have come to understand the potential of LMI neighbourhoods. By a proactive approach, CRA-related services (loans, mortgages, investments, etc.) may well become a source of income, a profit centre, instead of a cost item. Such a turn-about would be impossible without knowledge of local communities and problems of housing, economic development and quality of the living environment.

Citigroup

One bank with a positive approach to the Community Reinvestment Act is Citigroup. This provider of financial services supplies to some 130 million consumers, companies, governments and agencies in more than 100 countries a broad package of financial products and services, including 'consumer banking and credit, corporate and investment banking, insurance, securities, brokerage and asset management' (see www.citigroup.com). The concern carries such brands as CitiBank, CitiFinancial, Primerica, Salomon Smith Barney, and Travelers Insurance. Citigroup has its own foundation oriented to education, economic and community development, and quality of life. In 2000, Citigroup and the Foundation donated more than US$62 million to organisations in over 64 countries. The company also stimulates voluntary work among its employees.

Until 1998, Citibank considered the Act a cost item. There were hardly any rules at all about how the bank's officers had to deal with the Act. The approach was ad hoc and decisions were left to the branch offices. Like many other banks, Citibank lost money on CRA-related transactions. Moreover, the bank scored no more than moderately in the evaluations and came under heavy criticism when there was question of take-overs. Because Citigroup was constantly in search of take-overs,[1] and the media took not only Citibank (only one of the business units) but the entire group to account as to its social responsibilities, a change in strategy was necessary.

That change came in 1998, when the company decided to couple its CRA-related transactions to objectives of community development, and accommodated them in a new business unit: the Centre for Community Development Enterprise (CCDE). Simultaneously with the founding of that business unit, the concern committed itself to invest, in a period of 10 years, to lend a sum of US$115 billion in LMI households, LMI neighbourhoods and small businesses, in loans or otherwise (Citigroup, 2001). The unit provides to non-profit and for-profit organisations involved in community development, innovative, extensive and cost-effective financing packages that help them accomplish their projects. The Centre's primary concern is affordable housing, but increasingly it also invests in shops, day nurseries, care provisions and other services. In Harlem, the business unit has funded among other things the building of an office, a theatre and shops. It also provides credit to non-profit organisations that in an entrepreneurial fashion supply essential services in economically backward neighbourhoods. The Centre operates all over the United States – including, of course, New York – as well as in Puerto Rico.

The founding of the special unit appears to have been a great success. The turnover of the social investments has increased while the losses have been turned into a fair profit. In 2000, the unit loaned and invested US$762 million, 90 per cent more than in 1999; in the period from 1997 to 2000 the number of loans and investments of Citigroup (not just of the Centre for Community Development Enterprise) in LMI neighbourhoods increased by 125 per cent, from 8.5 to 19 billion dollars (Citigroup, 2001). That development is expected to continue in the coming years.

Keys to a successful CRA-strategy One key to a successful CRA-strategy is, according to Citigroup, collaboration with public and private partners. Sustainable relations with the most divergent partners are tried for, including parties not traditionally involved in community development. Together with the Local Initiatives Support Corporation (LISC, see 'Intermediary Organisations'), the New York City Department of Housing Preservation and Development (municipality) and 13 local non-profit Community Development Corporations (CDCs), Citigroup is working at the so-called 'Neighbourhood Homes Program'. Citigroup contributes a below-market-rate loan of US$16 million from CCDE and a gift of US$340,000 from the Citigroup Foundation. The programme intends to achieve high-grade but affordable housing in New York and to rehabilitate dilapidated buildings. The Centre's contribution is paid into a fund of the Local Initiatives Support Corporation (which totals US$100 million), from which Community Development Corporations can borrow at a low rate of interest, in combination with technical coaching.

Another success factor is the quality of the management. Citigroup has understood that the managing of the special business unit requires extraordinary knowledge and skills. That was reason for the concern to appoint somebody with much experience in the non-profit sector (and in particular affordable housing) to give shape and substance to the social investment policy.

EAB Bank

In February 2001, Citibank took over the European American Bank (EAB) from the Dutch ABN-AMRO Bank. The European American Bank dedicates itself to commercial and retail banking and has nearly 100 offices in New York and surroundings. Like so many other regional banks, it has a firm reputation of corporate community involvement. The bank is highly content with the take-over, because 'Citibank recognises and appreciates the relation which EAB through the years has built up with clients and the local community' (press communication, 12 February 2001, www.abnamro.nl). ABN-AMRO had shown understanding for·the social activities of EAB and accepted the legislation, but as the European bank was not accustomed to using social investments for public relations and strategic market development. Evidently, contexts are still different in Europe and the USA.

Through the EAB Community Development Corporation, the bank makes a valuable contribution to the revitalisation of city neighbourhoods such as Harlem by funding affordable housing and activities of economic development. Like other banks, this corporation works closely together with property developers, not-for-profit bodies (such as the New York City Housing Partnership and the Local Initiatives Support Corporation), social organisations, government bodies (such as the New York City Department of Housing Preservation and Development), and financial agencies.

The Bank of New York

The Bank of New York's way of dealing with Community Reinvestment Act is in many respects comparable with the approach of the Citigroup. This bank also has a separate business unit for community development: the Community Development Group (CDG). The Bank of New York holds the view that 'active collaboration with public, private and not-for-profit sectors is essential to the creation of strong and dynamic communities' (Bank of New York, 2001, n.p.). To that end, the Group engages in strategic partnership with social organisations, developers, companies and government bodies, offering them an extensive package of financial products such as loans, investments and financial services.

The underlying principle of its policy is that the bank has a social responsibility as a 'good corporate citizen', to contribute to the welfare of the community in which it operates. To achieve a substantial impact on the community, the company takes the stand that, in completion of the traditional 'grant making' (philanthropy), its core business should have a social dimension. By community development the bank understands the stimulation of affordable housing (and in particular house ownership) and economic development (especially small-scale enterprise), as well as the realisation of such provisions as day nurseries and youth clubs, and the donation of computers to schools and good causes to narrow the 'digital divide'.

In the year 2000, the bank invested US$1.3 billion in community development, affordable housing and loans for small businesses. Besides financial support the bank also continually supplies advice. In New York, the Community Development Group has developed several schemes jointly with social organisations. The bank has supplied US$21.6 million in building credits for 216 affordable dwellings in Manhattan, Brooklyn and the Bronx, and a loan of 2.5 million for the development of Harlem Centre, a shopping centre in 125th Street (Harlem's main street). Together with the European American

Bank, the Bank of New York has funded a shopping centre in the Bronx. The bank also participates in the New York Mortgage Coalition, which enables LMI households to become house owners (Bank of New York, 2001).

Legislation and Corporate Community Involvement

Legislation has helped to improve considerably the social behaviour of banks (in the USA, in New York). That observation raises the question how such legislation relates to the thesis that 'corporate community involvement is a matter of self-interest'. Why should a business company need the pressure of the law to invest in LMI neighbourhoods if that is anyhow (in theory) in that company's own interest? Possibly, legislation has woken the companies up to a self-interest that allegedly was 'not so obvious', and incited companies to develop creative and innovative products and services in collaboration with other organisations. From the experiences of Citigroup and the Bank of New York we can indeed deduce that innovativeness and collaboration are necessary conditions for a successful application of the Community Reinvestment Act.

Legislation can pull business across the line at which they were quite content with the way they were performing. The fact is that in actual practice entrepreneurs are not the 'rational actors' who maximise their long-term profit (shareholders' value, stakeholders' value). Now that companies, thanks in part to Michael Porter, have recognised the potential of LMI neighbourhoods and the self-interest has become obvious (the term 'emerging market' is gaining credit), a plea can be made for abolition of the Act. Those in favour of the Act point out, however, that the rules are still needed to see to it that all banks will go on investing in LMI neighbourhoods, even in times of a declining business cycle.

Business Improvement Districts (BIDs)

Another legal instrument to institutionalise the social interests of companies, is the so-called Business Improvement District (BID). The possibility of setting up a BID is laid down in the federal legislature. The Act enables local companies and property owners to form a tax district for the express purpose of reserving financial means to improve and promote that district. There are two kinds of BID: the property-based BID and the business-based BID. The first concerns an adjustable five-year programme that is annually evaluated, and is created by the majority of votes (more than half) of the commercial property owners within the borders of the district. The second is organised by local companies, with a minimum participation of 15 per cent of the companies in the district; subject to annual adjustment. The companies or property owners are free to choose the method of setting the level for the additional tax. Within property-based BIDs the criteria used are square area, storey (street level or higher), location on an important road or a byroad, and the proximity of improvements (projects). The initiators of a BID are expected to draw up to mutual satisfaction a programme and budget to be submitted to the District Council. As soon as the Council has approved programme and budget, the scheme is legally valid.

BIDs concern themselves on the whole with matters that are insufficiently cared for by the local government. Such matters are, for instance, the quality of street furniture, public lighting, parks and public gardens, parking, as well as increased safety and maintenance (over and above the public services). Business Improvement Districts have existed for more than 30 years and are found in Canada as well as the USA.

Supporters and Opponents

The BID concept has supporters as well as opponents. Opponents take the view that the additional taxes are, in the long run, harmful to private enterprise. Some argue that with this scheme, additional tax is paid for services that rightly should be supplied by the government. The most fundamental criticism is, however, that the concept promotes polarisation, since districts with much economic activity and rich property owners will have more generous budgets at their disposal than districts with little economic activities and relatively poor property owners.

Supporters of BIDs, however, have countered such arguments with persuasive success stories. The 34 BIDs in New York are allegedly co-responsible for the revitalising of a couple of 'ex-problem districts', such as Times Square, Grand Central and East Williamsburg in Brooklyn, by making them more attractive and safer for pedestrians and shoppers. The success of BIDs is ascribed on the one hand to the almost complete absence of red tape, and on the other to the priority given to such basic qualities as safety and hygiene. At the same time the experience has been that companies and property owners benefit from the additional tax. Owing to the additional investments, districts manage to attract more residents, companies and visitors, entailing rising turnovers for the suppliers of services, and rising land prices for property owners. Moreover, companies have less trouble recruiting manpower when the safety of the direct environment is ensured.

MetroTech BID

One of the 34 BIDs in New York is MetroTech BID, founded in 1992 to give substance to the revitalisation of Downtown Brooklyn. The investment programme of this non-profit organisation is oriented primarily to safety, hygiene (street cleaning) and economic development. A prominent player in the district is the polytechnical university.

This university was confronted in the 1970s with a drop in the student population, in part ascribable to an increase in crime and decay in the immediate environment. The university decided not to move out, but to work with the government at a masterplan for an office park to be called MetroTech Centre. At first, efforts to draw companies to the area were not very successful, despite the easy access (connections to the city-railway network) and the acceptable price level. By the installation of a BID, named after the office park, the greatest weaknesses of the area could be overcome, namely, the lack of safety and the mediocre quality of the living environment.

The enlisting of security officers – working closely with the municipal police (NYCPD) – has resulted for one thing in the spectacular reduction of crime by 84 per cent since 1991. Downtown Brooklyn can now claim to be one of the safest business districts of New York. In the sphere of hygiene,

Table 8.1 Budget of MetroTech BID

Revenues		Expenditure	
Additional tax	1,989,936	Public security	1,264,960
Not-for-profit contributions	109,020	Cleaning	165,100
Interest	22,500	Marketing/'outreach'	88,500
Gifts	66,500	Consultants	85,000
		Capital improvements	22,000
		Retail services	65,000
		Summer Jobs Program	9,000
		Garden Festival	50,000
		Administrative/general	539,515
Total revenue	2,187,956	Total expenditure	2,289,075

Source: MetroTech BID, 2001.

too, the district has achieved measurable results. By regularly sweeping the streets and instantly removing any illegal posters and graffiti, the cleanliness ratings have gone up a great deal.

Intermediary Organisations

A third instrument put in to unite the public and private sectors, is the intermediary organisation. Such non-profit organisations play an important part in the United States in the development of cities. The fact is that direct collaboration between the government and private enterprise often gets stuck against cultural, political and legal barriers. In New York, as elsewhere, the private sector tends to complain about bureaucracy in the government, while the government is much bothered by the commercial motives of the private sector. One of the principal intermediary organisations in New York is the New York City Partnership, to which the New York City Housing Partnership belongs. The New York City Partnership is closely involved in Restart Central, a joint initiative of the City and the state of New York to help the companies hit by the attack of 11 September, to pick up their business again. They can do so for instance with goods and services donated by private enterprise, individuals and non-government organisations. The partnership can do so with goods and services donated by private enterprise, individuals and non-government organisations, such as free counselling towards their recovery.

New York City Housing Partnership

The New York City Housing Partnership was founded in 1982 by bank manager and philanthropist David Rockefeller in cooperation with the New York City Partnership. The Housing Partnership envisages accomplishing, by the joint efforts of government, banks and other companies, affordable housing in New York, and stimulating private investments and redevelopment of vacant property in backward neighbourhoods. Thanks to the efforts of the partnership, between 1992 and 2001 some 22,000 affordable dwellings have been realised, spread across the five boroughs of New York. The first initiative of the organisation was the New Homes Program (operational since 1983): a partnership with the New York City Department of Housing Preservation and Development and the New York State Affordable Housing Corporation, whose purpose was to provide new, affordable dwellings for families buying their first home. On average, 1,200 houses are built every year with millions of dollars in public and private investments for permanent low-cost financing. As a complement to the New Homes Program, low-to-moderate income households have since 1993 had appeal to the Mortgage Coalition, a consortium of 10 mortgage lenders and eight social non-profit organisations, administered by the Housing Partnership. This coalition gives advice on mortgage and credit to potential buyers of houses in New York City, Long Island and Westchester, and coaches interested buyers through the proceeding of the mortgage application. Since its founding in 1993, the consortium has lent US$200 million against mortgage to thousands of individuals with low to modest incomes.

Another initiative is the Neighborhood Entrepreneurs Program, likewise a joint effort with the municipality (Housing Preservation and Development). This programme enables local companies to take over from the municipality the management, renovation and finally the ownership of sequestrated property[2] (on account of unpaid property tax). The renovation is financed by loans from private banks, permanent funding by the municipality, federal subsidies and low-income housing tax credits. An important criterion is that the companies and individuals taking over the management, shall give evidence of long-term involvement in the neighbourhood in question. The Neighborhood Entrepreneurs Program connects the entrepreneurs with the Housing Partnership, private banks and the municipality. The Housing Partnership coaches entrepreneurs through the jungle of red tape and serves as link between the companies and the municipal departments. Thus the intermediary – who is fluent in both languages – can lower cultural barriers.

Since the start of the programme in 1994, over 6,000 apartments in the South Bronx, Harlem and Central Brooklyn have been renovated. That success is due in part to the stimulating effect of the Community Reinvestment Act, which has made banks far more willing to participate in this kind of projects. Moreover, the risks are limited because the municipality and the Housing Partnerships operate a kind of safety-net construction in the event the fund does not fare too well.

New York City Investment Fund

Another initiative of the New York City Partnership is the New York City Investment Fund. Its spiritual father is Henry Kravis, one of the partners of Kohlberg, Kravis, Roberts & Co. This company invests in management buyouts on its own behalf and that of institutional investors such as the State, pension funds, banks and insurance companies (see www.kkr.com). The creation of this fund was inspired by the fear that the social division of New York would jeopardise the city's position in the rising knowledge and information economy. The fund's aim is to mobilise the potential of the city – in the shape of talent, money, diversity and ideas – to set up new companies and jobs in (budding) growth sectors (such as biotechnology and internet), and to offer all residents (in all neighbourhoods) the opportunity to participate actively in those sectors (New York City Investment Fund, 1999). As an offspring of the New York City Partnership, this fund provides (financial) support to companies and enterprising not-for-profit organisations that are supposed to have a multiplier effect on the local economy. The organisation serves as a catalyst, not only by direct investment in companies, but also by investing in other conditions for economic growth, such as a productive active population, research and education facilities, business-to-business networks, and financial products that fill up the gaps in the conventional supply.

More than 60 companies, among which AT&T, Bankers Trust and Pfizer, have come forward as investors in the fund. They invest US$1 million each, which they will receive back after 15 years – without interest. Besides giving financial support, the concerns are also prepared to give advice to promising entrepreneurs. The fund expects from investments in profit-oriented companies a share in the success on the same financial basis as other investors. Investments in non-profit organisations are assumed to be at least self-supportive. However, from a 'social fund' greater risks and lower returns than customary in the market are acceptable, notably from projects that help to overcome the social divide in the city. The fund diversifies its bets, across retailing, health care, media, and other industries at the local economy's core, imagining the city to be like a good balanced stock portfolio (*Business Week*, 1998).

The generous support among private enterprise for this initiative is ascribed in part to the charismatic leadership of Henry Kravis, whom many entrepreneurs are eager to meet in person. Participation in the fund not only offers opportunities for 'networking', but also gives people the gratifying feeling of doing something in return for the community.

Since 11 September, the fund has dedicated itself mainly to the companies who have suffered damage by the disaster. To that end, it cooperates closely with the city and the state of New York. Many businesses give free advice to the distressed companies of several sectors. The most attention goes to small businesses, which are highly vulnerable and have little self-regenerating capacity.

Local Initiatives Support Corporation

The Local Initiatives Support Corporation is another intermediary organisation with a prominent part to play in public-private collaboration. The principal difference with the New York City (Housing) Partnership is that this intermediary operates nationally. The Corporation was founded in 1980 and calls itself 'the nation's largest non-profit community development organization'. Its aim is to revitalise communities by supporting Community Development Corporations. The Support Corporation is convinced that these local organisations are best able to respond to the needs and priorities of boroughs and neighbourhoods.

The Local Initiative Support Corporation provides gifts, loans and capital investment to Community Development Corporations for neighbourhood revitalisation, notably in the sphere of housing and economic development. The organisation 'matches' locally generated funds with an equal amount towards the implementation of projects. It operates on three levels. Firstly, the organisation gives direct support to individual Community Development Corporations and operates as an intermediary for more than 900 companies and foundations that give technical and financial support to Community Development Corporations. The Support Corporation wants to give them a chance to grow into strong and stable bodies with an effective and fiscally responsible management capable of implementing a package of revitalising activities. Secondly, LISC aims to improve the environment in which Community Development Corporations operate by stimulating partnerships between local programmes, social organisations, local foundations, companies and authorities (state and municipality). A joint approach is considered necessary to achieve sustainable and substantial results. Thirdly, the intermediary aims to strengthen national support for community development by channelling subsidies to local programmes and encouraging the exchange of experiences among communities. It tries to convince governments of the importance of Community Development Corporations and a neighbourhood-oriented approach.

Abyssinian Development Corporation

One of the Community Development Corporations in New York is the Abyssinian Development Corporation, named after the Abyssinian Church. This organisation aims to enhance the quality of the living environment in Harlem through projects concerned with housing, employment, education, safety and other matters.

Through innovation and collaboration with other organisations, the Abyssinian Development Corporation tries to persuade companies of the potentialities of Harlem. Together with banks (among which the EAB Community Development Bank), the Local Initiatives Support Corporation and government agencies, the Abyssinian Development Corporation has succeeded in realising a large shopping centre, with supermarket Pathmark as principal attraction. To that end the organisation has made use of the Neighborhood Franchise Project of the Local Initiatives Support Corporation – actually sponsored by Deutsche Bank – which stimulates great retail chains to have franchise establishments set up in neighbourhoods like Harlem, on behalf of local employment and level of services. At the same time the corporation has succeeded, in collaboration with several parties – including banks stimulated by CRA – to raise the quality of life in Harlem. Decayed houses have been rehabilitated or replaced with new ones. By the increased input of the police (municipal policy) and neighbourhood surveillants, Harlem has been made a much safer place. Here, as elsewhere, safety is a major precondition for revitalisation.

The media have done a lot to enhance the image of Harlem. Thanks to positive articles in respected newspapers and journals, the borough enjoys increasing interest from residents, companies and tourists. A good communication strategy oriented to the acquisition of political and social support has proved a prominent condition for success. The positive results can also be ascribed to the leadership of the organisation as well as the associates. Strikingly, one of the key figures in this organisation has given up his job in the financial sector to give his full energy to his birthplace. His leadership is based on a combination of knowledge of the private sector on the one hand and great commitment to the neighbourhood of his roots on the other.

Pfizer and the Revitalisation of Williamsburg

Pfizer is a large pharmaceutical concern with establishments all over the world. The company was founded in the middle of the nineteenth century (1849) by German immigrants. Pfizer has a long tradition of philanthropy, which manifests itself in donations of money and products (medical compounds) and strategic partnerships in the area of education. In New York, Pfizer is best known, however, for its deep involvement in the revitalisation of Williamsburg (Brooklyn).

Immediate Cause

In the 1970s and 1980s, the neighbourhood Williamsburg – like so many other American town quarters – was confronted with great social-economic problems. The neighbourhood had acquired a one-sided demographic profile owing to the emigration of the white middle classes to the suburbs, leaving immigrants from all parts of the world behind. Many businesses decided to follow the example of the residents and also left for the suburbs. Pfizer as well was facing the 'should-we-stay-or-should-we-go' decision. Actually, the Pfizer headquarters had been moved to Manhattan back in the 1950s because it needed a larger office and wanted to be nearer to the financial district.

Unlike the companies that had left, Pfizer looked upon the local community as an asset instead of a weakness: 'We have a major investment there in people, plant and equipment, and customers' (Pfizer, undated, p. 4). To invest in the neighbourhood would in the long run contribute to the continuity of the company. It might not be a direct self-interest, but certainly a form of 'enlightened self-interest', with ethical motives (the corporate culture) playing a role. 'We believed we could benefit the community while meeting our responsibilities to shareholders, employees and customers' (ibid.). Moreover, the value of the charismatic performance of CEO Edmund Pratt must not be underestimated. For indeed, the risks were great and the alternative (move) enticingly easy.

Investments

In the early 1980s, Pfizer, together with the municipality, assessed what investments were needed to give a new lease of life to the area around the establishment. A clean and safe environment was considered indispensable for revitalisation. The municipality did its bit by cleaning up and fencing in vacant buildings. Pfizer then invested US$120,000 in upgrading the local city railway station and making it safer. The station is now constantly monitored. The security service in Pfizer's establishment keeps the situation in the station in sight and reports any disturbances instantly to the police. In improving the safety (outside as well as inside the station), Pfizer works closely together with the police. To smooth the input of more policemen, Pfizer has even put scooters at their disposal. All these investments have helped to reduce crime, to the benefit of residents and businesses alike. In addition, Pfizer suffers less than before from aggression against the business itself, now that it has built itself a good image in the neighbourhood.

Besides security, employment and housing were high on Pfizer's priority list. As a matter of fact, the residential neighbourhoods immediately surrounding the factory at the time showed all the symptoms of urban decay, including drugs, crime, prostitution, violence and vacancy. The company was very concerned about the situation in these neighbourhoods, since at the time almost two thirds of its employees had their homes within a radius of five miles from the factory. Moreover, the company would preferably maintain the area's traditional blend of residency and industry. For that reason, the company, together with the municipal Public Development Corporation, created the Broadway Triangle Urban Renewal Project. This project comprises the development of an industrial park in combination with housing for LMI-households in grounds partly owned by Pfizer and partly by the city. The company considers these investments as contributions to the reduction of unemployment, with an expected creation of 500 permanent jobs. Pfizer has itself given a good example by reinvesting in its local establishment.

Slowly but surely, more and more organisations have become involved in the revitalisation plans, including authorities, companies, and non-profit organisations. Thus, the Enterprise Foundation,[3] with the support of the Brooklyn Union Gas Company, American Express Company, the Federal National Mortgage Association and Pfizer, has realised two hundred dwellings for low-income groups in the immediate environment of its establishment. The Local Iniatives Support Corporation has in its turn renovated a large apartment complex on the edge of the area. At the same time, the utility companies Brooklyn Union Gas and Consolidated Edison Company of New York have given incentives for the renovation of houses in private ownership. In the context of the New Homes Program of the New York City Partnership and with the support of municipal department for housing preservation and development, a further 300 affordable owner-occupier houses are being developed.

The fourth pillar of the investment programme is education. The underlying philosophy is that job opportunities are useless when citizens lack the knowledge and skills required to fill them. In that line of thought, Pfizer became the corporate partner of a neighbouring highschool, in the framework of the municipal Join-A-School Program. Employees of the company act as mentors on a voluntary basis. Moreover, the company provides equipment and technical advice. As a matter of fact, the company has similar relations with other schools in the neighbourhood. However, Pfizer's most noteworthy relation is with a school that is the spiritual child of the Beginning With Children Foundation. This foundation aims to improve public education by means of public-private cooperation. The initiators of this foundation – Carol and Joe Reich – were in search of a suitable location, and at last literally bumped into Pfizer's.

Pfizer gave the foundation not only a building, but also US$500,000 to convert the building, which used to be the management's accommodation, into a suitable place for a school. The structural support of Pfizer to education in the immediate environment is evidence of a long-term self-interest in the sustainable development of the neighbourhood, and in particular in the proper education of future employees.

Success Factors

Pfizer's experiences prove that a company can make a structural contribution to the revitalisation of cities. In particular with respect to safety, housing and education the results of the efforts in Williamsburg are striking. Only in the area of employment there remains much to be done. Pfizer is doing its utmost to attract business to the area, but most companies seem to be wary of the risk. On the whole, Pfizer's efforts can certainly be called successful. What factors have helped to bring it about?

A fundamental condition for successful privately-supported area revitalisation is patience. Pfizer has learned that fast solutions are impossible in this type of undertaking. For such long-term investments, confidence in the potentialities of the immediate surrounding is crucial. A corporate culture in which social involvement is a core value, is helpful to acquire support from shareholders and other stakeholders for the kind of decisions Pfizer has taken. Besides, Pfizer's story confirms the importance of partnerships. The New York City Partnership and the Enterprise Foundation have provided essential contributions. Both organisations have many supporters among companies who want to contribute to neighbourhood revitalisation. Moreover these organisations lobby for the removal of legal barriers and the reform of an inflexible policy hampering private involvement in urban projects.

Pfizer's role in the revitalisation of Williamsburg is a clear example of corporate leadership. The company took a courageous initiative and stimulated others, involving them on the strength of an integral vision on the future of Williamsburg, with the indispensable political support of the City Council. The company moreover chose consciously to join forces with other organisations with superior knowledge of and expertise in the matters at issue. Anybody is free to contribute to the vision, as long as the principles are upheld. Pfizer looks upon the local government as a prominent and necessary partner for the revitalisation of areas. The company accepts, moreover (to a degree), the bureaucratic nature of the authorities, as well as the fact that all actors have different interests.

Conclusions

The impact of 11 September on corporate community involvement has two sides. On the one hand, the economic recession accelerated by the terrorist attack has strengthened solidarity, making government and private enterprise more inclined to join forces in the rebuilding of Ground Zero and reinstating the distressed companies (for instance through Restart Central and the New York City Investment Fund). On the other hand, the recession may induce companies to lose sight of their long-term social stakes and focus on their commercial short-term goals.

The case of New York confirms that the social involvement of private enterprise varies among sectors. In the USA (and notably in New York), banks are among the most 'social' sectors. Although in theory banks have a stake in a good relation with their direct environment (clients and employees!), legislation – as well as a degree of pressure from the media and scholars – have proved necessary to activate that self-interest in practice. Banks are increasingly aware of the need to deal more strategically with the local environment by developing creative and innovative products and services jointly with other organisations (authorities, non-profit organisations, and companies). Consequently, they no longer regard observation of the law as a form of social tax, but as a matter of self-interest, expecting investments in the local environment to contribute to the development of emerging markets and to enhance the corporate image. They also realise that a strategic approach makes demands on the quality of management: knowledge of the local circumstances becomes ever more important.

Another interesting phenomenon that we observed in New York is the Business Improvement District. This legal instrument institutionalises the local interests of companies in an appealing – and above all safe and clean – environment, and stimulates the development of partnerships between authorities, companies, social organisations and schools (universities). Business Improvement Districts distinguish themselves from other forms of tax levying in that the taxpayers have a direct influence on the programme and directly and demonstrably profit from the improved living and location environment. Moreover, they help to avoid bureaucracy. Despite the success of the concept in the USA, their chance of success in Europe remains questionable. Context differences still count for much.

The experiences of New York affirm the importance of intermediary organisations as brokers between public and private interests. The power of organisations of this type – which operate on several spatial scales – is primarily that they are familiar with both parties and show understanding for democratic and bureaucratic proceedings on the part of the government and non-profit organisations on the one hand and the commercial interests of firms on the other. The case of Pfizer bears evidence that one single company can take the initiative to the complete revitalisation of an area. The decision to invest in the local environment instead of moving to another location, was inspired by a combination of self-interest and personal involvement in the ups and downs of Williamsburg.

Notes

1 Citigroup has lobbied to take care that banks by an amendment would be allowed to merge with insurance companies. At once after that amendment, Citigroup availed itself of the opportunity to become the first bank-cum-insurance company in the United States.
2 Tax-foreclosed city-owned properties.
3 The Enterprise Foundation is a national non-profit organisation which, with the help of partnership, invests in affordable housing, safety, access to employment and day nurseries for low-income groups. See www.enterprisefoundation.org.

References

Bank of New York (2001), 'Strengthening Communities Through Partnerships'.
Berg, L. van den, E. Braun, J. van der Meer and A.H.J. Otgaar (1999), *De binnenstadseconomie in de eenentwintigste eeuw*, EURICUR, Rotterdam.
Business Week (1998), 'Henry Kravis ... Do-gooder? The LBO King is Raising Millions for Inner City NYC', Leah Nathans Spiro, 3 February, New York.
Citigroup (2001), 'Building Better Communities with People Around the World'.
Federal Register (2001), Vol. 66, No. 139, 19 July.
Fuchs, E.R. (1992), *Mayors and Money: Fiscal Policy in New York and Chicago*, The University of Chicago Press, Chicago.
MetroTech BID (2001), 'MetroTech Business Improvement District; Annual Report 2000–2001'.
New York City Investment Fund (1999), 'New York City Investment Fund: A Private Fund with a Civic Mission', New York.
Pfizer (undated), 'Pfizer in Brooklyn – A Redevelopment Story'.
Porter, M.E. (1995), 'The Competitive Advantage of the Inner City', *Harvard Business Review*, May–June, pp. 55–74.

Discussion Partners

S. Acosta, Program Director, Community Partnership Development Corporation, New York City Partnership

G. Armstrong, President, Housing Partnership Development Corporation, New York City Partnership

L. Brown, Senior Vice President, Bank of New York

A.C. Clark, Manager Supply Chain Projects, Pfizer Global Manufacturing

A. Ditton, Citicorp

S. Fainstein, Professor of Urban Planning and Policy, Rutgers University

G.S. Hattem, Deutsche Bank

G.D. Kaufman, Principal, New York City Investment Fund, New York City Partnership

Th.J. Kline Jr, Vice President/Team Leader Procurement and Distribution, Pfizer Global Manufacturing

R. Luftglass, Director U.S. Philanthropy, Corporate Philanthropy, Pfizer Inc.

R. Manson, Local Initiatives Support Corporation

P. Noonan, Senior Director Research and Policy, New York City Partnership and Chamber of Commerce

C. Roan, Manager Corporate Philanthropy, Corporate Affairs, Pfizer Inc.

R.J. Roberto, Senior Vice President, Community Development Division, EAB Bank/Citigroup

P. Rosenblum, Senior Vice President, HSBC Bank USA

D. Walker, Former Chief Executive Officer, Abyssinian Development Corporation

M.A. Weiss, Executive Director, MetroTech BID

K. Wylde, New York City Partnership

Chapter 9

Seattle

Introduction

By American standards Seattle is a city of no more than medium dimensions (with just over half a million inhabitants). Nevertheless, the city enjoys some international fame. Film fans will perhaps recall at once *Sleepless in Seattle*, while many music lovers know the city's name from such well-known bands as Pearl Jam and Nirvana. However, our attention to Seattle has some other reasons. For one thing, Seattle is the hometown of aircraft builder Boeing and coffee retailer Starbucks, two well-known companies with a reputation in community involvement. For another, the local government and other non-profit organisations seem very eager to develop partnerships with the private sector in order to stimulate a sustainable development of the city.

This chapter is organised as follows. The second section contains a profile of the city of Seattle. Next, we review the most important opportunities and problems, the response to them of (organised) enterprise, and the attempts to create cross-sector partnerships. The two sections which follow discuss the community involvement activities of Boeing and Starbucks, followed by the conclusions in the final section.

Profile

Seattle was founded in 1859 and is therefore one of the youngest cities of the United States. The city is situated in the extreme northwest of the United States, in the state of Washington, 182 kilometres south of the frontier with Canada and over 100 kilometres east of the Pacific coast. It is by far the most prominent city in King County, which houses over 1.6 million residents. The Greater Seattle area (as defined by the Office of Intergovernmental Relations of the municipality of Seattle) comprises three more counties (Snohomish, Pierce and Kitsap), which brings the population up to over three million (City of Seattle, 2000). This area is sometimes called the Puget Sound Region, after the Puget Sound, a 130-km long estuary of the Pacific.

Seattle is a prominent centre of high-grade technology for aviation, computer software, bio informatics, electronics and medical equipment. By far the largest employer is Boeing, the world's largest aircraft producer and one of the three main exporters in the USA. The Boeing associates in the region earn together about US$4 billion. A review of the 10 most important companies in terms of their share in regional employment is represented in Table 9.1.

Table 9.1 The most important employers in the Central Puget Sound Region

1	The Boeing Company	98,440
2	University of Washington	17,250
3	Microsoft Corporation	15,400
4	King County government	12,800
5	Safeway	9,851
6	Sisters of Providence Systems	9,423
7	Department of Defense	9,000
8	City of Seattle	8,870
9	Group Health Cooperative	8,800
10	United States Postal Service	8,500

Sources: Puget Sound Business Journal, 2000; individual companies; Economic Development Council of Seattle and King County, 2000; see also City of Seattle, 2000.

Microsoft, the world's number one software producer, is only one of the 2,500 software development companies in the region, which together employ some 30,000 people. Biotechnology and medical technology together generate US$2 billion and 15,000 job opportunities in 150 companies and non-profit organisations. Other important industries are: wood products, transport means, food, fish processing and clothing design. Table 9.2 shows a review of the employment structure in the Greater Seattle area.

Thanks in part to its geographical situation, Greater Seattle has always been a prominent centre of trade. Per head of population, the state of Washington exports more than any other state. At a growth rate of 4 per cent a year, international trade – at the time of writing providing one-third of total employment – is one of the fastest growing growth sectors of the state of Washington. The seaport of Seattle, 'the gateway to Asia', is the fifth greatest

Table 9.2 Employment structure in the Greater Seattle area (King, Kitsap, Pierce and Snohomish County)

Sector	Employees	%
Industry	240,100	14.3
Durable goods	185,600	11.0
Transport, including air transport	107,100	6.4
Other durable goods	78,500	4.6
Non-durable goods	54,900	3.3
Services	493,700	29.4
Wholesale/retail trade	396,490	23.6
Government	257,500	15.3
Banks, insurance companies, real estate	99,250	5.9
Construction	95,500	5.7
Transport/public services	94,920	5.6
Total	2,103,060	100.0

Source: City of Seattle, 2000, adapted by the authors.

container harbour of the USA. Seattle-Tacoma Airport, actually owned by the Port of Seattle, is (at 27.7 million passengers in 1999) a great hub of international connections with Europe and Asia.

Seattle offers a very attractive business location, as is known from several rankings and investigations (Economic Development Council of Seattle and King County, 2000). Some significant success factors are the well-educated active population, the quality of life, the diversified economic structure, the quality of education and care, the easy access to international and national markets, and the quality of the infrastructure.

Problems, Policies and Partnerships

This section analyses the main problems in the Seattle region as well as the policies of companies and governments to deal with these problems, and the partnerships that have been developed as a result of these policies.

Problems in the Seattle Region

The number one issue, not only in Seattle but also elsewhere in the United States, is education. The quality of the public schools in particular leaves very much to desire and until recently many schools did not meet a certain standard, simply because in many states there was no standard. Companies have for years shown their involvement with education, but the actions were mostly purely philanthropic, random and ad hoc ('random access kindness'). The donations were valuable but for lack of mutual adjustment failed to change the system.

For some years now, companies in Seattle have gradually made their commitment to education more strategic. Companies are prepared to invest more money in education because a well-educated active population is to their advantage. Some companies do more than just writing a cheque: they have taken to advising schools on better management, to breed not only better students but also better school leaders. That development has been signalled in the annual report of the non-profit organisation 'Alliance for Education'; local companies and individuals as well as national foundations are now recognising that support to education (in Seattle) is a good investment. That is due on the one hand to cyclical conditions, such as a tight labour market, and on the other to certain structural developments that have increased the importance of the labour factor. The rise of the service sector and the emerging information society are causing a growing need for higher-educated staff. Companies are discovering that the supply of jobseekers does not match their demand. More than ever before, companies are resorting to the so-called K12-system (from kindergarten up to Year 12), while before the emphasis was mainly on higher education (universities). Businesses have a stake not only in a well-educated active population, but also in minimising the costs caused by such social problems as crime and unemployment.

At the same time, however, companies are giving closer attention on the effectiveness of their investments. They are prepared to invest only if the would-be partners achieve fundamental changes. At the end of the 1990s, the strong leadership of the Seattle School Board and the superintendent (head of the school district) then in office paved the way for such changes in the Seattle region, stimulated by government initiatives such as the setting of standards for schools to meet, as urgently requested by private enterprise.

Accessibility

Another problem in the Seattle region relates to accessibility and the spatial distribution of people and activities. As far as its accessibility is concerned, the region has fallen victim to its own success. The pleasant location climate has in the past few decades invited a massive inflow of economic activity. The prosperous growth was in addition spurred by the rise of the information society, which thanks to Microsoft was of great profit to Seattle. Those developments have had great influence on the spatial spread of residents and activities. Land prices have soared, notably downtown. Many companies and residents have been compelled by the market forces to settle away from the centre. House prices have risen so much in the past few years that not only the low-income groups but also those with moderate incomes have difficulty finding a house they can afford. From 1970 to 1998 the average price of housing in King County rose from two to six times the average annual salary (Housing Partnership, undated). For a large portion of the population, house ownership is no longer within reach.

In combination with the strong dependency on private transport, the urban sprawl has led to serious congestion, especially on the roads to and from the centre. Remarkably enough, the traffic problems in the inner city are not too bad. Because Seattle is spread between several lakes and rivers, investment in new bridges and motorways is necessary. Equally urgent are investments in the quality of public transport, to reduce as far as possible people's dependency on private transport. To keep a check on urban sprawl, King County has drawn a circle around the city, within which to concentrate the urban growth. As space becomes scarcer within that circle, the interest in alternative housing formulas is rising. The public-private Housing Partnership encourages such alternative formulas by research and otherwise. This partnership – which is financed by the city of Seattle, the Port of Seattle and several companies (Boeing among them) – serves as intermediary between municipalities and developers who tend to have little trust in each other. Another ambition of the partnership is to convince municipalities and developers of the necessity of change, thus assuming the part of change agent. Both parties hold a fairly conservative attitude, which makes changes hard to carry through. Developers look first and foremost at short-term returns, which they may in fact need to survive, giving no thought to sustainable alternatives, which in the long term would yield them more revenue. The Housing Partnership points out that the parties involved must learn to work together. Lack of trust makes it difficult to find sustainable solutions for the housing problems. Only if and when all those involved recognise the urgency will a joint approach have a chance to take off (Housing Partnership, undated).

In recent years, Seattle's inner city has been confronted by the phenomenon of 'gentrification'. As in many other US cities, the centre of the city is enjoying a growing popularity as residential location, especially among high-income groups. These people are boosting the housing prices and thus the property tax, so that people with a relatively low income run into financial trouble and are more or less forced to move to cheaper neighbourhoods further from the centre. That development is worsening accessibility in the region. Of course, there are also positive effects of the inner city's reinforced housing function; for instance, the local government sees its tax base expanding after years of decline.

Much as companies are conscious of their own interest in the solution of transport problems, there is little willingness among them to take effective steps. Through the Chamber of Commerce, companies do lobby for investment in accessibility, but they do not consider co-financing by the private sector a real option. They argue that they already pay value-added tax, and that in their opinion accessibility is a purely public matter. Indeed, in the USA the public sector is responsible for the development of transport infrastructure. Perhaps a fully-fledged transport crisis would turn the tide, but for the moment that seems highly improbable. For one thing, people are very creative in solving their transport and housing problems (less so for educational problems), and for another, congestion apparently has come to be accepted as more or less normal. The matter is made even more complex by the legal constraints (in the state of Washington) on the formation of public-private partnerships. Public dollars must not, on the whole, benefit private investments.

Social Division

The third major problem in Seattle is the increasing gap between the poor and the rich (social division). The private sector has become very concerned about this problem, in particular after a protest march in 1993. This march was organised by citizens who thought the election of Seattle as the most liveable city of the United States by the journal *Money* was unfounded. In the eyes of the protesters Seattle was beset with grave social problems, such as crime, drugs, violence, poverty, racism and unemployment. The initiative for the march was taken by associations of citizens and small businesses. The march ended up at the Chamber of Commerce, where the 8,000 demonstrators expressed their urgent appeal to the social responsibility of private enterprise, and readily convinced the Chamber that their arguments were sound. Private enterprise, made aware of its own interest, founded the Urban Enterprise Centre (UEC), with financial support from several large companies, among which The Boeing Company. The Chamber invited one of the organisers of the march to establish the centre.

The Urban Enterprise Centre's aim is to raise the economic vitality of the central area and the Rainier Valley (two areas with relatively high rates of minorities, poverty and unemployment), and to prevent the inner city from passing through the same crisis as other North American cities. To that end, three pillars have been defined: job creation, forums on race (to stimulate mutual understanding), and business development (for instance, by giving advice to entrepreneurs).

In the matter of job creation, in 1994 the UEC jointly with the Rainier Job Service Center (RJSC) of the Washington State Employment Security Office and the Department of Social and Health Services (DSHS), drew up a scheme which was to make companies in Seattle enthusiastic for cooperation with social organisations and municipal agencies. The scheme stimulates companies to employ people from backward zones and underprivileged groups. The organisation aims to create jobs with a minimum annual income of US$18,000, to enable these people to buy their own home. The UEC wrote a letter to local companies asking them to employ people from the direct environment (the inner city). Thanks to that initiative, more than 6,000 benefits receivers have found a job. Companies are pleased, not only because they have been able to fill their vacancies, but also because they have hopes of tax relief provided that the government needs to spend less on benefits and crime control, and generates more resources through tax.

An illustrative example of public-private partnership is the Seattle-Preston Workforce Connection. In 1995 the managing director of the Bernard Development Company asked the UEC if it would be possible for companies situated in the I-90 Preston International Park to employ people from the central area and Rainier Valley. He also got in touch with the King County Department of Metropolitan Services for the purpose of analysing the prospects of a transport programme to meet the transport demands of employees and employers in the industrial park. A meeting of stakeholders followed, to consider the feasibility of such a programme and the willingness of employers to employ and support the envisaged workers. The meeting resulted in the formal founding of the Seattle-Preston Workforce Connection, and agreement on several objectives, such as to create cooperative relations and partnerships with public and private entities and business leaders in Preston.

The programme is client-oriented and creates a win-win opportunity for employers, employees and the participating organisations (Urban Enterprise Center and others, undated). The Seattle-Preston Workforce Connection enables employers to prepare to the changing labour market (an increasing proportion of non-whites, women and immigrants in the active population), and thus ensure the continuity of the company. There are two components; the referral and placement component which brings supply and demand together, and the supportive component which considers the overall needs of the employees (holistic approach). With respect to the former component, the roles and responsibilities of the partners: RJSC, DSHS, Private Industry Council, other community-based organisations, and employers, have been carefully considered. For example, the RJSC has been made the only point of address for employers in search of suitable workers; having all data at its ready disposal, it can answer questions of employers fast and well.

Employers are required to be deeply committed. Not only must companies chart their needs, they also have to set somebody free to act as contact person for the project and to inform the management extensively. Besides, companies are required to work with the transport organisation Metro King County to develop transport programmes for the employees. For too many employees, transport is an obstacle on the way to a job, as is the shortage of day nurseries and reception centres for elderly relatives. To remove such obstacles is the mission of the supportive component. Many large companies in the state of Washington have experience with special transport schemes (think for instance of carpooling and the use of company buses); indeed, if more than 100 employees start work between six and nine in the morning, they are legally obliged to draw up such a scheme.[1] Transport programmes are also in the interest of the companies themselves, because they help to attract new workers, retain existing ones and raise productivity by reducing stress, fatigue and sickness among the staff. The expenses for the employee are acceptable thanks to contributions from the employer and (occasionally) a concession ('match') from transport company Metro.

Partnerships are valuable instruments for the UEC. Collaboration has been established with the providers of services to the neighbourhood residents. In consultation with the local government and top managers of private enterprise, the Centre identifies opportunities and then stimulates a more effective allocation of public and private means. The underlying philosophy is that access to employment can break the vicious circle of structural poverty. Another important goal to strive for is to make residents once more proud of their neighbourhood. When the UEC was founded, the participants committed themselves to a mission statement that puts faith in the potentialities of backward regions and multi-cultural collaboration first.

As so often, to measure the results is a troublesome task. Since the start of the UEC, unemployment has gone down from 19 per cent (with peaks of 42 per cent) to 4 per cent (with peaks of 7 per cent), but that reduction can largely be ascribed to macroeconomic developments (notably the ICT boom). On the other hand, the UEC target areas have unmistakably become more attractive to companies as well as residents.

Toward a Sustainable Seattle

The municipality of Seattle is convinced that to solve the above-described problems, involvement of residents and companies is crucial. That is emphasised in one of its directive policy documents, 'The Comprehensive Plan, Toward a Sustainable Seattle'. The plan presupposes that inhabitants, social organisations, institutions and persons engaged in private enterprise will work with the municipality to find acceptable, advisable and innovative ways to attain Seattle's objectives by means of neighbourhood planning.

Sustainable urban development – reckoning with future generations – is the central aim of this plan. It was approved in 1994, as a response to the Growth Management Act (GMA) of the state of Washington, which enjoins upon counties and major cities to explain in plans how they intend to accommodate growth. The GMA is meant to diminish urban sprawl, stimulate future growth in urban areas already well serviced, maintain opportunities for transport, housing and open spaces, and protect the environment. Every town is obliged to explain how they propose to deal with the expected demographic growth by their policies of spatial planning, transport, housing, capital facilities, and services. The GMA wants cities not only to submit such an extensive plan, but also to take care that their future policy is consistent with it. The plans, which formerly had only an advisory value, were henceforward to have a stronger legal status. The state of Washington moreover attaches great worth to collaboration of cities on the county level, and enjoins upon the counties to draw so-called urban-growth boundaries to distinguish urban zones from rural ones.

A prominent part of the Comprehensive Plan is the urban-village strategy, which combines minor changes in the development pattern of the city with a more complete and competitive public-transport system, the well-considered use of housing assistance funds and planning instruments for the supply of desired and affordable houses, investment in facilities and service-delivery systems suitable for high-density neighbourhood, and decision making on the basis of priorities set by the local residents. The municipality looks upon neighbourhood planning as a mechanism for the implementation of the Urban Villages Strategy. Neighbourhood-oriented common-interest organisations of citizens and companies are invited to submit a plan for the construction of, for instance, a playground or park. Once a project has been approved, the municipal Neighbourhood Matching Fund matches the contribution of the community with voluntary work, materials, professional services or financial contributions. Most projects are indeed financed from public as well as private resources.

Evidently, then, the development of the neighbourhoods is left as much as possible to the residents and businesses in the areas in question: a grassroots approach. The neighbourhoods have a fair amount of freedom in choosing their approach, not only in planning, but also in the implementation. Some neighbourhoods leave the planning to the municipal staff; others farm it out to external consultants. The municipality believes that the approach has improved the relations between government, citizens and companies. In most neighbourhoods (associations of) companies have taken the initiative to the planning, evidently convinced of their stake in a pleasant environment. A disadvantage of neighbourhood planning is, however, that residents and companies tend to avoid awkward themes, such as spatial rearrangement, thus sometimes delaying structural solutions.

The municipality of Seattle works most with non-profit organisations by contracting out to them certain tasks. In 2001, the mayor of Seattle urged companies to make a contribution to social programmes. One concrete initiative from the private sector is to support a centre advising non-profit organisations on strategic planning. Another project, named Social Enterprise, helps non-profit organisations to operate more businesslike in order to achieve a higher budget. The mayor's idea to concentrate all contacts with private enterprise in one organisation has not yet been carried out. The departments prefer to keep their own contact with the private sector, for instance for co-financing some project. There is even some competition among the departments, who would rather see companies undertake projects with them alone.

Boeing

Boeing is not only the world's largest producer of aircraft (both commercial and military aircraft), but also the most important supplier of the NASA. In terms of turnover, Boeing is the largest exporter in the United States. The company can without hesitation be counted as a global company, with customers in about 145 countries, employees in more than 60 countries and establishments in 25 states of the USA. Nevertheless, there is still a distinct concentration in the region around its birthplace of Seattle, with nearly 100,000 employees divided among three establishments. The aircraft builder has long been of eminent importance to the regional economy. As long as things went well with Boeing, things went well for Seattle. When in the early 1970s Boeing had to carry through economies and dismissals, that was one cause of a stagnating economic development and a drop in the population of the city.

The developments shocked private enterprise into awareness of the need for diversification, and gave rise to the founding of the Economic Development Council for Seattle and King County.[2]

Boeing sets much store by good corporate citizenship, as is evident for instance from the company's mission statement. In that mission, the company gives evidence of its efforts to provide a safe workplace, to protect the environment, to promote the health and well-being of employees and their families, and to work with the local communities by volunteering and financially supporting education and other worthy causes. The philanthropic policy is coordinated by the Boeing Company Contributions Committee. This committee acts not only from a charitable conviction, but also in the interest of the shareholders, employees and the communities where Boeing does business and where its workers live and work. The philanthropic policy thus has been given a strategic dimension and is more and more integrated with the company's core business. Since the merger with McDonnell-Douglas (headquartered in St Louis), the company has developed a common vision on local involvement. A holistic and integral approach was thought necessary to help solve structural problems in the community. In the eyes of the company, such an approach cannot succeed without strategic relations with partners in the non-profit world.

Policies and Activities

Boeing's philanthropic policy addresses four themes: 1) education; 2) health and human services; 3) art and culture; and 4) environment and community (Boeing, 2000). The company is very conscious of its (enlightened) self-interest in being actively involved in these themes. Boeing not only wants to instil in children and young people enthusiasm for science (mathematics, physics, and chemistry, subjects required for many jobs within the company), but also to help raise the overall quality of education. In the end that results in better workers.

The company supports relief and development organisations at home and abroad (such as United Way and CARE), because it has a stake in healthy employees and the relief of structural poverty. Investments in art and culture help to bring about the pleasant living environment appreciated by the well-educated employees that the company needs so badly. By the same motive, Boeing also donates money to organisations eager to stimulate the environmental consciousness of citizens without jeopardising long-term economic growth, in other words, organisations that are in favour of a sustainable development of the (local) economy. Boeing spends at most 2 per cent of its profit before tax on philanthropic goals. The company wants to be the philanthropic leader, not so much through the highest financial efforts, but by functioning as a catalyst to make other companies more involved. The underlying thought is that structural problems can never be solved by one single company. Broad social support is indispensable. So, Boeing has initiated discussions with other companies, politicians and superintendents (leaders of the school districts) about the future of public schools. The joint conclusion was that all schools should meet some standard (which indeed varies from one state to another).

Commercial and social interests also come together in a special scheme for managers. Boeing lends out its managers full-time and with full pay to help non-profit organisations gain knowledge and skills. On the one hand this scheme produces more efficiency and effectiveness among the non-profit organisations, and on the other it offers managers an opportunity to acquire new skills, such as how to motivate volunteers.

Boeing has as much as possible decentralised the decision-making on how to achieve local involvement. The distribution of the funds among the regions is related to the number of local employees and Boeing's significance for the community. In every place where there is a Boeing establishment, one person is responsible for establishing relations with social organisations and for assessing needs and necessary actions: the focal point for community activities. These coordinators meet regularly to exchange experiences and knowledge. The company has invested a lot of time and money in the retraining of employees for strategic cooperation with social organisations. Boeing managers in several cities have been instructed in the Boeing philosophy of corporate citizenship and in the main concerns of the community (problems of education, for instance). They have been familiarised with the available instruments, such as donations, supply-chain management (dealing with suppliers and customers), voluntary work and the establishment of partnerships. When considering opportunities for partnership, managers are supposed to understand the motives and considerations of the envisaged partners. The participating managers will have been informed of initiatives that with Boeing's help have effectively taken off. Regrettably, the fact must be admitted that so far, hardly any strategic partnerships with cities have been achieved. One of the main obstacles, Boeing states, is the quality of managers on the part of the envisaged partners. They often lack the skills needed to work with private enterprise. Social organisations sometimes have no understanding for the needs of a company, which makes a trustful relation hard to achieve.

Another obstacle to partnerships is the lack of objective measuring instruments to chart the effectiveness of corporate community involvement.

Boeing has always been very actively involved in the well-being of the city, as has been manifest mostly from donations and sponsorships. For instance, Boeing is one of the greatest corporate sponsors of the Alliance For Education. Boeing has also contributed US$250,000 to the new neighbourhood centre in Holly Park. Its commitment to the theme 'accessibility' is somewhat disappointing. Like many other companies, Boeing seems to assume that the infrastructure is the government's responsibility, although its stake in it is undeniable and comparable to that in education.

Lift-Off

One of the projects in which Boeing is involved is Lift-Off. Together with the City of Seattle and the Chamber of Commerce, the company has played a leading part in the realisation of this project. Lift-Off envisages providing effective and affordable (after-school) childcare for children in Seattle and King County. The demand for care (about 41,000 places in King County) considerably exceeds the supply. One-quarter of the parents cannot find day care for their child (under 12), or are not entitled to or cannot afford it. Moreover, the available childcare centres are often of inferior quality. Lift-Off is a dynamic partnership with community and business leaders, schools, governments, private funders, community-based groups, parents, and faith-based groups. The target group has been the focal point of the concept development. Hundreds of parents, children and other community members have been approached to give their view of (after-school) childcare facilities. These views and models of successful schemes elsewhere in the USA have been the basis for an ambitious blueprint for change. Action teams consisting of representatives of common-interest organisations, businesses, grantmakers, authorities and religious organisations are working on concrete projects in the entire county. The projects are concerned with early learning (the hosting of young children under school age) as well as the provision of activities for school-age children outside the school, before and after school hours.

From Seattle to Chicago

Recently, Boeing decided to move its headquarters to Chicago, to give it a neutral location in respect of the other operational establishments. Boeing wants to prevent its top managers being influenced in their decision making by personal contacts with the people who will be adversely hit by any negative measures, such as retrenchments and economies. Opinions vary about the consequences of the departure of the Boeing hierarchy. At any rate, no more than some 500, admittedly very high-grade, jobs will be lost for the moment. Boeing has more or less promised that the move will have no consequences for the company's commitment to the city, in terms of sponsoring and philanthropy. Nevertheless, the departure might make the aircraft builder's role on the sponsoring and philanthropy market less dominant, and incite other companies to become more active on that score.

Starbucks

Starbucks Coffee Company came into being in 1971 with its first establishment on Pike Place Market[3] in Seattle. In 2001, the number of establishments mounted to over 5,000 in 24 countries, predominantly in North America, Asia, and the United Kingdom. The establishments of Starbucks offer the visitor a very extensive range of coffees and teas, small delicacies, and coffee- and tea-related accessories. The company's ambition is to develop Starbucks into one of the best known and most celebrated brands, among other things by further expanding the number of establishments. As well as in its own retail establishments, the firm sells coffee beans, coffee beverages and tea through supermarkets and its own website.

The company's mission bespeaks attention for all stakeholders. The six guiding principles are: 1) to provide a good workplace and encourage respect and dignity in interaction (employees); 2) to welcome diversity as an essential feature of the management (employees, customers); 3) to maintain the highest standards in buying, roasting and fresh delivery of the coffee (customers, suppliers, buyers); 4) at all times to make the customers content (customers); 5) to make a positive contribution to the communities where the company is active, and to the environment (neighbourhood residents, employees, customers, etc.); and 6) to recognise that profitableness is an essential element of future success (shareholders). The fifth principle will have most of our attention, but obviously the principles are interwoven.

The initiatives springing from the fifth principle (corporate community involvement) fall apart into three categories: environmental matters, commitment to coffee-producing areas, and community building. In the matter of general environment protection, the company has drawn up an environmental mission statement that envisages environmental leadership in all its activities. In coffee-producing areas the company wants to help solve social and ecological problems, to protect the people and the territories that are vital to the coffee production. To that end, the company stimulates organic methods of coffee growing (that is to say, without synthetic pesticides, herbicides or fertilisers), and the culture of coffee in a shady environment (to spare the trees and keep the ecosystem in balance). Starbucks also defends the welfare of small coffee growers by issue of the Fair Trade certificate. This certificate helps small farmers by organising them in a cooperative which delivers directly to coffee importers and roasters. Starbucks works with several organisations to give substance to this form of social involvement. Among the partners are the relief and development organisation CARE (about which more below), and Conservation International, which gives technical assistance to growers to improve the quality of their coffee and to reduce environmental damage (conservation of biodiversity and notably the control of deforestation). Starbucks started out by giving financial support to Conservation International to make the theme more publicly known. When that appeared to be successful, the company proceeded to the effective purchase of the sustainable coffee. Starbucks wants to be an example for other players on the coffee market to follow.

Community Building

Starbucks' role in Seattle depends mostly on its third guiding principle, community building. Unlike the relationship with CARE, most initiatives on the local level are purely philanthropic and hardly strategic. That Starbucks has formed so few strategic partnerships on the local level is largely due to the relative smallness of a branch establishment. Starbucks expresses its commitment to its birthplace in gifts, for instance to the public libraries (to promote literacy, among other things), to a school (the Zion Preparatory Academy) which receives a portion of the profit of a local shop, to parks and the Seattle Symphony. Like many other North American companies, Starbucks has set up a foundation, the Starbucks Foundation. This foundation, created in 1997, has a well-defined clear objective, namely to promote literacy in America. Local associates of Starbucks are stimulated to apply to the Foundation for subsidy on behalf of local literacy organisations.

Recently the Foundation committed itself to a four-year partnership with Jumpstart, a non-profit organisation providing one-to-one education notably to children from the federal Head-Start programmes. The children involved are so-called pre-schoolers who have a great chance of running into trouble at school. Jumpstart sees to it that these children have already acquired some basic skills (reading, communicating, social skills, etc.) before going to school. Moreover the organisation assists parents to help the learning process of their children along. Jumpstart makes grateful use of about 1,000 students who thus learn how to teach and gain skill in coaching young children.

The Jumpstart approach is proving successful. Participants to the programme appear to score better than their pairs who have not taken part. The Starbucks Foundation has promised Jumpstart an amount of US$1 million for a period of four years, so that the programme can be carried out in still more cities. Naturally, Jumpstart receives financial support from many more companies, foundations and individuals. However, with Starbucks the involvement goes deeper than just writing a cheque. The company encourages partners (managers of branch establishments) to do volunteer work for Jumpstart, and to that end informs staff and customers of the work of Jumpstart. Starbucks has a stake in the collaboration with Jumpstart because it has an interest in a well-educated active population and new customers. The corporate input remains limited to financial means, however, because in this case there is no direct relation with the core business (which is to make and sell coffee).

Starbucks considers corporate social responsibility a feature of its corporate philosophy. Within the company 14 people are part of the CSR team, for instance in the realms of community relations, environment, and business practices. This group of persons work on internal cross-functional teams to integrate corporate social responsibility as part of each programme developed. Often, direct support from the top management is decisive in that respect.

The social policy of Starbucks aims at involving local partners (among whom are branch establishment managers) in several ways in the company's local initiatives. The selection of good causes is left to the branch managers and local associates. Some branches donate unsold foods to social organisations. The company encourages voluntary work by matching every hour of it with a donation to the local non-profit organisation concerned. A similar matching principle is operated for donations to local community organisations. Besides, the company incites managers to make their expertise available to non-profit organisations, for instance by taking a seat on an advisory board.

That the company is aware of its own interest in a healthy environment is most evident from its cooperation with basketball player Earvin 'Magic' Johnson and his Johnson Development Corporation. Here we see two companies, united in the joint venture Urban Coffee Opportunities (UCO), opening establishments of Starbucks with pictures of Magic Johnson in relatively poor neighbourhoods. For its investment decisions, the UCO tends to estimate the potential of a neighbourhood somewhat higher than conservative analysts would. The fact is that the disposable income in these neighbourhoods often turns out to be higher than many people would think. Besides, the establishment, by creating employment, may well cause the negative spiral to turn, and thus enlarge the disposable income. Such investment is by no means philanthropic, but is a well-considered, strategic corporate decision based on the assumption that citizens can create their own prosperity. UCO combines the retail power of the coffee merchant with Johnson's business acumen and knowledge of underserved neighbourhoods. The collaboration enhances the image of Starbucks as an employer, and expands its circle of customers, especially in neighbourhoods where shops (and hence competitors) are scarce. UCO does its utmost to make the staff in these establishments mirror the local population (a policy comparable, in that respect, with that of McDonald's; see Chapter 4).

Starbucks has learned that an active social policy is often attended by intensified alertness of social organisations. On the other hand, the company profits from its good social image. A recent development resulted in the residents of a low-income neighbourhood becoming indignant because a white policeman had shot a black resident, and therefore targeted Starbucks as the venue to demonstrate their discontent with the corporate world and the police. However, the media and community leaders convinced the residents that they had chosen the wrong target, since the Starbucks company was very much socially involved (as witness, for instance, the branches with Magic Johnson).

Starbucks and CARE

Although the alliance between Starbucks and the relief and development organisation CARE has nothing to do with the Seattle region, this alliance is very much worth a closer look. CARE is one of the world's greatest private international relief and development organisations. It was founded after the Second World War to offer relief to survivors of the conflict in the shape of so-called CARE Packages (food parcels). In the course of the years CARE has developed into an organisation that supplies food, assistance after catastrophes, care, education and other forms of relief to poor families in the Third World. Nowadays CARE puts the crossbar a few notches higher: its ambition is to help families in poor communities to beat poverty for good (structural solutions). The principal weapons in the fight against poverty are empowerment, equity and sustainability. CARE tries to activate the potential present in all people, for instance by investing in elementary education (notably for girls) and coaching people in setting up in business or expanding it. The organisation regards strategic partnerships as instruments to achieve those goals.

In his book *The Collaboration Challenge*, Austin (2000) analyses the success and failure factors of some partnerships, among which are those between Starbucks and CARE. On his analysis, the alliance has proved very lucrative for both parties. The two organisations found each other more or less by chance in 1989, when Peter Blomquist, director of CARE, was drinking a cup of coffee at one of the establishments of Starbucks. While reading the brochure 'Where Starbucks gets its coffee', he was amazed at the overlap between the provenance areas of Starbucks and the countries where CARE had been (and still is) active. The first contact may have been fortuitous, but after that, planned action was called for. The director of CARE got in touch with Dave Olsen, Starbucks' coffee purchaser. Austin concludes that one must be alert and take action as soon as the opportunity arises. At the stage of getting acquainted, communication is of the essence. Parties should get to know each other thoroughly before putting concrete proposals on the table.

The connection between the two organisations rests not only on common interests (Starbucks and CARE both have a stake in the welfare of the population in coffee-producing countries) but also on mutual trust, both personally and corporately. Getting acquainted requires mutual willingness to invest time in the learning process. It is necessary to know the potential partner organisation well to estimate the possible value of partnership as well as the possible risks involved. Thus, Olsen has studied the activities of CARE. Austin points at the importance of due-diligence process, each would-be partner diligently trying to create support among their rank and file by bringing people in contact with one another (notably on the top level) and exchange information. To win CARE's support was very necessary, because this organisation is understandably very cautious in selecting (private) partners. Negative publicity about its partner is awkward for any organisation. To avoid losing credibility, non-profit organisations should at all times maintain their independence. On their part, companies need to be critical in choosing a partner. Starbucks believes that to be an eligible partner, a non-profit organisation should have experience in working with companies. The would-be partner must have understanding for the commercial targets of the business; the quality of its associates is another factor not to be underestimated. Yet another condition for success is long-term commitment. Starbucks has shown understanding for the fact that results of CARE's activities will not be perceivable until the medium term. Long-term loyal partners offer moreover room for a flexible approach, in which the exact contents (input and output) need not be fixed beforehand.

The alliance between CARE and Starbucks has developed in the course of time from a purely philanthropic to an integrated form of collaboration, in the terminology of Austin (2000). It all began with the composition of a parcel with three kinds of coffee from countries where CARE operates. Of each parcel sold, US$2 went to CARE, which yielded the organisation US$62,000 in 1992. Starbucks used the expertise and infrastructure of the company to generate funds for CARE. CARE in turn gave Starbucks positive publicity by bestowing upon it the Northwest International Humanitarian Award in 1992. In 1993 the collaboration was intensified. Starbucks donated US$100,000 for a project in Ethiopia, a coffee-producing country. Furthermore, the company sponsored a concert whose revenues benefited CARE. The collaboration now showed the features of a cause-related marketing partnership, in other words, an alliance in the transactional phase. By the partnership with CARE, Starbucks' corporate values were made explicit. The relation with the relief organisation has made the employees proud of their company. In 1994 and 1995 the intensity of the relation increased further. Starbucks donated US$500,000 for a period of three years and gave CARE a central part in the in-store and mail-order communication and promotion efforts. The exchange of staff members fostered an even better acquaintance of the two organisations, and harmonised their missions and values. By the time of writing, Starbucks has become the principal private donor of CARE. When activists in Guatemala accused Starbucks of not having helped the coffee plantations there, CARE advised Starbucks on how to deal with awkward social questions. A framework for action for coffee suppliers was then developed.

The collaboration between CARE and Starbucks is a clear example of common interests. The alliance has enabled Starbucks to build up a strong image, so that the company has become more than a run-of-the-mill coffee retailer. On the other hand, Starbucks has profited from CARE's knowledge of the political, economic, social and ecological situation in coffee-producing countries. CARE is grateful for the enormous publicity (such as information about CARE printed on the coffee mugs), thanks to which the organisation has become known to far more people than before. The partnership has met a prominent condition for successful collaboration, namely a balanced distribution of the benefits. Latterly, however, the situation has changed somewhat, as Austin points out. Starbucks has experienced tremendous growth, with considerable red tape as unavoidable result. As Starbucks has grown and gained more resources, it has allowed the company to develop more partnerships with various non-profit organisations, including Conservation International. So, lately, the collaboration has lost some of its intensity. Austin concludes that long-term relations risk becoming too complacent, being taken for granted. The challenge to both parties is now to develop new initiatives.

Conclusions

The strategic involvement of Seattle companies is manifest primarily in their collaboration with non-profit organisations on behalf of education (the number one concern) and employment. These themes are highly topical, for there is a lack of skilled workers due to the structural problems in education and the ensuing mismatch between supply and demand on the labour market. Companies give substance to their stake in a well-educated active population in different ways. On the whole there is a distinct shift from pure ad-hoc philanthropy to a strategic and businesslike relation, with companies giving more than before heed to the effectiveness of their investments. Businesses in Seattle are not (yet) prepared to make a substantial contribution to the solution of general problems of housing and accessibility. Only for their own workers have companies set up transport schemes, but in most cases not so much of their own free will as because it is legally enjoined upon them.

Although philanthropy and strategic policy converge in certain respects, the internal organisation of companies is not keyed to the combination. Boeing as well as Starbucks make a clear distinction between the donation policy and strategic decisions. The decision of Boeing to leave Seattle is a clear example of a relatively hard-headed, businesslike and strategic decision which seems hard to reconcile with the social role the company has for years played in the region. Although hardly any employment will be lost in the first instance, in the future the head office might easily decide to cancel jobs or move an establishment to elsewhere. The consequences of Boeing's departure cannot yet be estimated. The relation between the aircraft builder and the city will probably become more businesslike, because Seattle has lost its status aparte. Partnerships with non-profit organisations will more than ever get a strategic flavour, both parties wanting to receive return on their investments. On the other hand, the expectation is that other businesses will show more initiative towards non-profit organisations once Boeing has lost its dominance.

The partnership of CARE and Starbucks confirms the importance of several success and failure factors in cross-sector partnerships, such as mutual respect, the maintenance of independence (notably for the non-profit organisation), and long-term commitment. Somewhat frustrating – at least for economists – is the conclusion that this type of partnerships cannot take off unless the two parties hit it off. The alliance owes much to the interaction between Peter Blomquist and Dave Olden. Sociopsychological factors and the 'chance' factor must not be underestimated.

Notes

1 By the Community Trip Reduction Law of the state of Washington.
2 The Economic Development Council for Seattle and King County tries to attract and retain companies, and collects statistics about the economic development of the region.
3 Pike Place Market is a permanent, daily market with local and international food, art and craft, restaurants, clothing, antique shops and trendy boutiques. The market draws residents and tourists.

References

Alliance For Education (2000), '2000 Annual Report'.

Austin, J.E. (2000), *The Collaboration Challenge: How Non-profits and Businesses Succeed Through Strategic Alliances*, The Drucker Foundation, Jossey-Bass Publishers, San Francisco.

Boeing (2000), 'Citizenship Report 1999'.

City of Seattle (2000), 'The Greater Seattle Datasheet', Office of Intergovernmental Relations.

Economic Development Council of Seattle and King County (2000), '2000–2001 Demographic and Economic Profile of Seattle and King County, Washington'.

Education Week (2000), 'College Students Help Jump-Start Preschoolers' Learning', Linda Jacobsen, 13 December.

Housing Partnership (undated), 'It's about Families: It's about the Quality of Life: It's about Jobs: Housing: It's Everybody's Business'.

Puget Sound Business Journal (2000), January.

Seattle Times (2000), 'The Center of Seattle: Seattle Center is Convincing Evidence that a Government can do well', O. Casey Corr, 20 August.

Urban Enterprise Center (2000), 'Strategic Plan'.

Urban Enterpise Center (undated), 'Business Incubator Feasibility Study'.

Urban Enterprise Center (Greater Seattle Chamber of Commerce) and The Bernhard Development Company (undated), 'Seattle – Preston Workforce Connection'.

Discussion partners

T. Bailey, Vice President Community and Local Government Relations, The Boeing Company

B. Center, President, Washington Council on International Trade
D. Cline, Director Strategic Planning Office, City of Seattle
M. Curry, Seattle Planning Commission, City of Seattle
R. Du Pree, Human Services Department, City of Seattle
E. Huttman, Senior Director of Development, Care
L. Kohn, Director Office for Education, Strategic Planning Office, City of Seattle
M. Luis, The Housing Partnership
C. McCoy, Economic Development Council of Seattle and King County
H. McKinney, Vice President Urban Affairs, Greater Seattle Chamber of Commerce
W. Marsh, Economic Development Council of Seattle and King County
S. Mecklenburg, Director Environmental and Business Practices, Starbucks Coffee Company
I.H. Moncaster, Director Northwest Office, Care
R.K. Pasquarella, President, Alliance for Education
T. Robinson, Executive Director, Seattle Center Foundation
P. Sommers, University of Washington

Chapter 10

St Louis

Introduction

This chapter describes the state of corporate community involvement in the city of St Louis, or, more accurately, the St Louis region. After a concise profile of city and region, there follows an analysis of the local involvement of private enterprise. This analysis consists of two parts. The first part reviews the various intermediary organisations that deal with the public interests of the private sector. The second part concentrates on the social involvement of some active companies established in St Louis: energy producer Ameren UE, Bank of America, and deliverer of postal services UPS. Some tentative conclusions from this case study conclude the chapter.

Profile[1]

St Louis is situated in the state of Missouri, south of the spot where the Missouri and Illinois rivers flow into the Mississippi. The city of St Louis lies on the border between the states of Missouri and Illinois. The metropolitan area is a so-called bi-state region comprising 12 counties, of which five are in Illinois and seven in Missouri.

The city has played a prominent role in American history. In the nineteenth century St Louis developed into a trade and commerce centre that drew many immigrants in search of a better life. The fast growth of the city was due in part to its favourable location near the great rivers. By the end of the nineteenth century, St Louis was the fourth city of the USA. In 1904 it was the proud host of the World Exhibition and the Olympic Games.

Urban Sprawl

After the Second World War, however, employment as well as population plummeted. After 1960 the number of residents diminished to less than half, from 750,000 to (by estimation of the Bureau of Census) 366,000 in 1996 (see Table 10.1). In the same period the county of St Louis and the metropolitan area grew considerably in population and activity. St Louis is a classic example of a central city suffering from the phenomenon of 'urban sprawl' and attendant desurbanisation: the outflow of people and jobs to the 'green' suburban municipalities. The same problem has hit other American cities, but St Louis suffered more because its borders date from 1876. St Louis is moreover in the exceptional position of being enclosed by the St Louis county but forming no part of it.

Table 10.1 Population of St Louis, 1960–96

Area	1960	1970	1980	1990	1996
Missouri	4,319	4,676	4,916	5,190	5,306
City	750	622	453	396	366
County	703	951	973	993	1,005
Metropolitan area	2,161	2,429	2,377	2,444	2,552
Share of city in metropolitan area	34.7%	25.6%	19.1%	16.2%	14.3%

Source: Bureau of Census, US Department of Commerce, State of Missouri, in Rosentraub, 1997.

The outflow, first of people and then of jobs and purchasing power, jeopardised the economic basis of the city. Moreover, manufacturing industry, strongly represented in the city, suffered from fundamental changes in the economy, such as the globalisation and de-industrialisation of western economies. Another development that frustrated the economy was the retrenchment in the federal defence budget, which plunged regional suppliers into difficulties.

Present Situation

The urban region of St Louis is today a vast area (16,573 square kilometres), with more than 2.5 million inhabitants, ranking eighteenth on the list of urban regions in the United States in terms of population. Some commuters have to travel more than 40 miles to their work in the city. Others have found employment in the smaller cities that have grown in economic importance. The region has become polycentric, as is clear among other things from the emergence of large shopping centres along the motorways. The population of thc city is still on the wane, by 1 or 2 per cent a year. Seventy per cent of those population groups that count as minorities live in the city. The proportion of African-Americans in the city amounts to more than half in some neighbourhoods, against 17.5 per cent in the region (Bureau of Census, 1994).

The present economic structure of metropolitan St Louis is that of a modern service city. The share of manufacturing industry in total employment (including construction and mining) amounts to one-fifth. The region has a name to defend in the production of motorcars and aircraft (and related products) in particular. The state of Missouri is still the second largest producer of cars after Detroit. The construction of aircraft and related parts is associated with the presence of McDonnell-Douglas, which has its roots in Missouri. Now that this aircraft builder has merged with Boeing, the region no longer accommodates the headquarters, which first moved to Seattle and then to Chicago (see the section about Boeing in Chapter 9).

Despite the outflow of people and activity, St Louis still is an important factor in the American economy. The city is the home base of 11 companies from the Fortune 500 (Ameren among them, see below) and nine from the next lower group of 500. St Louis thus holds the fourth position among centres for headquarters of major companies.

Table 10.2 Employment in metropolitan St Louis

Sector	Absolute	Relative
Services	413,592	32%
Transport, communication and utilities	82,825	6%
Government	153,083	12%
Wholesale and retail trade	310,792	24%
Banks, insurance and real estate	81,508	6%
Construction and mining	68,217	5%
Manufacturing industry	196,125	15%
Total	1,306,142	100%

Source: Missouri Department of Labor and Industrial Relations and Illinois Department of Employment Security, 1998.

The average unemployment rate in the metropolitan area is relatively low: 4.1 per cent. In the city and the county of St Louis there are, however, some neighbourhoods where there are considerably more unemployed people than elsewhere, up to 10 per cent (Missouri Department of Labor and Industrial Relations, 1998).

Intermediary Organisations

As has already become clear from other North American cases, the government plays but a modest role in the American community. Many hold the credo 'the less government, the better'. The lack of such general provisions (in the form of subsidies and benefits) as are common in Europe, has induced companies and citizens to take initiatives themselves. They have created several social organisations that dedicate themselves to good causes. Companies have their own foundations to which every year they transfer a certain percentage of pre-tax income to spend on good causes. Most companies take an active part in the many non-profit organisations (NPOs), which serve as a kind of intermediary between demand for and supply of 'philanthropic funds'. These NPOs have a private character, are mostly privately or public-privately financed, and have a social objective in mind. To make a profit is not a primary object. In recent years an increasing tendency has been observable among companies and NPOs to proceed strategically and proactively when spending money on good causes.

The Metropolitan Association for Philanthropy (MAP)

In St Louis, the Metropolitan Association for Philanthropy (MAP) – the regional association of 'grantmakers' – plays a prominent part in philanthropy. The association was founded in 1970 by some companies and foundations eager to make their donations more effective. The association counts some 60 members (companies and foundations) who on the basis of their own agenda donate money to projects that enhance the quality of life in St Louis and surroundings. The association aims to stimulate philanthropy in the region and make subsidies more effective. The organisation acts as an intermediary between foundations and companies. The Metropolitan Association for Philanthropy coordinates, brings parties together, provides information, and stimulates effective philanthropy in the region by: 1) recognition and promotion of the value of partnerships between sponsors and NPOs; 2) development and maintenance of essential sources of information; 3) the supply of educational facilities and professional development opportunities in an environment with like-minded people; 4) encouragement of cooperation; and 5) stimulation, diversification and improvement of communication within the philanthropic society (Metropolitan Association for Philanthropy, 1999).

The association respects the individual autonomy of sponsors as to their good causes policy, but itself pursues a proactive approach. A number of attention points have been defined and efforts are made to arrange partnerships of members around them. Besides, the organisation stimulates its members to donate money more strategically, so that philanthropy lines up with the core business. However, that does not seem straightforward in actual practice. Many companies consider 'grant making' (granting subsidies) not as a source of profit nor as a form of marketing. Because most firms spend at most 5 per cent of their pre-tax income on good causes, shareholders tend to a passive attitude towards the allocation of philanthropic dollars. In other words: they do not judge the expenditure by its possible return on investment.

Because of their shareholders passiveness, companies are slow to show enthusiasm for comprehensive plans for the sustainable development of the city. That is notably true of companies that have no clear-cut interest in the prosperous development of the city. Banks and utilities (see the sections on Ameren and Bank of America) are among the few companies that have a direct interest and therefore are sooner inclined to participate in large-scale, integral projects. Strategic social involvement is most likely shown by the large corporations that are represented in several intermediary organisations (among which is Civic Progress, see below). On the assumption that the major companies are unlikely to raise their contributions to NPOs, any growth of the overall budget can be achieved only by persuading the smaller businesses to take their responsibility. Such companies tend to proceed less strategically; their commitment often takes the form of writing out cheques ad hoc at cocktail parties (the so-called cocktail giving). That way of corporate social responsibility is hardly effective, either to the community, for lack of focus and mutual adjustment, or to the company, for lack of a relation with the corporate strategy.

The question is, then, who can be the initiator of large-scale, integral projects in St Louis. Local authority is sadly splintered. Not only does the metropolis of St Louis fall apart into several municipalities and other tax-levying authorities; even within these bodies red tape prevails. The fragmentation hampers the drawing up of integral plans by the government. In practice, in the region of St Louis any initiatives appear to be taken not by the government but by private enterprise, whether or not through the well-organised NPOs. Unfortunately, however, the NPO activities are badly adjusted: there is much overlap and little exchange of knowledge. In actual fact, many NPOs look askance at one another, fearing competition. The bad fragmentation – both in the demand for and the supply of charitable dollars – spoils the effectiveness and efficiency of the philanthropic activities. A ray of hope is that the main grant-makers have recently taken to consulting with one another.

An additional problem is the lack of leadership in the city of St Louis. That lack must be blamed not on the qualities of the mayor, but mostly on the way decisions are reached in the city. The mayor has less decisive authority than his colleague in Chicago (see Chapter 4). The quality of the municipal management is another adverse factor. What with the small population and weak administrative body, St Louis has difficulty attracting, or keeping, skilled urban managers. The private sector has recognised that problem, and through the medium of Focus St Louis has undertaken to finance the training of managers for the various municipal departments.

Civic Progress

One of the intermediary organisations that meet the desire of major companies to express their social involvement in a strategic way, is Civic Progress. This organisation was founded in 1953 to keep St Louis on its feet in the competition with other major cities. Civic Progress serves as a forum where chief executive officers (CEOs) of major companies in the region of St Louis, together with representatives of government and university, spend their time and resources on projects intended to improve the regional economy, the educational system and the living environment.

Until recently, Civic Progress was a reactive organisation, responding to requests for funds. A few years ago the organisation reconsidered its own position, and embraced a more proactive procedure, by which Civic Progress itself identifies important problems, decides in which of them to play a part, and whom preferably to join to solve the problems identified. The major companies have a strategic interest in an improved living and location climate. Participation in Civic Progress is useful for the company (although direct benefits are hard to identify), but also for the CEO himself, who in this way gives substance to his personal social commitment. It is the CEOs themselves who reserve time for employing their knowledge and experience for social objectives.

Objectives

Civic Progress intends to develop, together with other organisations in the community, strategies and plans that help implement measures which: 1) improve schools; 2) reduce the racial and economic division; 3) encourage regional cooperation; 4) lead to a better system of infrastructure; 5) take care that St Louis remains an appealing location; and 6) contribute to a high-grade community life.[2] These six sub-objectives have been allotted to as many committees. The members of Civic Progress do not themselves draw up the agenda (since it is not a political organisation), but sets out to define themes together with the community. Cooperation with other community organisations ('civic entities') is thought important to launch large-scale undertakings.

Civic Progress differs in several respects from the Regional Commerce and Growth Association (RCGA). This regional Chamber of Commerce represents all business companies (including small and medium-sized ones) as well as employees' associations. RCGA is occupied with the companies' commercial (often short-term oriented) interests, while Civic Progress focuses on their (often long-term oriented) social interests. Admittedly, the private sector in St Louis – represented by RCGA – has lately displayed an increasing interest in the region's sustainable and balanced evolution. The companies are in favour of checking further deconcentration – urban sprawl – by investing more in the inner city. Reurbanisation could boost the level of services in the city. In comparison with other cities, St Louis is in an unfortunate starting position, however, with a mono-functional inner city that lacks liveliness.

Some Projects in which Civic Progress takes Part

To stimulate the development of so-called charter schools is one object of Civic Progress in the realm of education. These schools receive the same amount per student from the government as public schools do, but may shop for supplementary funds through businesses and other organisations. In addition, these schools need not observe all the rules imposed on public schools.

One initiative involving the infrastructure committee is 'Build Up Greater St Louis' (BUGSL). This initiative was launched in 1996 to assess the infrastructural needs of the region, set priorities, and serve as catalyst for concrete actions. The scheme is managed by RCGA jointly with several other parties, among which the transport departments of Illinois and Missouri. Civic Progress favours expansion of the airport (Lambert Airport), and supports an RCGA-scheme for economic development of the grounds around the airport.

To relieve racial and economic division is one of the greatest challenges confronting St Louis. Civic Progress is aware that a favourable economic situation (with an all-time low unemployment rate in 2000) offers chances to save unemployed minorities from their downward spiral by helping them to find employment. The Civic Progress committee appointed to that end together with others in the community seeks opportunities to contribute to 'racial economic progress'. The first need is for schemes of job creation, recruitment, capital provision, technical aid and opportunities for contracts and purchases for companies led by minorities.

The St Louis Inner City Competitive Alliance

Among the most interesting projects aimed at sustainable urban development is the Inner City Competitive Assessment and Strategy Project, because it is so comprehensive and involves so many parties. Its object is to let underprivileged citizens and communities share in the benefits of economic progress. Since June 1999, representatives of the private and public sectors and from the non-profit sector have been in consultation to draw up an action-oriented agenda for the revitalisation of the inner city of St Louis. Together they form the St Louis Inner City Competitive Alliance. Some companies with seats outside the inner city also participate in the initiative in the conviction that sustainable regional development depends to a high degree on the economic vitality of the urban core.

The approach chosen by the coalition of representatives is distinguished by its market-orientation. Its objectives are: 1) to make the inner city more appealing for existing and new businesses; 2) to raise the income, welfare and professional opportunities of inner-city residents; and 3) to make a contribution to the efficiency, growth and vitality of the overall regional economy. To chart the economic potential of the inner city, the Initiative for a Competitive Inner City (ICIC)[3] was commissioned to carry out an investigation into the competitive advantages of the St Louis inner city.

The investigation report contains 14 recommendations for the improvement of the location climate and the stimulation of four growth clusters. The improvement of the location climate should be achieved by reinforcement of the labour supply ('workforce readiness') and improved local government services. Four spearhead clusters have been selected from 14 (potential) growth clusters identified by a cluster analysis. The four clusters, metal industry, transport, logistics, and construction, all reasonably match the labour supply in the inner city, and can at short delay offer employment to a total of 3,050 low-skilled people (ICIC, 2000).

The project was officially started in September, 2000, so that conclusions cannot yet be drawn. For the moment, the companies seem willing to support the plan; managers of prominent companies have committed themselves to the development of one of the clusters. The alliance has consciously chosen to farm out the effective development of clusters to company managers, who from their knowledge and experience are to compose teams of experts. Together they are seeking for lacking actors, relations and communication lines in the cluster concerned. The management of the alliance has been kept very small (two persons) and confines itself to the overall coordination.

Strikingly, the so-called 'black leaders' also have expressed confidence in this private initiative. Some of the wide support for the project seems to be due to its private nature. Evidently, the private sector enjoys more credibility than the public sector. Another explanation for the massive support from private enterprise is that more and more stakeholders understand the necessity of action; indeed, only joint efforts can turn the negative spiral of de-concentration and disinvestment into which St Louis finds itself.

St Louis 2004

Another intermediary organisation eager to play a role in the sustainable development of the city, is St Louis 2004. This organisation was founded in 1996 on the initiative of Civic Progress, to be a catalyst for improvements in the region. St Louis 2004 (2000) wants to bring together people, organisations and funds to transform the region into a better place to live, work and recreate (St Louis 2004, 1999). To realise that, the organisation tries: 1) to involve residents in the identification of problems, chances and solutions; 2) to accomplish sustainable improvements by stimulating the joint implementation of projects; and 3) to motivate the community to actions likely to inspire regional pride. The year 2004 serves as an artificial deadline for 13 action plans, and is a reminder of the successful year 1904 (Olympic Games, World Exhibition). The underlying philosophy is that a deadline tends to motivate people and serve as a catalyst for the collection of (financial) resources.

The action plans focus on: 1) revitalisation of the inner city (downtown); 2) clean drinking water, safe parks, and secure foot- and cyclepaths; 3) reduction of youth crime ('Cease Fire'); 4) diversity of the active population; 5) reduction of hatred and prejudices; 6) sustainable neighbourhoods; 7) easy access to day nurseries and education courses; 8) easy access to care providers; 9) easy access to education; 10) stimulation of entrepreneurship among minorities and women, as well as stimulation of internet use in backward regions; 11) stimulation of redevelopment in backward regions by means of the Greater St Louis Land Development Fund; 12) stimulation of the technology-based economy (ICT); and 13) the staging of events in 2004.

St Louis 2004 is an ambitious organisation, which through the above mentioned programmes can undoubtedly contribute to the sustainable development of the region. The organisation is financed by some 30 companies and foundations, among which the Bank of America and Boeing. St Louis 2004 has to a degree been successful in achieving a more integral and less fragmented approach to problems. More cannot and must not be expected from an organisation that will abolish itself in 2004. On the other hand, St Louis 2004, like other organisations, is resisted on account of its regional approach, which nevertheless seems essential for this very region.

Highly Involved Companies

In metropolitan St Louis, the following companies are among those who profess a pro-active attitude to corporate community involvement: Ameren UE, Bank of America, and UPS.

Ameren UE

Ameren UE (Union Electric) and Ameren CIPS (Central Illinois Public Services) are both parts of Ameren Corporation, an energy producer with headquarters in St Louis. This company is the result of the 1997 merger between Union Electric and CIPSCO Incorporated. This merger was made possible by the liberation of the American energy market, which actually is proceeding at different rates in the federal states. The social activities of Ameren have been accommodated with two departments. Their activities are closely integrated and some initiatives have been undertaken by the two departments together. Their managers report to one person, the vice president for Corporate Communications and Public Policy.

The department of economic development proceeds according to commercial rules, concentrating on investments that make a demonstrable contribution to the company's long-term profit. Social considerations are secondary. As a utility company, Ameren UE has a direct interest in the sustainable development of the regional economy: the more businesses and inhabitants, the higher the turnover and the higher also the profit (at diminishing average expenses). The company practises, among other things, strategic planning on the regional level, and giving location advice to businesses. Ameren is able to steer the developments somewhat, for instance by granting discounts on energy prices, but is forbidden by law to take on an active developer's role in projects. Moreover, Ameren supplies numerous complementary services that are in range with the core business and by which the company shows its social commitment. An example is the operation of easy payment conditions for the handicapped and the elderly.

The department of corporate communications and public policy acts on the principle that Ameren wants to be a good citizen so as to keep the loyalty of consumers. This department handles the donation policy, concentrating on the themes of education, services to young people, services to the elderly, and environment. Besides, over a four-year period (1998–2001) Ameren is granting scholarships to a total value of US$1 million for students at colleges and universities in Missouri and Illinois.

Bank of America

Banks belong to those sectors that have a natural bond with their direct environment, since investment in the quality of that environment will in time enhances their profitability. That natural inclination is reinforced by federal legislation (the Community Reinvestment Act) that encourages the local commitment of banks (see Chapter 8). Its principal implication is that banks are not allowed to exclude people from financial services (such as mortgages and loans) by so-called red-lining, that is, for the sole reason of being residents of certain neighbourhoods. Banks are obliged to report the geographic and social distribution of their services. The social performance of banks is tested by the federal government.

Bank of America is generally regarded as one of the banks that deal with the Community Reinvestment Act in a proactive manner. Initially, Bank of America – like so many other banks – considered the Act an irritating obstacle. At present, strict observance of the Act is looked upon as an opportunity to distinguish oneself from other providers of financial services. It is a means of public relations and brand building. Moreover, the bank can profit from a good social image because one third of its clientele consists of non-profit organisations. Another motive for corporate community involvement is the concentration trend in the banking business. Mergers and take-overs will eventually result in a market with just a few mega-banks (about five, is the expectation) and a variety of small niche banks. Banks that aspire to the former group will do well to observe the Community Reinvestment Act, lest they run into trouble with mergers and take-overs they might envisage.

The philosophy adopted by Bank of America is one of integrality. That not only the top managers but also the executives on lower levels should take social responsibility is considered essential, since the latter decide whether or not citizens are granted a loan or a mortgage contract. To stimulate executives to deal proactively with the Community Reinvestment Act, the bank offers courses in diversity training to make the sale of financial services geographically and socially more diversified. Besides, associates are rewarded for providing services to underprivileged population groups and neighbourhoods.

The social involvement of Bank of America is manifest firstly in its support to the St Louis Equity Fund, which offers tax credits for financing affordable housing. Another very active supporter of this fund is energy producer Ameren. Secondly, the bank helps to revitalise backward neighbourhoods by investing in projects, organisations and financial intermediaries who provide affordable housing, services and jobs. The bank's aim is to create 'healthy neighbourhoods' that are capable of sustainable development. Thirdly, the bank stimulates companies run by minorities, women and handicapped persons through the Minority Business Development Council.[4] All these activities are not only socially responsible, but also commercially justified: they reinforce the core business.

UPS

United Parcel Services (UPS) renders its services all over the world and is rightly called a global company. Its headquarters are in Atlanta, Georgia. The local involvement of UPS is inherent in the corporate culture and included explicitly in the mission. All employees (not just managers) are supposed to be committed to the community. The social involvement of the company is in particular concerned with the weaker members of the community: the elderly, the handicapped and the lower-income groups. The company wants to help those people and give them skills, irrespective whether they use them in or outside the company.

Local involvement is to UPS of strategic importance for its image towards consumers and employees, the slogan being 'the community is our customer'. UPS enables its employees to participate in social projects, for the sake of team-building and also to make a contribution to sustainable urban development.

For 25 years UPS has participated in schemes to help youngsters and adults to prepare for and hold on to a job. A long time before President Clinton's call to business companies to cooperate with the government to reform the social benefits, UPS was involved in effective school-to-work and benefit-to-work programmes all over the country. For these programmes candidates are selected for work and training in cooperation with local organisations. The programmes differ in type of candidates (problem teenagers, students, drawers of benefits) and in the cooperating organisations (government, NPOs). UPS also works together with organisations able to remove certain barriers on the path to work, such as educational agencies, transport companies and day nurseries. The programmes are beneficial not only to the community but also to the company.

Education is a crucial factor with UPS. Every employee may enrol in the education programme, UPS paying for the training. The schooling proceeds through in-house training and mentoring groups, but even a full university study including bachelor's degree is an option. Managers with UPS can learn through a mentorship to be a different kind of leader (a mentor rather than 'the boss'). The philosophy is that by stimulating people to enrol in an education, you can release them from the negative spiral; a philosophy that is the more true as the tendency to be unemployed threatens to be transferred from one generation to the next.

In the past few years, UPS has given more and more substance to its local commitment, encouraged by the economic growth and the tight labour market. The company will enter history as an 'employer of choice' and hopes in this way not only to attract (young and mobile) people but especially to keep them (for young people are inclined towards job-hopping). The offer of education in combination with a five-year contract can help slow down the turnover of staff. One half of the employees avail themselves of the education programme. To UPS this type of social enterprise is a matter of pure self-interest. In the past year, UPS was pronounced 'employer of the year'. In the journal *Forbes*, UPS held fourth place among the 'most admired companies'.

Conclusions

More and more companies and non-profit organisations in the region of St Louis recognise that corporate community involvement demands a strategic and proactive approach. That is clear on the one hand from the tendency of pure philanthropy to give way to 'strategic philanthropy', and on the other from the changed role of intermediary agencies such as Civic Progress, which now take a proactive instead of a reactive attitude. Local community involvement is shown notably by companies that have a natural and direct interest in the sustainable development of the region, among them banks (Bank of America) and utility companies (Ameren).

The St Louis case illustrates that corporate community involvement requires an integral approach throughout the organisation. Many companies confine themselves to rhetorics at the top. Bank of America is a good example of an organisation which teaches social responsibility down to the executives. Special training courses and incentive rewards can contribute to a better social performance.

The greatest obstacle which hampers St Louis is the bad fragmentation, both on the regional (the lack of regional adjustment) and the municipal level (the massive red tape). Fragmentation also occurs among the NPOs. There is a distinct need for an 'orchestrator' who unites the parties and lays out the road to sustainable evolution.

Notes

1 Borrowed in part from Van den Berg and Braun, 1998.
2 By investment in community life is understood expenditure on behalf of art and culture, and sports.
3 The Initiative for a Competitive Inner City is a national not-for-profit organisation, founded in 1994 by Professor Michael Porter, associated to the Harvard Business School.
4 See www.bankofamerica.com.

References

Berg, L. van den and E. Braun (1998), *From Gelredome to a Gelredome Complex: An International Investigation into the Role of Domes in Urban Revitalisation*, EURICUR, Rotterdam.

Initiative for a Competitive Inner City (ICIC) (2000), 'St Louis Inner City Competitive Assessment and Strategy Project: Creating Jobs, Income and Wealth in the Inner City', St Louis Inner City Competitive Alliance.

Metropolitan Association for Philanthropy (MAP) (1999), '1998–1999 Annual Report'.

Missouri Department of Labor and Industrial Relations and Illinois Department of Employment Security (1998), 'Non-Farm Wage and Salary Employment'.

Rosentraub, M.S. (1997), *Major League Losers: The Real Costs of Sports and Who's Paying For It*, Basic Books, New York.

St Louis 2004 (2000), *Go Public: An Investment in the Community; March 1999 to March 2000 Annual Report.*

Discussion Partners

S.M. Bell, Senior Community Relations Supervisor, Ameren Services

K.S. Cahill, Chief Operating Officer, St Louis Inner City Competitive Alliance
J.A. Cavato, Managing Director, Bank of America
J.R. Jordan Jr, Administrative Director of Civic Progress
D.A. Joyner, Senior Vice President, Commerce Bank
M.S. Kearney, Manager Economic Development, Ameren Services
M.K. Martin, Supervisor Customer Service, Ameren Services
F.H. Perabo, Acting President, St Louis Metropolitan Association for Philanthropy
J.B. Sauter, Human Resources Supervisor, UPS, Missouri District
P.G. Sortino, President of St Louis 2004

Chapter 11

Synthesis

Introduction

The purpose of the present chapter (the synthesis) is to identify the (potential) implications of corporate community involvement for the development of cities and metropolitan regions. To that end we confront the research framework developed in Chapter 2 (based on an extensive literature study) with the case studies of Chapters 3 to 10.

The second section of this chapter introduces the concepts of corporate community involvement and corporate social responsibility (CSR) and identifies the developments that stimulate companies to be involved in their communities. The third section analyses the implications of these developments for the behaviour of companies towards the communities in which they operate. After that, we concentrate on the relation between companies and one specific community, the city. Next we discuss the added value of cross-sector partnerships in view of a sustainable development of cities. The barriers in the development of such partnerships are then identified.[1] The chapter concludes with some final remarks on the implications of corporate community involvement for managers of cities and companies.

Corporate Community Involvement

Many agree that the attention to the social responsibilities of companies has increased in the 1990s, not only among scholars but also among businessmen and politicians (see, among others, Goyder, 1998; Burke, 1999; Chatham House Forum Report, 1996). In the literature we observe growing support for stakeholder theories, according to which companies are accountable to people and organisations who influence the continuity of the firm (Douma and Eppink, 1998; Post et al., 1999; Karake-Shalhoub, 1999; De Waal, 2000). At the same time, the classical shareholder approach (companies have only one objective, that is to maximise shareholder value) is more and more subject to criticism (Goyder, 1998).

According to the stakeholder approach, companies have an interest in acting in a socially responsible way, because good citizenship is needed to secure the social viability of the firm (Douma and Eppink, 1996; Davis, 1960). Several authors (including Elkington, 1997; De Waal, 2000; Boudhan et al., 1996; Burke, 1999; Goyder, 1998) claim that some fundamental developments stimulate companies to give more attention to their social responsibilities and interests. They regard the increasing attention as the result of changes in production processes (labour becoming important), in preferences of consumers and employees, in the role division between public and private sectors, and in the power of media (increasing transparency caused by innovations in information and communication technologies).

The last decades many terms have been introduced to put the (supposed) broader interests and responsibilities of companies into words. One of the most popular terms is the triple-p bottom line, which states that companies have to account for their social, ecological and financial performances (people, planet, profit) (Elkington, 1997). Increasingly, firms give an account of their social and ecological performances through the internet or (chapters in) annual reports. One of the examples is the 'Shell Report', which is explicitly based on the triple-p bottom line concept (Shell, 2000). Some other commonly used expressions are corporate social responsibility (CSR), corporate social involvement, socially responsible enterprise (SRE), corporate sustainability, corporate citizenship and corporate community involvement. In principle, all concepts are more or less based on the assumption that companies have an interest to build and maintain relations with their relevant stakeholders. However, it seems that some terms are mostly associated with ecological challenges (notably corporate sustainability), while other expressions are often related to ethical questions, for instance in the field of human rights (particularly CSR and SRE). Because our investigation concentrates on the relation between the company and the city in which it is located we prefer to use the terms corporate community involvement and corporate citizenship.

Changing Corporate Behaviour

In practice, companies adopt different approaches to corporate community involvement. Strategies can vary from passive to proactive (Eilbert and Parket; 1973, Carroll, 1979; Boudhan et al., 1996; Burke, 1999). In the case studies of our investigation, we were mainly in search of companies that act in line with the proactive approach, according to which community involvement is an opportunity to achieve competitive advantages. By means of desk research (including information on the internet) and the help of (local) experts we have been able to select and interview some frontrunners in the field of corporate community involvement. Table 11.1 gives an overview of the companies that were involved in our research.

All companies investigated recognise the importance of corporate community involvement. The majority considers good citizenship an integral part of their corporate culture. The Rabobank Group expresses its wish to contribute to economically and socially desirable developments in the communities in which it operates (Rabobank Group, 2000). McDonald's acts in line with the vision of founder Ray Kroc, who thought it his duty to give something back to the community. One of the guiding principles of Starbucks' mission is to make a positive contribution to the communities where the company is active. Boeing promises that the firm will work with its communities by volunteering and financially supporting education and other worthy causes.

Table 11.1 Companies in our investigation

Case study	Companies
Netherlands	ABN-AMRO, Ahold, ASN Bank, ING, McDonald's, Nuon, Philips, Rabobank Group, Randstad, Shell
Chicago	McDonald's, Sara Lee, the Shaw Company
Leeds	Leeds United, HSBC, Westfield Health Scheme
London	Centrica, Deloitte & Touche, Diageo, Lattice
Munich	BMW, Siemens, Stadtsparkasse München, Vereinsbank Victoria Bauspar
New York	Citigroup, Deutsche Bank, EAB Bank, the Bank of New York, Pfizer
Seattle	Boeing, Starbucks
St Louis	Ameren, Boeing, Commerce Bank, UPS

Companies make a range of contributions to the communities (cities) in which they are located. Without any doubt, the most valuable contribution stems from regular business activities (business basics, core business) which produce employment, products or services, and taxes. On the one hand, these regular activities may generate positive external effects, for instance by contributing to the creation of clusters of related firms or by attracting firms and people to the benefit of others. On the other hand, basic activities may produce negative external effects such as nuisance, congestion and pollution. Furthermore, core business decisions (including investments and disinvestments) can affect the socioeconomic development of neighbourhoods and cities (both negatively and positively). Core business activities make up the basis of the pyramid model (depicted in Figure 11.1), a tool used by the London Benchmarking Group to value corporate contributions to communities.[2]

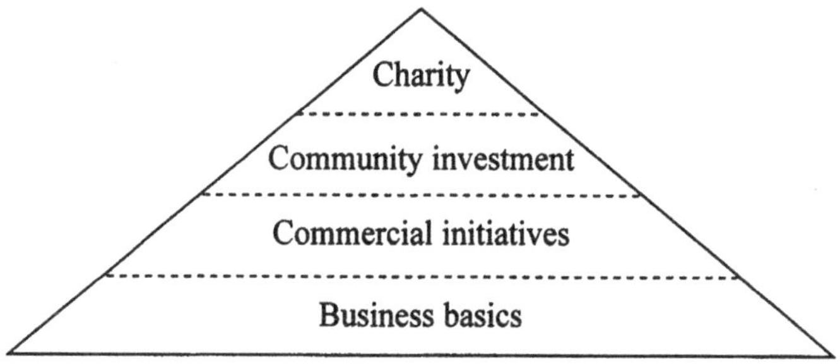

Figure 11.1 The London Benchmarking Group model

Source: Logan and Tuffrey, 1999.

Optimising the External Effects of Business Basics

Our research confirms that companies increasingly attach importance to optimising the external effects of their business basics. The trend of CSR makes firms more aware of their interaction with the community as a stakeholder, which has led to policies aimed at improving their social and ecological performance. These policies may concern various aspects of the regular activities, such as the internal production process, supply chain management (including the selection of providers) and human resources management. Proactive companies use such policies to distinguish themselves from competitors and to build sustainable relations with their (local) environment. A good example concerns the staff policy of McDonald's. This company stimulates franchise holders to match the composition of their staff to the demographic structure of the community. In this way the fast-food chain seeks to obtain a good reputation and broad support for its activities in the communities in which it operates.

The impact of corporate behaviour on communities particularly comes to light when a firm modifies its presence through strategic investment or disinvestment decisions such as openings, closures, moves, reductions and expansions of operations. Naturally, financial-economic indicators still dominate such strategic decisions. However, proactive companies tend to reckon with the implications of these decisions for society, understanding the mutual interaction between the firm and its local environment. Diageo is clearly an example of such a company. The firm helped to set up an organisation to regenerate a Scottish region, after its inevitable decision to close one of its factories in that region.

Proactiveness may also reveal itself in a stronger belief in the potential of particular (low-income) neighbourhoods, implying the acceptance of higher risks, lower (expected) profits and longer recuperation terms. The Dutch supermarket chain of Albert Heijn is willing to open or expand stores in such areas, having strong confidence in the medium and long-term future. The most important contribution of pharmaceutical concern Pfizer to Williamsburg (Brooklyn, New York) has definitely been its decision to stay and even to expand its activities. *A posteriori*, that decision can be characterised as fairly risky, showing an enormous amount of trust in the development potential of a multi-problem district. Another interesting example relates to the investments of coffee retailer Starbucks in underserved areas. The firm estimates the potential of these (inner-city) neighbourhoods higher than conservative analysts would. Starbuck argues that the disposable income in these neighbourhoods is often higher than many people think, while the creation of employment may help to turn the negative spiral and thus enlarge the average income.

'Strategic Philanthropy'

The private sector can also contribute to (sustainable) urban development by non-basic activities, such as making donations (charity), investing in the community and sponsoring (commercial initiatives).

The case studies demonstrate that proactive companies tend to shift the emphasis of their non-basic community involvement activities from charity to community investments. Most companies have adopted a more strategic and proactive approach to, what used to be called, philanthropy. They are using their community activities to gain competitive advantages by building strong relations with relevant stakeholders and by improving their location environment. The strategic approach notably reveals itself in the way philanthropy is organised. Large (and especially US) companies no longer leave the decisions to the CEO ('cocktail giving'), but to a special business unit or organisation. Some of them (including Boeing, Citigroup, Diageo, Lattice, Sara Lee, Shell and Starbucks) have set up their own foundations to channel corporate and private donations.

Another development, closely related to the institutionalisation trend, concerns the increasing use of a thematic approach instead of ad-hoc and random philanthropy. Furthermore, our investigation shows that philanthropic activities are more and more related to core business activities. Both developments are put into words by Diageo, producer of beverages and one of the most proactive companies in the UK in the field of CSR. The company considers focusing on a limited number of themes that are connected with the core business of the company as one of the principles of corporate philanthropy (Diageo, 2001).

Many firms that we investigated have adopted a thematic and or core-business related approach to corporate philanthropy. For example, the foundation of foodstuff producer Sara Lee (a company named after its female founder with many female employees and customers) supports the fight against hunger and initiatives that take the interest of women to heart. UK energy supplier Centrica aims its community activities at (among other themes) support to elderly (and handicapped) customers, because many of their problems are energy-related (many senior citizens die of cold in the UK). The philanthropic policy of aircraft producer Boeing addresses four themes: education, health and human services, art and culture, and environment and community (Boeing, 2000). Each theme can be related to the basic activities of the company. Boeing wants not only to instil in children and young people enthusiasm for science (mathematics, physics, and chemistry: subjects required for many jobs within the company), but also to help raise the overall quality of education.

Strategic philanthropy also implies that companies more and more base their community investment decisions on the expected financial and non-financial benefits for company and society. Many firms investigated admit that they have an 'enlightened self-interest' to be involved in philanthropic activities. Energy supplier Centrica considers its donations as instruments to enhance its image and to promote its brands. According to Diageo, social investments should contribute to the long-term viability of the firm. The foundation of infrastructure manager Lattice responds to clear business needs such as the need for a good workforce. Many US firms – including Boeing, Starbucks and McDonald's – acknowledge that their contributions to initiatives in the field of education are mainly based on expected long-term benefits (a better educated workforce).

The strategic approach may also have consequences for the amount of money companies are willing to spend on 'philanthropy'. Theoretically, the willingness to make investments (to incur costs) increases as the benefits grow. In practice, however, we observe that most proactive companies limit the amount of philanthropic community investments to a fixed percentage of the pre-tax profit (1 or 2 per cent). Therefore, a growth in the total amount of donations is more likely to be realised by stimulating other companies to invest in their communities. Some proactive companies (and their foundations) already act as catalysts to involve other companies and individuals. For example, the Diageo Foundation takes initiatives, makes people aware of a particular problem, and tries to bring persons, organisations and financial resources together.

Companies and Local Communities

The main conclusion from the previous section is that in general, companies become more aware of their relation with communities. In this section we concentrate on the relation between companies and local communities such as cities and villages. We discuss the spatial dimensions of corporate community involvement, aiming to identify companies with a relatively strong interest in local communities.

The Spatial Dimensions of Corporate Community Involvement

Stakeholder theories assume that companies have to reckon with groups or individuals who are able to withdraw the company's license to operate. It is common to make a distinction between primary and secondary stakeholders (Douma and Eppink, 1996; Post et al., 1999; De Waal, 2000; Karake-Shalhoub, 1999). Primary stakeholders are employees, customers, financiers (shareholders) and suppliers. They are directly involved in the production process. Examples of secondary stakeholders are governments, media, interest groups (NGOs) and neighbouring residents. They determine the social acceptance of the company and thus affect the behaviour of primary stakeholders. The division between primary and secondary stakeholders is not clear-cut. In practice, individuals and organisations hold several stakeholder functions towards several companies (Goyder, 1998). For instance, governments can also act as customers, as in the case of aircraft builder Boeing.

Communities can be defined as the geographic areas in which (particular) stakeholders are located. They can range from a neighbourhood to the entire world (Goyder, 1998). In theory, every group of stakeholders has its own community. For example, Burke (1999) identifies the employee community, the area in which the (potential) employees live, and the fenceline community, in which neighbouring residents live. The dimensions of these stakeholder communities depend on the characteristics of the company, and in particular the products it delivers and the sales, purchase, capital and labour markets on which it is active.

Our research confirms that companies are willing to invest in cities (through core business, sponsoring, community investments and philanthropy), as long as they are convinced of their (enlightened) self-interest. The case studies teach us that corporate behaviour to the benefit of the development of cities and the well-being and prosperity of citizens is often related to the need of companies to build and maintain good relations with employee and customer communities. The more stakeholders are concentrated in the city or metropolitan region, the more interest a company has in a well-balanced and sustainable development of the city. In 1984, Brooks, Liebman and Schelling observed that many American companies had become aware that the quality of the living environment in cities and the quality of infrastructure affect their own continuity. Our impression is that also many European companies increasingly recognise their interest in an attractive urban environment. After all, an unappealing environment can jeopardise the continuity of a company, for instance because it becomes harder to recruit the right kind of staff, as Baumol had already remarked in 1965.

The Employee Community

Private initiatives in the sphere of corporate involvement in local communities can be regarded as the result of self-interest in building a good relation with the employee community. In all cities investigated, the private sector is very much concerned about the quality and quantity of the available workforce. Some firms complain that the quality of (public) education leaves much to be desired. In their opinion the adaptation of curriculums to the needs of the labour market is insufficient. Another problem is that particular population groups (minorities, immigrants, low-income groups, the disabled, single mothers) do not enter the labour market, while companies do need them, especially in times of economic growth (tight labour markets).

Employee-community driven projects may give the enterprise a good reputation among present and future employees and secure access to a well-educated workforce. The case studies confirm that workers pay more and more attention to the social reputation of the firm. For instance, energy supplier Centrica found that its community activities contribute to a good corporate image among job seekers. In addition, many companies use community projects as instruments to motivate employees. Siemens, Boeing and UPS have developed programmes that offer their employees the opportunity to gain knowledge and experience from working for social organisations. The city functions in such projects as a training ground for gaining real-life experience (Kanter, 1999; see also Mutz, 1999).

The relation between a company (or a business unit) and its local employee community depends on the type of employment provided (function, wage and maximum acceptable home-work distance), the situation on the labour market (tightness) and the importance of labour in the production process. The group of companies investigated can be divided into industrial and service companies.

Our sample of industrial companies includes producers of electronics, oil, food and beverages, energy (infrastructure), medicines, cars and aircrafts. In general, these firms have a limited number of business units (production, distribution, marketing, etc.) with their own employee communities covering a limited number of metropolitan regions. The dimension of one employee community depends on the type of business unit, the type of labour and the average wage. Understandably, Boeing aims its community involvement activities at the communities around its plants, paying special attention to the cities with strategic business units such as St Louis, Seattle and – after the move of its headquarters – Chicago. Local budgets are based on the number of local employees and the significance of that plant for the local economy. More than 40 per cent of the total budget is reserved for initiatives to improve education and to promote science. In addition, the firm also makes donations to cultural facilities to contribute to an attractive living environment for its (well-educated and well-paid) employees. Foodstuff producer Sara Lee also supports facilities in the region with a view to attracting and retaining well-educated employees. Another example of employee-community driven involvement refers to electronics concern Philips. In its home country The Netherlands, this company concentrates its community activities (in particular the Philips Employment Scheme, which aims at fighting unemployment) on the metropolitan regions where the company has plants. Oil company Shell confirms that, within the Netherlands, it has a natural affiliation with the metropolitan regions that house establishments and employees, including Rotterdam (production and storage), The Hague (headquarters) and Amsterdam (research).

The second group includes banks, employment organisations, and chains of stores and restaurants. These firms do not have a special relation with one city, but they do have an interest in nearly all cities (as employee communities) because many of their branches are located in urban environments. In general, their branches (not their headquarters or other supporting units) recruit employees from a relatively small area, such as a neighbourhood or a town quarter. The average home-work distance of these companies' employees is relatively low, which is not only related to low education and wage levels, but also to the fact that are often more branches in the region, enabling internal optimisation of home-work distances. McDonald's is one of the companies that are very much aware of their relations with local employee communities. The company prefers to call itself multilocal rather than multinational, stimulating franchise holders to develop good relations with local stakeholders (employees and customers) (see the section about optimising the external effects of business basics). McDonald's has no special relationship with Chicago, where its headquarters are located. In a similar way, coffee retailer Starbucks encourages its local partners to be involved in their communities through participation in non-profit organisations and the selection of good causes, giving the company a good reputation among employees and customers in the neighbourhood. The relationship between Starbucks and its birthplace Seattle is not really distinctive.

The Customer Community

The case studies demonstrate that many examples of proactive corporate community involvement stem from the wish of companies to develop good relations with present and future customers. Firms are involved in local customer communities for several reasons, such as securing their reputation, developing new products and exploring new markets. The relation between a company (or a business unit) and its customers community depends on the products or services it delivers (distribution of products or direct contact with the customer) and the markets on which it is active. Among the firms in our sample are global industrial companies (distributing products across the world), global service companies (delivering services across the world using a network of branches, often located in metropolitan areas), regional industrial companies and regional service companies.

The relation between companies and local customer communities is particularly relevant when the customer has to travel to a business unit, located in a metropolitan area. In that case, the company has a clear interest in an attractive and accessible location, often being part of a spatial cluster. For example, Dutch supermarkets chain Albert Heijn acknowledges its interest in attractive shopping centres (clusters) and the well-being and prosperity of surrounding neighbourhoods (customer communities). Therefore, the firm is highly active in the Consultation Platform for Urban Renewal that aims to regenerate backward neighbourhoods in the Netherlands through investments in shopping centres and the quality of the living environment in surrounding neighbourhoods.

To many companies that we investigated, the city (and its neighbourhoods) represents opportunities to explore new markets. US banks increasingly recognise the market development potential of inner-city neighbourhoods, being stimulated by US law (Home Mortgage Disclosure Act and Community Reinvestment Act). They now understand that an integral approach to community development is needed to make investments in affordable housing and small-scale enterprise profitable. Like many other US banks, Citigroup, EAB Bank, The Bank of New York and The Bank of America have established special business units to look after community development. These units issue loans for affordable housing, small businesses, shopping centres, day nurseries, care provisions, youth clubs, schools and other services to make neighbourhoods more attractive.

The local involvement of the Rabobank can also be regarded as an instrument to gain a competitive advantage in the development of 'new markets'. The Rotterdam branch of this Dutch bank participates in a neighbourhood development company that aims to regenerate backward neighbourhoods in Rotterdam. In the case of success, the bank has good opportunities to sell its financial products (notably mortgages) to the local residents. The social investments of Randstad are also driven by future customer communities. This Dutch employment organisation looks upon special employment programmes (such as the ArenA Initiative) as pilots for the development of commercial services. A special business unit (Randstad Employment Services) has been established to manage these pilots.

Finally, the local customer community is very important to companies whose customers are concentrated in one specific metropolitan region (regional companies). A good example is the city bank of Munich (Stadtsparkasse München). This firm has a stake in the regional economy as most of its clients live in the region. The same applies to football club Leeds United and energy companies Ameren and Nuon, although the customer communities of both companies tend to grow as the result of various exogenous trends such as the internationalisation, professionalisation and commercialisation of football, and the liberalisation of the energy market.

The Added Value of Cross-sector Partnerships

Because cities are increasingly confronted with changes, diversity, fragmentation and a lack of consensus, the need for partnerships grows, especially between government and non-public organisations (Miller, 1998). The (future) prosperity of metropolitan regions depends to a high degree on organising capacity, which is the ability of urban management to get actors together (in strategic networks) and to develop and implement policies that respond to fundamental developments and create conditions for sustainable development (Van den Berg et al., 1997). As more and more companies recognise their interest in developing good relations with local stakeholder communities (as discussed above), new opportunities to develop partnerships between private and non-private organisations arise. One of the most important pre-conditions for the creation of such coalitions is that cooperation produces added value that benefits all participants (Henton et al., 1997). In other words: partnerships require that the actors recognise their mutual dependence (Stone, 1989; Klijn and Teisman, 2000).

Public Authorities

In most cities investigated, public authorities seem to be aware of the need to cooperate with private actors. The majority realises that companies play a crucial role in accomplishing a long-term vision and strategy. They agree that collaboration with the private sector may help to attract additional resources and to exchange knowledge and expertise (see also Gribling et al., 1999; Cahn, 1999). The city of Seattle, for instance, claims that the involvement of companies is crucial in the realisation of its comprehensive plan towards a sustainable Seattle.

In the UK, local strategic partnerships – bringing together authorities, companies and social organisations – play an important role in the national City Challenge programme. The British government sets great store by the involvement of the private sector because companies are buyers and suppliers of local products and services, play a part in the prosperity and welfare of neighbourhoods, and possess knowledge and expertise (DETR, 2001). Local city governments are requested to involve the private sector in the vision-development process. Stimulated by national urban policies, local government in London and Leeds is now in a process of developing more strategic partnerships with the private sector. In the future, the London Development Agency wants to stimulate maximum leverage of private and public funds by jointly setting priorities (LDA, 2001). Leeds City Council wants to involve companies in the implementation stage of the Vision for Leeds within the framework of the Leeds Initiative. The municipality acknowledges the added value of joint planning, coordinated lobbying and the exchange of knowledge and ideas.

Companies

Our research demonstrates that proactive companies in the field of corporate community involvement acknowledge the added value of partnerships. Companies admit that cooperation with governments and non-profit organisations is often needed to deal with local challenges in a structural and integral way. They reason that the required knowledge, power and resources are distributed among various organisations and sectors (see Bryson and Crosby, 1992). Local governments are usually regarded as key actors, being responsible for the general, long-term and integral development of the local community (see Brooks et al., 1984).

For example, participant organisations in the ArenA Initiative (Amsterdam) and the Seattle Preston Workforce Connection understand that the fight against structural unemployment demands an integral approach aimed at taking away obstacles to reactivation of the unemployed, for instance in terms of education, mobility, child-care and culture. Both partnerships include governments, companies, employment agencies, schools, transport companies, day nurseries, and organisations that defend the interests of ethnic minorities. Each participant controls a part of the solution.

What is more, US banks regard collaboration with public and private actors as a key success factor in their community development activities (see, for instance, Citigroup, 2001; The Bank of New York, 2001). They reason that the revitalisation of communities demands an integral approach, requiring efforts from public and private actors to make housing more affordable, to reduce crime, to create jobs and firms, and to increase the level of services. Their community development units cooperate with social organisations, developers, companies and authorities, and offer them special financial products.

Medicine producer Pfizer also acknowledges the added value of partnerships. To make the Williamsburg neighbourhood more attractive, the firm acts in conjunction with organisations that hold knowledge or expertise in a particular area. Among the partners are the police (in the area of safety), the municipality (housing, employment, education), and schools (education).

Furthermore, front runners in corporate citizenship are aware that partnerships can generate external resources which otherwise might not have been made available to any individual partner (see Miller, 1998). Many companies and their foundations try to get other actors (companies, foundations, governments, individuals) involved in their social activities. They act as a catalyst, trying to gain optimum profit from the leverage construction. One of them is football (soccer) club Leeds United. The 'football company' uses its brand, image and the natural appeal of sports in general and football in particular, to generate additional resources. The rule is that every pound invested by the club should attract at least one more pound from corporate sponsors (such as clothing sponsor Nike and home banker HSBC) and governments.

Barriers to the Development of Partnerships

It turns out that corporate community involvement offers new opportunities for partnerships between public and private actors. We have identified a number of areas in which interests of companies and non-private institutions are converging. Moreover, it appears that representatives from both sectors acknowledge the added value – and in some cases even inevitability – of cross-sector collaboration in the process towards sustainable urban development. However, in spite of these favourable conditions, the number of public-private partnerships that ensue from corporate community involvement seems disappointing. In our view the discrepancy between opportunities on paper and actual results can be explained by analysing the barriers in the process of coalition forming. These barriers refer to the process of interaction between stakeholders and the economic, political, cultural and spatial conditions in which the stakeholders operate.

By means of literature research we have identified three factors (or groups of factors) that play a part in the development of cross-sector partnerships. These three factors are determinants of organising capacity (Van den Berg et al., 1997) and the animation of local economic development processes (Bennet and Krebs, 1991). Firstly, the process of coalition forming depends on the presence and quality of strategic networks and support, solidarity, trust and loyalty among relevant stakeholders (see also Austin, 2000; Borys and Jamison, 1989; Kouwenhoven, 1991; Klijn and Teisman, 2000; Miller, 1998). Secondly, the willingness to cooperate hinges on the incentives that arise from local opportunities and threats (the local agenda) (see also Miller, 1998). Thirdly, interaction between stakeholders is influenced by the skills of individuals (leadership and the quality of human resources) (see also Austin, 2000).

Strategic Networks and Support

Our investigation confirms that the quality of strategic networks in metropolitan regions is an important success factor in the process of coalition forming. It appears that the development of joint initiatives benefits by the presence of formal and informal consultative structures, as well as the efforts of intermediary organisations functioning as a bridge between sectors. Strategic networks are needed to gain support among stakeholders, to make them aware of their interests in society and to take away cultural barriers between stakeholders. In addition, the creation of partnerships depends on internal networks and internal support, that is within the partner organisations.

Intermediaries and Platforms

In all cities investigated we have identified (several) intermediaries and platforms that facilitate the process of forming cross-sector partnerships. These organisations differ in spatial scope (see below), functions (see below), fields of activity (housing, employment, education, poverty, business development, quality of the living environment, or combinations), manner of funding (membership fee, donations, public money), and leading sector (business-led, government-led, non-profit-led).

Intermediary organisations and platforms have the potential to stimulate interaction between stakeholders in several ways. Firstly, they can create support for collaboration by making organisations and individuals aware of the importance of a particular issue, and their interests and responsibilities in that matter. Secondly, they can act as initiators by presenting a vision, a plan or another reaction to a particular problem to motivate and activate other organisations. Thirdly, they may function as a 'cultural' bridge between sectors by increasing mutual trust and understanding among partner organisations from different sectors. Fourthly, intermediaries are capable of lending assistance during negotiations, that is the elaboration of the vision into a strategy, the allocation of roles to the various partners and the setting of concrete goals.

In terms of organising capacity, intermediary organisations show leadership. The case studies confirm that leadership comes in different disguises. Table 11.2 reviews a selection of the intermediaries featuring in each case study. The list shows a variety of organisations, including development corporations with a social objective, business associations and platforms, advocates of philanthropy, and a limited number of cross-sector (public-private) platforms. Not included in the list are companies and their foundations (see Table

11.1), although they also have the opportunity to fulfil (some) intermediary functions. For example, Leeds United stimulates its sponsors to participate in the club's social projects, while Pfizer developed a vision and convinced other organisations of their interest and the need to work together, in its effort to revitalise Williamsburg.

Table 11.2 Selection of intermediaries and platforms

Case study	Intermediaries
Netherlands	Consultation Platform for Urban Renewal (OPS), The ArenA Initiative, Amsterdam Zuidoost Business Association
Chicago	The Commercial Club of Chicago (The Civic Committee, Leadership for Quality Education, World Business Chicago, Chicago Metropolis 2020), Metropolitan Planning Council
Leeds	Business in the Community Yorkshire and Humber, Leeds Initiative
London	Local Strategic Partnerships, Business in the Community London, London First
Munich	The Inzell Consultation, Mobinet, Switch
New York	Business Improvement Districts, New York City Partnership (NYC Housing Partnership, NYC Investment Fund), Local Initiatives Support Corporation, Community Development Corporations
Seattle	Alliance For Education, the Housing Partnership, Urban Enterprise Center (Seattle-Preston Workforce Connection), Johnson Development Corporation
St Louis	Metropolitan Association for Philanthropy, Civic Progress, the St Louis Inner City Competitive Alliance, St Louis 2004

Spatial Scope

The spatial scope of intermediary organisations ranges from neighbourhoods (for example, the ArenA Initiative and the Seattle-Preston Workforce Connection) to cities (for example, Leeds Initiative, St Louis 2004, New York City Partnership) and countries (for example, Local Initiatives Support Corporation and the Consultation Platform for Urban Renewal). However, nearly all platforms agree that local problems demand local solutions, and that a local approach helps in the quest for support among stakeholders. Business in the Community is a good example of a national organisation that is in the process of giving shape and substance to a more regional approach, not only through regional departments but also by means of strategic cooperation with local stakeholders.

In London, this idea finds expression in intensive collaboration between BITC and the more locally operating business platform of London First. In many other UK cities (including Leeds and Bradford), BITC set up local '... Cares' programmes (for example, Leeds Cares, Bradford Cares), by which employees invest time in the improvement of the living quality in their neighbourhoods (Business in the Community Yorkshire and Humber, 2000).

The spatial scope of an intermediary can be considered a factor of importance in the process of gaining support. Our impression is that it is easier to get actors involved when the spatial scope of a platform coincides with the spatial work area of the most relevant stakeholders. For instance, participants of the ArenA Initiative agree that this platform owes its success in part to the uniform delimitation of the area envisaged: the administrative borough of Southeast Amsterdam.

Instruments to Obtain Support

The experiences teach us that intermediary organisations make use of several instruments to gain support among stakeholders. For one thing, they often hold data (knowledge, information) that can convince others of their interests and responsibilities. For instance, the Local Initiative Support Corporation convinces great retail chains of the potentialities of backward neighbourhoods. Likewise, Johnson Development Corporation (set up by basketball player Magic Johnson) has made it clear to Starbucks that neighbourhoods with a low average income can still be promising locations. Another instrument is (physical) confrontation with problems and solutions, or 'Seeing is Believing' in the terminology of Business in the Community. The importance of tangible results also comes up in the case of the ArenA Initiative: the opening of a collective establishment of commercial employment agency Randstad and non-profit organisation Employment Services (the first 'real' action) is considered crucial in the efforts to gain support among companies.

Additionally, intermediaries organise informal and formal meetings to bring stakeholders together, to exchange visions and ideas, and to promote the development of personal networks between individuals. In the framework of the ArenA Initiative, breakfast and luncheon sessions not only result in new projects but also add to the support for existing projects. In London and Leeds, Business in the Community (BITC) regularly convenes meetings, stimulating companies to adopt a more strategic approach to corporate citizenship, with increasing attention to collaboration with the government and the non-profit sector. Moreover, BITC makes use of 'leadership teams' as instruments to involve companies more actively in social activities. In these teams, representatives of companies are supposed to give direction to the projects.

Moreover, intermediary organisations frequently make use of promotion and publicity as instruments to get actors involved. Suitable communications means are (electronic) newsletters and the internet. Like many other platforms, Business in the Community (UK) prefers a positive approach, which implies that they put leaders of corporate citizenship in the limelight, instead of blaming less active companies. Furthermore, several case studies demonstrate that an important condition to utilise external communication instruments is a good reputation of the intermediary organisation. After all, negative publicity about an intermediary is damaging, not only for himself but also for the partners involved. Therefore, BITC does everything in its power to protect the 'Business in the Community' brand. How important reputation and image are is also evident from the role of Leeds United. That company has created, through its association with (professional) football, valuable support among other companies (sponsors), social organisations, and public authorities.

Internal Networks and Internal Support

Several cases confirm that the process of coalition forming and obtaining support starts within the partner organisations. As coalitions run into more strategic and interactive forms of cooperation – the integration phase according to Austin (2000) – the need for support and active involvement of all units (departments) of the partner organisations tends to grow. In general, the obtainment of internal support is a task of the business unit (department, foundation) charged with social activities under the heading of philanthropy, public relations or community affairs. Obviously, it helps when this unit is backed up by the organisation's board (of directors). Furthermore, intermediaries can be helpful: Business in the Community UK wants to advise its corporate members on the implications of corporate citizenship for the internal organisation and the interaction between departments in particular.

One of the companies that have changed their internal organisation to acquire internal support is Centrica. This company has taken steps to get the marketing department and the department for corporate community involvement match their activities better. Another good example is the foundation of Lattice, which is considered a business unit acting in the interest of the company. The budget of this unit (allotted by the company!) is not a fixed percentage of the profit, but is set each year anew on the basis of concrete needs and plans. Another 'instrument' to obtain internal support is the corporate culture. Many proactive companies have a strong corporate culture which holds corporate citizenship as one of its values. Such values are often anchored in a mission description. Important determinants of the corporate culture are the history of the firm, and the culture of the country where it (or its headquarters) is located. Because of their status as former public utilities, service providers such as Centrica and Lattice are naturally involved with the community. Football clubs like Leeds United likewise have a strong tie with their direct environment, which indeed produces both the football players and the fans. Many American companies have a long tradition of philanthropy which is in fact an element of the American culture.

Incentives from Local Opportunities and Threats

According to the concept of organising capacity, shared opportunities and threats can increase the willingness to cooperate significantly (Van den Berg et al., 1997). Opportunities and threats manifest themselves on various geographic levels, ranging from global to local. As we have already discussed the global developments that stimulate corporate community involvement, we will now concentrate on local conditions that facilitate the creation of cross-sector partnerships ensuing from corporate citizenship.

The investigation demonstrates the importance of at least two 'local conditions': 1) serious problems that threaten the viability of cities and hence, the viability of firms located in cities (common threats); and 2) measures of the government that affect the behaviour of individuals and organisations, stimulating stakeholders to cooperate (political incentives).

Common Threats

As a rule, the willingness to cooperate grows as problems get more serious. The experiences in European and US cities confirm that cross-sector initiatives in the field of corporate citizenship tend to develop around issues that people are really worried about. In all cities investigated stakeholders are willing to participate in projects in education and employment as these themes are high on the agenda of nearly all politicians, citizens and business managers. As far as other issues are concerned, differences between cities (local conditions) need to be taken into account.

In the case of the ArenA Initiative, companies faced the threat of a damaged reputation, as local residents called in the media to protest against the opening of the Amsterdam ArenA football stadium. This demonstration was a reaction to the growing gap between the business district and the residential area, and in particular the fact that the creation of employment did not benefit local citizens. The establishment of Business in the Community UK (a platform to get UK companies involved in society) is generally considered a direct result of serious social problems and disturbances in UK cities in the early 1980s. In a similar way, the birth of Leeds Initiative (a joint programme to revitalise the city) in 1990 can be ascribed to the economic problems and the weak image of Leeds at that time. In the case of London, serious accessibility problems stimulated local business to set up London First, a business platform that promotes corporate community involvement as an instrument to develop London in a sustainable way. Many initiatives in New York have arisen from grave problems in the sphere of crime (safety) and the quality of the living environment. In Seattle, a protest march about the 'wrongful' selection of the city as most liveable in the US resulted in the founding of the Urban Enterprise Centre, a business platform that aims to revitalise the local economy.

Political Incentives

The research demonstrates that local and national governments can create favourable conditions for cross-sector partnerships to develop. Policy measures such as taxes, subsidies and other regulations may increase the (perceived) added value of cooperation and thus stimulate stakeholders to change their behaviour. One of the possibilities for governments is to encourage cross-sector collaboration by making specific demands in the application of budgets. In the UK, the national government finds it important to relate the distribution of the urban revitalisation budget to the degree of cross-sector cooperation, not only during the development of a vision but also at the stage of implementation. The municipality of Seattle uses the matching principle to promote corporate citizenship. Community initiatives that correspond to the urban strategy can count on additional resources from the Neighbourhood Matching Fund.

Some governmental inventions go one step further as they almost force actors to change their behaviour, thus making cross-sector cooperation more attractive. The Community Reinvestment Act and the Home Mortgage Act are clear examples of this type of policy instruments. Both laws – passed in the 1970s and activated in the 1980s and 1990s by amendments – oblige banks to meet the credit demands of low-to-moderate income neighbourhoods. In cases of poor performance indicators, banks run the risk of negative publicity, while they are not allowed to merge with, or to take over other banks. This national policy can be regarded as an incentive to cooperate with local stakeholders.

The legislation has stimulated banks to develop innovative and creative products and services, in close cooperation with local stakeholders, including companies, authorities and non-profit organisations. Like many other banks, the Bank of New York, Deutsche Bank, EAB and Citibank now understand that a joint approach is needed to make investments in low-to-moderate income neighbourhoods profitable.

Another policy instrument that facilitates the development of partnerships is the possibility to create official bodies, which institutionalise the common interests of the organisations in question. In the USA and Canada, for instance, the legislator offers companies or property owners in a particular area to activate a Business Improvement District (BID). BIDs are installed if more than fifty percent of the companies or property owners vote in favour. In a BID, all companies or property owners pay an additional tax to raise the quality of the living environment. There are no free riders.

Individual Skills

In the end, the outcome of the coalition forming process depends on the interaction between people. The case studies confirm the importance of individual skills, not only in terms of leadership, but also with regard to the quality of human resources in the three sectors (public, private, non-profit).

Many discussion partners agree that the efforts of one or more individuals are decisive in the process of interaction between stakeholders and the creation of strategic coalitions. People involved in the ArenA Initiative praise the input and enthusiasm of four key players: the project leader (who is also director of the local business association), the alderman of the borough council, the director of Employment Services, and the director of the Amsterdam Medical Centre. Pfizer's courageous decision to invest in Williamsburg instead of moving out, can be credited to the account of the CEO then in office. His charismatic conduct has considerably broadened the support for the plans, both inside the company and among other parties.

The functions and instruments of leaders are nearly identical to those intermediaries. They take initiatives, develop a vision, create support (wake up others to their self-interest), bring people and funds together, and supervise the evolving of a strategy. One of the main challenges leaders are confronted with, is to reduce the cultural barriers between sectors and to improve mutual understanding and respect. In many cases, we observe a low perception of the qualities of possible partners causing a lack of mutual trust and a low estimate of the added value that cooperation can produce. The companies in the cities we have reviewed hold a rather biased impression of the public sector. Most of them experience bureaucratic and democratic processes as a brake on coalition building. Pfizer, however, is convinced that collaboration with the local government is necessary to improve the immediate surroundings. They consider bureaucratic and democratic processes inevitable and inherent to public authorities.

Among many companies the opinion prevails that the government takes a too dominant attitude, taking away the control of their projects. Some companies are bothered by the broader approach which local governments tend to adopt. The case studies have revealed that companies prefer projects in a relatively small area (city district or neighbourhood), or projects with a specific theme. Local governments often practise an urban or regional approach embracing numerous themes. Some companies maintain that people employed in the public sector or the non-profit sector distrust the private sector, suspecting it of (hidden) commercial motives.

The investigation shows that proactive companies – that recognise the added value of collaboration with public authorities and non-profit organisations – invest in human resources. The Bank of New York has recruited someone with experience in the non-profit sector to lend shape and content to its policy towards low-to-moderate income neighbourhoods. Boeing invests much time and money in the retraining of managers to make them acquainted with problems in the community, and to inform them about the possibilities of (cross-sector) strategic partnerships. Quite a few companies – notably in the USA – encourage their managers to gain experience in social organisations. At the same time, many business managers say that they would applaud investments in the quality of public and non-profit human resources. In their opinion, managers in these sectors need to acquire more knowledge about the specific commercial and social interests of companies.

Challenges for Managers of Cities and Companies

Managers of cities and companies face the challenge to translate their common interests into joint initiatives. That is by no means a simple feat of translation. Several barriers hamper the formation of cross-sector coalitions. To bring public and private actors together for the sake of social projects is thus a very complicated process.

The investigation teaches managers of cities that companies are only prepared to participate in social projects if their self-interest is clear. It is true that companies have a stake in an attractive city, but that does not automatically mean that they are willing to contribute to its realisation. There is every reason to believe that companies prefer participation in small-scale projects (on the level of a city district or a neighbourhood) and projects with a special theme (education, employment, safety, etc.). The municipal management can anticipate by, on the one hand, translating integral plans on the level of city and region into clearly delimited projects, and on the other, approaching private enterprise with knowledge and understanding of the specific commercial and social interests of individual companies.

Another observation is that companies would rather take the initiative themselves than participate in an initiative of the public sector. That is why local governments would be wise to encourage and facilitate initiatives from the private sector, for instance by subsidies (matching) and other incentives. Besides they would be well advised not to present initiatives from the public sector as such but to involve companies at a very early stage, so that the companies have a sense of ownership.

Managers of business companies learn from the investigation that a strategic approach to corporate community involvement can help businesses to attain commercial objectives. An increasing number of companies regard collaboration with non-profit organisations (and public authorities) as an indispensable component of such an approach. Companies are facing the necessity to learn more about the problems existing in society, and to develop methods for charting the return on investments in their solution.

Moreover, the investigation has shown that corporate community involvement has implications for the internal organisation of businesses. The more strategic cross-sector partnerships become, the greater will be the need for a broad internal corporate support for social involvement and for the development of relations among departments in order to give shape to social activities.

Finally we conclude that the cultural differences among private companies, public authorities and non-profit organisations hamper the formation of coalitions. Managers of city and enterprise alike face the challenge to learn more about the norms and values of the (envisaged) partners. Companies that recognise their stake in collaboration with public authorities will be wise to accept to some degree the bureaucratic and democratic processes, which are inherent to the public sector. Public authorities on their part should accept the fact that the objective of companies is to earn profits.

Notes

1 The sections 'The Added Value of Cross-sector Partnerships' and 'Barriers to the Development of Partnerships' are implicitly related to the process of coalition forming, as depicted in Figure 2.4. The former concentrates on added value; the latter deals with the importance of support, incentives and people.
2 The general principle underlying the model is that charitable gifts are given with only minimal concern for a return to the business – it is seen as the right thing to do. A community investment strategy is much more carefully focused to secure some long-term returns to business, while a commercial initiative in the community must give some direct competitive advantage to the company and its brands. The lower down the triangle, the stronger the pressure becomes for an accounting of the business benefits (Logan and Tuffrey, 1999 and 2000).

References

Austin, J.E. (2000), *The Collaboration Challenge: How Non-profits and Businesses Succeed Through Strategic Alliances*, The Drucker Foundation, Jossey-Bass Publishers, San Francisco.

Bank of New York (2001), 'Strengthening Communities Through Partnerships'.

Baumol, W. (1965), *Welfare Economics and the Theory of the State*, rev. 2nd edn, Harvard University Press, Cambridge, Mass.

Bennet, R.J. and G. Krebs (1991), *Local Economic Development: Public-private Partnership Initiatives in Britain and Germany*, Belhaven Press, London.

Berg, L. van den, E. Braun and J. van der Meer (1997), *Metropolitan Organising Capacity: Experiences with Organising Major Projects in European Cities*, Ashgate, Aldershot.

Borys, B. and D.B. Jemison (1989), 'Hybrid Arrangements as Strategic Alliances: Theoretical Issues in Organizational Combinations', *Academy of Management Review*, Vol. 14, No. 2, pp. 234–49.

Boudhan, B., I. Vonk and F. Nelissen (1996), 'Maatschappelijk Ondernemen: Dienen en verdienen', Stichting Maatschappij en Onderneming, Informatief, SMO–96–5.

Brooks, H., L. Liebman and C.S. Schelling (1984), *Public-private Partnership: New Opportunities for Meeting Social Needs*, American Academy of Arts and Sciences, Ballinger Pub. Co, Cambridge, MA.

Bryson, J. and B. Crosby (1992), *Leadership for the Common Good: Tackling Public Problems in a Shared Power World*, Jossey-Bass, San Francisco.

Burke, E.M. (1999), *Corporate Community Relations: The Principle of the Neighbor of Choice*, Quorum Books, Westport, CT.

Business in the Community Yorkshire and Humber (2000), 'Leeds Cares for the community by the Community'.

Cahn, A. (1999), *PPPs Risk Management for Big Transport Projects*, Spanish Ministry of Civil Works and The Spanish Railway Foundation.

Carroll, A.B. (1979), 'A Three Dimensional Conceptual Model of Corporate Social Performance', *Academy of Management Review*, Vol. 4, pp. 497–505.

Chatham House Forum Report (1996), 'Unsettled Times', p. 9.

Citigroup (2001), 'Building Better Communities with People Around the World'.

Davis, K. (1960), 'Can Business Afford to Ignore Social Responsibilities?', *California Management Review*, Vol. 2, pp. 70–76.

Department of the Environment, Transport and the Regions (DETR) (2001), 'Local Strategic Partnerships: Government Guidance'.

Diageo (2001), 'Corporate Citizenship 2001 Guide'.

Douma, S. and J. Eppink (1996), *Ondernemingsstrategie*, Kluwer, Deventer.

Eilbert, H. and I.R. Parket (1973), 'The Current Status of Corporate Social Responsibility', Business Horizons, Vol. 16, pp. 5–14.

Elkington, J. (1997), *Cannibals With Forks: The Triple Bottom Line of 21st Century Business*, Capstone, Oxford.

Fosler, R.S. and R.A. Berger (1982), *Public-private Partnership in American Cities: Seven Case Studies*, Lexington Books, Lexington, MA.

Goyder, M. (1998), *Living Tomorrow's Company*, Gower Publishing Ltd., Aldershot, UK.

Gribling, M., M. van Vliet and F. Go (1999), 'Ondernemend besturen: Publiek-private samenwerking bij toeristische flagship projecten', Management Report No. 26–1999, Erasmus University, Rotterdam.

Henton, D., J. Melville and K. Walesh (1997), *Grassroots Leaders for a New Economy*, Jossey-Bass, San Francisco.

Kanter, R.M. (1999), 'From Spare Change to Real Change', *Harvard Business Review*, 1 May, pp. 122132.

Karake-Shalhoub, Z.A. (1999), *Organizational Downsizing, Discrimination, and Corporate Social Responsibility*, Quorum Books, Westport, CT.

Klijn, E.-H. and G.R. Teisman (2000), 'Appearances of Public Private Partnerships: PPP as Governance Arrangement and the Management Problems', Paper for the International Research Seminar on Public Management in Rotterdam.

Kouwenhoven, V.P. (1991), *Publiek-private samenwerking: Mode of Model?*, Eburon, Delft.

Logan, D. and M. Tuffrey (1999), *Companies in Communities: Valuing the Contribution, The Corporate Citizenship Company*, Charities Aid Foundation, Kent.

Logan, D. and M. Tuffrey (2000), *Companies in Communities: Assessing the Impact, The Corporate Citizenship Company*, Charities Aid Foundation, Kent.

London Development Agency (LDA) (2001), 'Success Through Diversity: London's Economic Development Strategy'.

Miller, C. (1998), 'Partners In Regeneration: Constructing a Local Regime for Urban Management?', Policy and Politics, Vol. 27, No. 3., pp. 343–58.

Mutz, G. (1999), 'Strukturen einer neuen Arbeitsgesellschaft: Der Zwang zur Gestaltung der Zeit', *Aus Politik und Zeitge-schichte*, Bundeszentrale für politische Bildung, B 9/99.

Post, J.E., A.T. Lawrence and J. Weber (1999), *Business and Society: Corporate Strategy, Public Policy, Ethics*, Irwin/McGraw-Hill, New York.

Rabobank Group (2000), 'Jaarverslag 1999'.

Shell (2000), 'The Shell Report'.

Stone, C. (1989), *Regime Politics: Governing Atlanta, 1946–88*, University of Kansas Press, Lawrence, KA.

Waal, S.P.M. de (2000), *Nieuwe strategieën voor het publieke domein: maatschappelijk ondernemen in de praktijk*, Samson, Alphen aan den Rijn.

Index

Note: bold page numbers indicate figures and tables. Corporate Community Involvement is abbreviated to CCI.

For Product Safety Concerns and Information please contact our EU representative GPSR@taylorandfrancis.com Taylor & Francis Verlag GmbH, Kaufingerstraße 24, 80331 München, Germany

T - #0112 - 160425 - C0 - 219/152/12 - PB - 9781138711433 - Gloss Lamination